BILINGUAL LEGACIES

Bilingual Legacies

Father Figures in Self-Writing from Barcelona

ANNA CASAS AGUILAR

UNIVERSITY OF TORONTO PRESS
Toronto Buffalo London

Toronto Buffalo London
utorontopress.com

ISBN 978-1-4875-4500-0 (cloth)
ISBN 978-1-4875-4501-7 (EPUB)
ISBN 978-1-4875-4502-4 (PDF)

Toronto Iberic

Library and Archives Canada Cataloguing in Publication

Title: Bilingual legacies : father figures in self-writing from Barcelona / Anna Casas Aguilar.
Names: Aguilar, Anna Casas, author.
Series: Toronto Iberic ; 74.
Description: Series statement: Toronto Iberic series ; 74 | Includes bibliographical references and index.
Identifiers: Canadiana (print) 20210352817 | Canadiana (ebook) 2021036095X | ISBN 9781487545000 (hardcover) | ISBN 9781487545017 (EPUB) | ISBN 9781487545024 (PDF)
Subjects: LCSH: Fatherhood in literature. | LCSH: Fathers in literature. | LCSH: Sex role in literature. | LCSH: Families in literature. | LCSH: Biography as a literary form. | LCSH: Spanish literature – Spain – Barcelona – History and criticism. | LCSH: Spanish literature – 20th century – History and criticism. | LCSH: Catalan literature – 20th century – History and criticism.
Classification: LCC PQ6072 .A38 2022 | DDC 860.9/352510904–dc23

We wish to acknowledge the land on which the University of Toronto Press operates. This land is the traditional territory of the Wendat, the Anishnaabeg, the Haudenosaunee, the Métis, and the Mississaugas of the Credit First Nation.

Publication was made possible by a grant from the Scholarly Publication Fund, under the auspices of the Vice-President, Research & Innovation, and the Provost and Vice-President, Academic, University of British Columbia.

University of Toronto Press acknowledges the financial support of the Government of Canada, the Canada Council for the Arts, and the Ontario Arts Council, an agency of the Government of Ontario, for its publishing activities.

Funded by the Government of Canada
Financé par le gouvernement du Canada
Canada

Contents

To Ben

Acknowledgments

Numerous people, institutions, and research initiatives have been supportive of this project. I first need to thank my colleagues at the University of British Columbia, where I am fortunate to have found a top-notch human and intellectual community. Thank you to Ralph, Rita, Raúl, and André for their trust. Thank you, Bri, for being the most welcoming colleague and friend one could wish for. Thanks for their friendship to Kim, María, Malala, Andrea, Olga, and Stephanie. To Olga, thank you for sharing your passion for motherhood as an intellectual endeavour and for all the life advice. Thank you to Jon for being an inspiring colleague and model at work. Thank you, Nancy and Alessandra, for your sincerity and for always knocking on my door to ask if I am doing well. Thank you, Tammy, for your trust and spontaneity. Thank you, Marie-Eve, for arriving when you did, full of energy and projects. Thank you, Gao, Luisa, Sima, Arturo, Patrick, and Anne, for continuing to make the department the place I want to work in. Thank you, Michael, Carole, and Emanuela, for making our work possible every day. Thank you, Joël, for your hard work to make the Department of French, Hispanic and Italian Studies thrive. I am blessed that I go to the office with an immense sense of good fortune when I think of seeing you all.

I am also extremely lucky to have Mary Chapman close by. She has been an illuminating presence, offering constant support, advice, and care on issues ranging from grant applications to childcare and institutional navigation. She and her husband, Jeffrey, are in every sense models to follow. Thank you to our dear Zoe, who has brought us closer. I also need to thank Xana for her enthusiasm and love for Gabriel and for us as a family and Mirta who, when we talk, always makes me connect with the passion for research. Thanks to many in the history department for their indispensable friendship as well: Tristan, John and his family, Heidi, Bill, Hicham, Tara, and Sebastian.

A very special thanks goes to the Wall Institute for Advanced Studies and my unforgettable cohort. Becoming a Wall Scholar in 2018–19 not only shaped my intellectual life but also gave this book much-needed time and resources for completion. I want to thank Philippe Tortell and the committee that awarded me the scholarship for believing in this project, as well as Emma McEntee for her warmth. Through a grant from the Wall Institute, I was able to organize a book workshop in October 2018 that pushed me to finish a first draft of the manuscript and to invite several scholars to give me feedback on it. This feedback was priceless. Thank you to Jo Labanyi, Alberto Medina, Jon Beasley-Murray, Mary Chapman, and Bill French, as well as Ben Bryce, for being part of this workshop.

I also want to thank Mark Thompson for his impeccable work and the three reviewers for so generously pushing me towards a clearer and more concise expression of what I wanted to say. I also need to thank Nancy Jean Ross for her careful, well-thought-out translations, Anneliese Schultz for patience when editing my work, as well as the librarians at the University of Northern British Columbia and at UBC for their help.

Before I joined UBC, at Wright State and Dayton I was lucky to be able to count on Hope Jennings, Rocío, Fede, and David Navarro. At Whitman College, Ian and Alvaro and later Stiliana from Oberlin formed a formidable reading group. Annaliese Baker and Elyse Semerdjian were caring presences during my time in Walla Walla. At UNBC, Zoë, Karima, and Jacqueline were invaluable at a crucial point in my career. I want to thank them for, first, welcoming us when we arrived in Prince George and, second, for their help when Gabriel was born. Thank you particularly to Zoë and her family, Calista, and Chad for their support for our long-distance relationship, from hosting Ben to welcoming all of us when we were back in Northern BC. Maintaining two academic careers in different institutions and two households with a little one was the biggest challenge I faced during the writing of this book, and I would not have made it without the help of our friends and colleagues in Prince George or without the support of my colleagues at UBC and my parents and sister, the trust of Alyssa Cantarutti, my family doctor, as well as the support of Jill and Bob. Jill, thank you for your unconditional friendship, your closeness, and your words of experience. Bob, you have not only been a model of intellectual and critical thought but also a rock and a friend; thank you for always being there. I am also deeply grateful to The North American Catalan Society, where I have met inspiring scholars, particularly to Aurélie, Rosi, and Mario for their warmth and mentorship. I also want to thank Sharon Keefe Ugalde and

Anne Pasero, two women who served as models when I started my graduate studies, as well as those with whom I worked at the Centre Dona i Literatura, particularly Anne Marie Poelen, whose friendship is one of the biggest treasures I have.

I am infinitely beholden to my family. Rafael Casas's and Glòria Aguilar's encouragement has guided me all these years. My sister, Natàlia, can dissipate my fears and frustrations with her irony and sense of humour. I thank them for their tireless support with Gabriel, for always offering their time, and for their energy and love, which allowed me to go to the library to do research, write, and work. I feel lucky that two of my grandparents, Gloria Panadés and Isidre Casas, were here almost until the end of this project. Isidre Casas, the only grandfather I met, died just as I was doing the last revisions of this book, in October 2020. My grandmother, Gloria, knows that I would like for her to stay here with us forever. My son Gabriel has been fundamental in helping me to see the need to finalize this project and to maximize time. I also want to thank Nick, Deborah, and Rowan for welcoming us when we arrived in Vancouver and for giving us a much-needed sense of belonging. Thank you as well to our neighbours at the Pacific Heights Co-op. Gabriel, Ben, and I are lucky to have found such a lively community. I have also been lucky to meet a wonderful group through the Casal Català de Vancouver. My friends in Barcelona, Natalia Villaverde, Joana Gaspar, Ángeles Rodríguez, and Mònica Junyent, my extended family in Spain and Canada (els Casas, els Aguilar i els Bryce), as well as my godmother, Conchita Rambla, have always helped us in our multiple moves. From Toronto I want to mention Rosa Sarabia, Ximena Bereocochea, Pamela Fuentes, Alice Jonathan, and Paulina Dabrowski, greatly missed since I left the city.

Finally, thank you, Ben, for all your support. I look up to you every day for your constancy, willpower, work ethics, and intellectual curiosity, of course hoping that some of it will rub off. Ben, you are the cornerstone that allows for many projects to come to fruition, and therefore I dedicate the book to you.

BILINGUAL LEGACIES

1 Filiations

Five days after Francisco Franco, instigator of the Spanish Civil War (1936–9) and Spanish military dictator for 36 years, died, the Spanish intellectual Juan Goytisolo (1931–2017) published, from self-exile in Paris, an article entitled "In Memoriam, F.F.B. 1892–1975." This article appeared in *Ruedo ibérico* (Iberian Bullring), a Spanish-language political journal based in France, and in it Goytisolo denounced the moral genocide that Franco had inflicted upon those who, like Goytisolo, were children during the war and grew up under Franco's regime. In this article, Goytisolo portrayed Franco as an arbitrary and castrating father, a monstrous head of the family who obliged Spaniards to abandon their own principles (162). Goytisolo described the dictator as a person "cuya sombra ha pesado sobre mi destino con mucha mayor fuerza y poder que mi propio padre" (163; whose shadow has weighed over my destiny with much greater force and power than my own father). Despite Goytisolo's impassioned words in "In Memoriam," the writer's two autobiographies, *Coto vedado* (1985; Forbidden Territory) and *En los reinos de taifa* (1986; Realms of Strife), reveal a more complex idea of paternity: While father and dictator are both bound to the author's perception of censorship and law, two inhibiting presences from which Goytisolo wants to liberate himself, the father does not map onto the figure of Franco completely. In fact, it is the biological father who is primary for Goytisolo in explaining his familial origins, his childhood memories, and his affective relationships to languages and in constructing an authorial figure in accordance with the above.

Goytisolo is not the only Spanish author who grew up under Franco's dictatorship and who described the biological father as crucial to understanding the self and projecting this self as an authorial figure. In reality – and logically – fathers in autobiographical works published after Franco not only diverge from the figure of the dictator but offer an image of paternity that challenges the one promoted by the regime. Through a close reading of autobiographical texts published in Spain between 1975 and 2005 and written by four authors born in Barcelona – Juan Goytisolo (1931–2017), Carlos Barral (1928–89), Terenci Moix (1942–2003), and Clara Janés (1940–) – I argue that the father shaped these four writers' conceptions of gender and their relationships with the Spanish and Catalan languages and literary traditions. In so doing, I demonstrate the central place of father figures when reformulating gender and linguistic consciousnesses in Spain after Franco and how the intersection of paternity and language, whether Spanish or other languages such as the Catalan, shaped literature in Spain in the late twentieth century.

Paternal Shadows

The superimposing of Franco and the biological father in Goytisolo's "In Memoriam" responds to a very specific discourse experienced by those who grew up under Franco's dictatorship: During Francoism, the family was a sacred institution and a source of social stability. The family resembled the hierarchical organization of the State, in which the dictator was an unquestionable father, head of the household, and ruler responsible for the nation. As a model of society in microcosm, the family was "commanded by a patriarch just as Franco commanded the 'family' that was Spain" (Grugel and Rees 133). An ideal of family – united and conservative – was essential to impose gender models and transmit "appropriate" roles to future generations. In this context, the father was an authoritarian, unyielding figure, a model linked to the Regime's ideas of virility and emphasizing control, discipline, honour, and nationalism. In 1945, Franco's regime reintroduced the 1889 Civil Code with the "Fuero de los Españoles" (Lex fori of the Spanish people). This law proclaimed the family as the natural institution and foundation of society and reinforced male authority, stressing the father's power over children and women and his responsibility for them. The "Fuero de los Españoles" "gave legal status to the male head of the household (*cabeza de la familia*), making the father officially in charge of all other family members and the representative of the family in the public sphere" (Grugel and Rees 134). Aurora Morcillo points out how the *patria potestad* (custody) of children was in the hands of the father and was only transferred to the mother if/when the father died (144). The "Fuero de los Españoles" claimed that married women "ought to be subjected to their husbands, as they are subjected to the Lord; because the man is the head of the woman as Christ is the head of the Church" (39).

Catholicism was indeed fundamental in this regard: Franco understood his relationship to Spain in parallel with Christ's position as a cornerstone of the church and saw biological fathers as well as religious fathers as indispensable when passing the church's precepts on to the younger generations. Through the foundational weight of "Nacionalcatolicismo," core ideas of the Catholic patriarchy were adopted by the regime as a way of organizing society. Ana Luengo comments on the family as an institution "cristianamente bendecida e inamovible" (blessed and steadfast in a Christian manner) and notes how following God's commandments, "no poner el nombre de Dios en vano, honrar a los padres – eran las bases de la sociedad" (26–7; not using the Lord's name in vain, honouring one's parents – were the foundations of society). Christian morals turned the family into a model of heteronormative and traditional values "sin fisuras, sin desvíos, sin 'puntos de ausencia'" (29; with no loopholes, no deviations, no "room for failure"). Thus, the dictatorship established control over society and enforced a particular idea of the paternal figure in multiple ways.

The Francoist notion of fatherhood fused precepts of Roman Law and Christianity: The *pater familias* – in Roman law, both the father and the owner of the family – was important to first distinguish and later connect and fuse the public and private spheres. John Borneman explains in the *Death of the Father* that the term *father* first excluded "the relationship of physical parentage, referring instead to 'a permanent qualification of the supreme God'. *Father* was a classificatory term that indexed a universal source of authority" (4); later, the term was "employed to describe kinship, indexing an individual relationship to a particular person. This linguistic shift has, in turn, affected political leadership … By investing the relation to political authority with paternal affect, that is, with emotional qualities such as love, honour, loyalty, and fear, this authority partakes in both the power and the fragility of an intimate bond" (4). Francoism created a purposeful image of the Caudillo as a figure of control and protection, the one who enforced rules and laws, and the provider of shelter and responsibility. Franco was idealized as victor of the crusade against the Communists and protector of the nation, making use of a Christian narrative of salvation. Some of these elements aligned Franco's Spain with other fascist, totalitarian, and authoritarian regimes in which there was an unquestionable cult of personality focused on a man.[1] According to Morcillo, Franco's image was that of the iron surgeon cutting out the cancer of chaos and anarchy. The official propaganda proclaimed the Caudillo's leading role in bringing the country back to its time-honoured natural form of government, the traditional Catholic monarchy (16). The Caudillo became "the medieval warrior-crusader, defender of the faith and restorer of Spanish national greatness, with his relationship to the Church as an important plank in the theatrical panoply" (58). Miriam Basilio examines how the dictator appropriated symbols of royal power and authority to create cohesion and to promote his self-appointed role as saviour, "embodying national unity as his figure created a nexus between the words Fatherland, State and Leader" (68–9). Alberto Medina explains that the media consistently presented an image of a paternalistic Franco doing everything for the good of Spain (17). In this way, Franco became the model for identification and controlled the country's ideological apparatuses (Medina 17–18). The dictator's omnipresence was reaffirmed in the Francoist newsreels, the *Noticiarios y Documentales* (Kim 23) projected from their beginnings in 1943 at the start of each film in movie theatres. Franco's power and legal authority was also applied through cultural control, censorship, and repression in the media and the realm of education. In schools, "[n]ot only did Franco's portrait hang in every classroom, but numerous illustrations of the dictator appeared in material specifically directed at children to establish a personality cult" (Harvey 110). Franco himself was aware of the importance of the family when allegorizing the nation and his role in it: In Franco's 1892 novel *Diario de una bandera* (*Diary of a Flag*), a young officer in Morocco meets his long-lost father, and the soldier is caught in a moment of vulnerability (see Pavlovic, 25 as well as Julio L. Fernández's *Los enigmas del Caudillo* (The Enigmas of the Caudillo)). In Franco's 1942 film *Raza* (*The People*), the Spanish Civil War is allegorized through the conflict between two brothers whose father is dead.

In parallel with the regime's discourse, families appeared in numerous films and writings as representations of the Spanish nation and, after Franco's death, the paternal imagery took a turn: Teresa M. Vilarós affirms that "Franco lleva por los cuatro costados la firma del padre" (46; Franco is imbued from head to toe with the signature of the father), and, following his death, Spaniards confronted something that they had never expected: Franco's legacy (37). The dictator's absence produced, according to Vilarós, withdrawal symptoms, revealing that Spaniards had become *addicted* to the regime's repressive and totalitarian structure (45). In *Exorcismos de la memoria* (Memory Exorcisms), Alberto Medina relates Franco's death to the death of the father of the horde as described in Freud's *Totem and Taboo* (53). For her part, Cristina Moreiras Menor highlights Franco's death as a starting point for Spaniards to express and represent other identities in which diversity and difference could take place (*Cultura* 149). When Spaniards constructed these new identities, however, the figure of the dictator as a father remained a ghost, a spectral presence not completely buried (150). In *La estela del tiempo* (*The Wake of Time*), Moreiras Menor reiterates how the Francoist apparatus continued under the authority of King Juan Carlos (120). In *Tramas, libros, nombres* (*Plots, Books, Names*) José-Carlos Mainer explains that "[l]a estructura familiar, hecha de silencios y chantajes, parecía ser, en 1975, la metáfora por excelencia del gran círculo concéntrico que el franquismo trazaba alrededor de treinta millones de españoles en minoridad forzosa" (75; the family unit, composed of silences and bribes, seemed to be, in 1975, the metaphor par excellence of the great concentric circle that the Franco regime drew around thirty million Spaniards in a forced minority). Mainer points out how, in this context, David Cooper's *The Death of the Family* (1971) was an influential book for the generation that grew up under the dictatorship, a generation that tried to cast out the phantasms of authoritarianism, capitalism, Franco, their educators, fathers and partners, and even sons and daughters. For this generation, all of these elements were part of the same chain (Mainer 300).

There are numerous cultural representations from Spain in which the family can be read allegorically as the country and the father as an allegorical representation of the dictator or as his shadow, particularly after Franco's death. José Carlos Mainer points to Carlos Sahagún's *Primer y último oficio* (1979; First and Last Purpose), Manuel Vázquez Montalbán's poetry, or Ramón Irigoyen's *Cielos e inviernos* (1979; Skies and Winters) and *Los abanicos del Caudillo* (1982; The Caudillo's Ranges) as examples in which we see the son's rebellion against a castrating father who is associated with Franco (73–4). Vilarós eloquently explores the Oedipal tension in the newspaper articles and autobiographies of Juan Goytisolo, Jaime Gil de Biedma's poems in *Las personas del verbo* (1975; The Subjects of the Verb), Francisco Regueiro's *Madregilda* (1993), and Gabriel Ferrater's poetry (see Vilarós 27, 32, and 57). Other examples are Saura's films: *El jardín de las delicias* (1970; The Garden of Delights), *Ana y los lobos* (1972; Ana and the Wolves), *La prima Angélica* (1973; Cousin Angélica), *Elisa, vida mía* (1977; Elisa, My Love), and *Deprisa, deprisa* (1980; Hurry, Hurry). All feature authoritarian, weak, or non-existent father figures that can be interpreted as references to the dictator and that attest to the underlying influence of Freudian imagery in the works of the director. *Cría cuervos* (1976; Breeding Ravens) is probably the movie that most clearly states this affinity between the father and Franco: In the film the protagonist, Ana, repeatedly expresses her desire to kill her father, a general on the Nationalist side. The references to two Anas (the child and the adult) and Jeannette's song "Porque te vas" (Because You Leave) associate the protagonist with a generation ready to see authoritarianism and censorship fade away. Ana María Moix's *Julia* (1970), Víctor Érice's *El espíritu de la colmena* (1973; The Spirit of the Beehive), José Luis Borau's *Furtivos* (1975; Poachers), Francisco Regueiro's movie *Padre nuestro* (1985; Our Father), and Adelaida García Morales's *El Sur* (1983; South), which inspired the movie by Érice with the same title, are other examples of films and texts in which the preservation of familial unity, authoritarianism, silence, or fratricidal violence turn out to be "metáforas de una sociedad convalesciente de largos años de autoridad, minoridad moral e hipocresía" (Mainer 68; metaphors for a society convalescing from many years of authority, moral minority and hypocrisy).[2] Thus, in the cinema and literature produced at the very end of the dictatorship and after Franco's death, family dynamics and the relationship between sons or daughters and paternal figures often appear shaped by the dictatorship. The generational tensions transmit a sense of incarceration, repetition, or fracture between new and old cultural frames.

Jaime Chávarri's film *El desencanto* (Disillusionment), released in 1976, is one of the most-discussed examples in this regard: The film exemplifies the importance of the deceased father as well as how academics diverged on how to read the cultural production of the transition. In this documentary about the dead Falangist poet Leopoldo Panero, both his wife Felicidad Blanc and his sons speak about the poet as husband and father. Vilarós considers the film to be "uno de los textos más fuertemente edípicos en la muy edípica narrativa española" (47; one of the most strongly Oedipal texts in the very Oedipal Spanish narrative) and points out how intergenerational dialogues are characteristic of the historical moment of the transition (42). Moreiras Menor reads the father in *El desencanto* as an "absence" that becomes structural in order for self-reflection to take place (*La estela* 126) and points out the correlation between the two movies about Panero (*El desencanto* and *Después de tantos años* – the last one released in 1994 and directed by Ricardo Franco) and the historical moment: "Aunque ni *El desencanto* ni *Después de tantos años* son documentales sobre la historia en general o sobre el franquismo y la Transición en particular, la historia de estos 'momentos históricos' es parte central de su puesta en escena" (*La estela* 147; Even though neither *El desencanto* nor *Después de tantos años* (After So Many Years) are documentaries on history in general or on the Franco regime and the Transition in particular, the history of these "historical times" is a central part of the mise-en-scène). Moreiras Menor notes reoccurring elements in the two movies, "[m]emoria, huellas, ruina, transición de generación a generación, narrativas derrotadas de una promesa (que da lugar a un duelo imposible, el de Michi, empeñado en traer los fantasmas al centro; a una melancolía paralizante, la de Juan Luis)" (147; memory, traces, ruin, transition from generation to generation, defeated narratives of a promise (which leads to an impossible mourning, that of Michi, who is determined to bring ghosts to the centre; a paralysing melancholy, that of Juan Luis)). Defined both by mourning and paralyzing melancholy, the movie is interpreted as a work of art that clings to Spain's past.

Other critics take exception to the allegorical reading of the father as Franco and his legacy when looking at *El desencanto*. Jo Labanyi has argued that "Convertir al poeta Leopoldo Panero, muerto en 1962, en símbolo de Franco como gran padre muerto es hacer caso omiso de la cronología" ("Los fantasmas" 74; To convert the poet Leopoldo Panero, who died in 1962, into a symbol of Franco as the great deceased father is to entirely ignore chronology). In her interpretation, where she highlights the importance of the son – the writer Leopoldo María Panero and the wife, Felicidad Blanc, also a writer, Labanyi warns of the dangers of doing a "national psychoanalysis of Spain" (77), particularly when looking at the transition to democracy: "¿A qué deseo obedece esta tendencia reiterada a explicar la Transición – e incluso los años posteriores de una democracia plenamente asumida – en términos de un mono, una melancolía, un trauma ocasionado por la muerte del Padre?" (82; To what desire can we attribute this repeated tendency to explain the Transition – including the later years of a fully adopted democracy – in terms of withdrawal symptoms, depression, a trauma brought on by the death of the Father?). Juan Egea is also critical, stating, "[l]as narrativas edípicas son ciertamente frecuentes en la producción cultural del franquismo y de la transición; pero el acercamiento edípico a la cultura de la posguerra y la transición es igual de frecuente y, a estas alturas, hasta hegemónico" (85; Oedipal narratives definitely occur frequently in the cultural production of the Franco regime and the transition; but the Oedipal approach to postwar culture and the transition is just as frequent and, at this point, even hegemonic). Egea claims the need to end what he calls an "omni-explanatory model" of reading Spain's Oedipal narratives (80, 85) and urges readers to "ocuparse de la figura del padre como algo más y algo menos que el trasunto simbólico del dictador" (79; to concern themselves with the figure of the father as something more and something less than the symbolic representation of the dictator). Similarly, in *Anatomía del desencanto* (Anatomy of Disillusionment), Santiago Morales Rivera considers the symbolism of the dead father to be "un simbolismo sobredeterminado" (22; an overdetermined symbolism): "O, dicho en otras palabras, el duelo irresuelto por la muerte de Franco se ha erigido en la alegoría más repetida en España para explicar la perplejidad que experimenta ese país conforme termina el siglo XX" (22; Or, in other words, the unresolved mourning for the death of Franco has become the most often repeated allegory in Spain to explain the bewilderment that this country is experiencing at the end of the twentieth century). Morales Rivera questions the use of psychoanalytical terms such as addiction, trauma, repression, mourning, and melancholia to interpret the cultural production of Spain post-dictatorship (69) and adds that "a los ojos de buena parte de los hispanistas la ficción española de los últimos cuarenta años se transformará en un *historial clínico* de la depresión experimentada por la sociedad española tras morirse el dictador" (72–3; in the minds of a good number of Hispanists, Spanish fiction of the last forty years will become a case study of the depression experienced by Spanish society after the death of the dictator). In a similar vein, although he is not specifically speaking of *El desencanto*, Ángel Loureiro criticizes the use of psychoanalytical terminology when interpreting Spain's contemporary culture, in which the past "haunt[s] Spanish politics and society in various ways, resulting in a pervasive malaise in Spanish culture that is diagnosed with predictable monotony – trauma, melancholy, the return of the repressed, a tumour, an open wound" ("Pathetic Arguments" 225). Indeed, we can look at Leopoldo Panero, whose literary works were at the service of the Francoist regime, as an authoritarian father under the authoritarian rule of Franco, but there are other readings of *El desencanto*: Both in *El desencanto* and in *Después de tantos años* (1994), undoing the paternal legacy translates into a form of artistic productivity and a web of materials where fatherhood appears in layers. In these films but also in Leopoldo María Panero's texts *El lugar del hijo* (2000; The Place of the Son) and *Papá, dame la mano que tengo miedo* (2007; Papa, Give me your hand, I'm scared), we are presented with a family of writers for whom literature is an inescapable present reality and one deeply connected to family.

Bilingual Legacies offers another consideration to the omni-explanatory model already criticized by Egea to show what happens when one approaches "la figura del padre como algo más y algo menos que el trasunto simbólico del dictador" (79; the figure of the father as something more and something less than the symbolic representation of the dictator). My study provides a way to understand paternity in Spain beyond the shadow of the dictator, as a crucial link in the chain of generational change and in the processes of loss, inheritance, and legitimacy of other languages and cultures within the country as well as the transformation of gender identities and gender models during the transition to democracy. The psychoanalytical framework continues to be important – given that it is a framework that influenced these four authors – but not binding: The four authors I study were part of Barcelona's intellectual elite, and, by the time they started publishing their autobiographies in the late 1970s and until 2005, they were acquainted with psychoanalytical precepts and may even had considered them as somehow outdated. In fact, my reading of the primary texts notes how a psychoanalytical framework (particularly the Freudian) can fall short on many occasions and is purposively subverted in these authors' writings. In this regard, one needs to mention that psychoanalysis had a dissimilar impact in Spain during the twentieth century, being, as Federico Allodi points out, directly related to one's particular sociocultural context.[3] Francoism was opposed to psychoanalytical precepts that stress the importance of the subconscious and sexuality and that criticize religion, family, and tradition.[4] The church was also pivotal when articulating a criticism against psychoanalysis.[5] The only Spaniards brought up after the Civil War who knew Freud's work were those able to travel outside of Spain (for instance, Goytisolo) or who could get a hold of banned books. As Jordi Gracia and Domingo Ródenas point out, Freud's texts were not common reading in Spain, "dada la fobia católica por el análisis del inconsciente o más genéricamente las pulsiones y recovecos irracionales (por definición inmorales en términos normativos y doctrinales)" (*Historia* 184; given the Catholic phobia of analysis of the subconscious or, more generically, the irrational impulses and depths (by definition immoral in legal and theoretical terms)). That said, the psychoanalytical framework is useful when interpreting texts published after 1975 that, indeed, were influenced by psychoanalysis and making allusions to this framework, often in a deliberate and critical way.

The works studied attest that the Oedipal triangle is often at play but that it is also insufficient to understand the complexity of the father–son and father–daughter relationship as it appears in self writings. Sigmund Freud stressed the importance of the father in terms of rules, ambivalent feelings, castration, and gender identification. In *Totem and Taboo*, Freud talks about the father of the horde, an all-powerful figure whom sons finally kill. The murder of this father is followed by the emotion of guilt, the rise of brotherhood, and the creation of social rules and totems. The death of the primal father is necessary to create fraternity and community. In *The Ego and the Id* and in *Civilization and its Discontents*, Freud speaks of another father, the one situated in the Oedipal process. Although the father within the Oedipus complex is not opposed to the one in *Totem*, as both are related to guilt and are woven into the norms of civilization, Freud links this father of the Oedipal process with the *superego*, the punitive internal structure that establishes limits and controls the instinctual drives of the "Id."[6] According to Freud, the Oedipal process structures the self, as it is the process through which the *superego* is enforced and thus is how the subject incorporates authority. The *superego* performs the paternal function within the subject's psyche through internal guilt, fear of external authority, self-regulation, and self-control. It is through the Oedipus complex that Freud explains how gender identity is formed: The father steps between mother and child, prohibiting the child's taking the mother as an object of desire. The father thereby inspires rivalry in the child; the child wants to eliminate the father, but, because of this thought, the son feels guilty. The Oedipus complex is dissolved when the child accepts the father's prohibition: The son infers that one day he will take the father's place. In the case of the daughter, she needs to accept, not without feeling envious and frustrated, that she is castrated in a double sense – physically because she discovers that she lacks a penis and symbolically because she will never inherit the father's place.[7] The result of the first identification establishes the ambivalence towards the father that remains – sometimes repressed – in adulthood, in which the feelings of imitation, admiration, and veneration are fated to change into despair, guilt, and resentment.

In Goytisolo's autobiographies, for instance, we see the explicit use of Freudian terminology and concepts – pulsion, repressions, and instincts – but also a narration where the space, the body of the father, the autobiographer's sexuality, and the revision of the relationship with the father after his death are all essential in creating a writing subject. For his part, Terenci Moix subverts Freudian precepts to demystify and mock the father, particularly through his body. In Barral's *Memorias*, we find descriptions of a desired, nonpatriarchal father,[8] closer to what Julia Kristeva proposes in *Tales of Love*: An imaginary father and a fusion between the father and the mother that is also a response to the Freudian or Lacanian father as bearer of the law. In Clara Janés's case, the father is a figure that the daughter looks upon with fascination (and that is presented as fundamental to establishing heterosexuality and a feminine identity), but notions such as "castration anxiety" would reduce the ways in which Janés becomes conscious of her literary authority and the place of the father and his death in this process. The case of Janés also highlights the intricate relationship between feminism and fatherhood: Feminist scholars critique the notion that paternal prohibitions give coherence to culture against the instinctual gratifications of the mother-child.[9] Some feminists have questioned how in psychoanalysis the father is a signifier of patriarchal authority, the law that defines one's place in culture and women's place as subordinate to men, as the father has been tied to law, culture, language, responsibility, and sacrifice and imagined as the one who ensures processes of inheritance, legitimacy, and lineage; transmits his surname; and maintains kinship structures.[10] Indeed, according to Lacan, following Freud, the father breaks the primary dyad between mother and child. The baby believes that he or she is one with the mother, a figure who fulfils all of the child's desires and necessities. The father interrupts this union by introducing the third element, differentiation, the signifier, the Phallus, incest, prohibition, and, consequently, desire. For Lacan, the father introduces the child to the world of language and meaning. Through his Name and his Law, the father makes possible the separation between the child and the maternal body and gives the child the possibility of developing both a physical and a psychic ego. Accordingly, Lacan sees the father as liberating the child (from the mother) and as crucial in the connection between the subject and the acceptance of social norms and institutions.[11] While Lacan considers the father to be the one who gives access to the world of language to the child, philosophers such as Luce Irigaray answer this by stating that the father castrates the desire for/of the mother: "Desire for her, her desire, that is what is forbidden by the law of the father, of all fathers: fathers of families, fathers of nations, religious fathers, professor-fathers, doctor-fathers, lover-fathers, etc. Moral or immoral, they always intervene to censure or to repress, the desire of/for the mother" (36). For her part, in *Revolution in Poetic Language*, Kristeva proposes the "semiotic" as the prelinguistic and pre-Oedipal drives, rhythms, and tones that come before the world of signifiers. With the semiotic, Kristeva questions the symbolic paternal power and proposes that the advent of language is not purely founded in the rupture with the mother, thus questioning Lacan's irrevocable union between father and language. In *Revolution*, Kristeva offers the concepts of the "semiotic *chora*" as a maternal space where the subject has contact with the mother's regulations, a law before the law (see Oliver, *Reading Kristeva*, 46–7). As Ramírez-Christensen explains, the father is an "ubiquitous reference point in the narratives of desire" (7); he is also defined as the signifier of satisfaction and guarantor of meaning in the symbolic order (Copeland 6, 7). Feminist critics call into question the way in which the father is associated with progress and civilization while women and mothers apparently destroy this order. In *Sovereign Masculinity*, Bonnie Mann similarly points to the link between fatherhood and sovereignty, writing that "the figure of the father is a figure of sovereignty, whether hard and punitive or benevolent, that evokes certain forms of awe. The fathered child is in the frame, is whole. The unfathered child has a hole in his soul, an open, irreparable wound" (161–2).

The relationship between fathers and sons and fathers and daughters on the one hand and feminism and patriarchy on the other speaks to the great complexity of gender construction as well as to the variety of individual cases and how are they reflected in autobiographical works. Clara Janés illustrates not only how women relate to the autobiographical genre as interlopers (to use Sidonie Smith's word) but also that how they account on fatherhood often differs from the way in which the paternal figure is seen by men. Janés's work, in this regard, connects with other seminal texts as well films of contemporary Spain where the daughter–father bond is explored, such as Adelaida García Morales's short novel *El sur* (1985; The South) where the father's and the daughter's access to knowledge are interconnected or Carlos Saura's *Elisa, vida mía* (1977; Elisa, My Life), which explores fatherhood and the Spanish literary canon as interwoven. In Catalan, Teresa Pàmies's *Testament a Praga* (1971; Testament in Prague) merges historical memory with filial responsibility and betrayal as the protagonist, Terensa Pàmies, is given a tape where her father explains his memories of the war and exile, a tape that she transcribes, often changing the father's memory by intercalating her own thoughts and disagreements.[12]

One of the clearest examples of how the primary texts do not always match with psychoanalytical theories on the father is the issue of the representation of bodies. The fathers' bodies are of primary importance in the four authors' descriptions, and these bodies are neither abstract nor absent but, on the contrary, present even after the father's death. The father's physical absence, as Jane Gallop points out in *The Father's Seduction*, is bound to his power to legislate and is aligned with the binary between body and mind that places women in relation to the body. Gallop states that "[b]y giving up their bodies, men gain power – the power to theorize, to represent themselves, to exchange women, to reproduce themselves and mark their offspring with their name. All of these activities ignore bodily pleasure in pursuit of representation, reproduction, production" (67). André Green explains that the idealized father is "une entité de pouvoir illimité, tyrannique, ignorant la frustration, protecteur" (11; a being of unlimited power, tyrannical, unaware of frustration, a protector).[13] Psychoanalyst Simone Korff differentiates between "Dieu le père et les pères terrestres" (282; God the Father and earthly fathers) by citing Benveniste's dictionary on Indo-European institutions; she explains, as does Borneman's previous quotation, that "le mot *pater* est la qualification permanente de Dieu et en renvoie jamais à une paternité physique, le père qui élève l'enfant le père nourricier étant désigné en latin archaïque par la terme atta" (282; the word *pater* is the perpetual qualification of God, and never refers to physical paternity; the father who raises the child, the foster father, was designated in archaic Latin by the term atta). Conceived as a "structural absence" (Con Davis 7) or a vertical presence (Mékouar 35), this abstract father tied to a deity is also a place in our consciousness, an idea that supports religious and political institutions by stressing hierarchies within each of them. Kelly Oliver highlights in *Family Values* that the father is present as an abstraction in the Western imagination, and his absent body turns him into the representative of abstract authority. For Oliver, this absent father is essential to our image of paternity, as this absence permits him to be associated with the law and authority (4–5). Certainly, the father's lack of physical presence contrasts with the way in which mothers are permeated with bodily issues; as Andrew Parker explains in *The Theorist's Mother*, following Freud, the term "materia" derives from "mother" (19). This physical absence of the father is in fact a paradox, given that it is precisely the strength that comes from the body that gives power to men. This is only one example of what psychoanalyst Silvia Tubert calls the "radical asymmetry" (9) between conceptions of fatherhood and motherhood in her introduction to *Figuras del padre* (The Father Figures), where she points out that motherhood and fatherhood need to be studied as complementary concepts that change together. In contrast, the paternal body is indispensable in these four authors' descriptions of the father: The sick body of Juan Goytisolo's father, the paternal body mocked by Terenci Moix, or the destroyed body of Clara Janés's father are examples that attest that, like the maternal body, the paternal body is, in its concrete and corporeal aspects, fundamental for the self.

That said, the body of the father is directly linked to the authority of the autobiographer over his/her life and over the text. In *The Madwoman in the Attic*, Sandra Gilbert and Susan Gubar consider that it is precisely the lack of certainty about the father's paternity that produces storytelling, interlinking paternity, language, and sexism: "A man cannot verify his fatherhood by either sense or reason, after all; that his child is his is in a sense a tale he tells himself to explain the infant's existence. Obviously, the anxiety implicit in such storytelling urgently needs not only the reassurances of male superiority that patriarchal misogyny implies" (5). In this context, paternity has been imagined as founded on a physical void, on a fear of lack of evidence. Levinas speaks about fatherhood within his conception of subjectivity and ethics in *Totality and Infinity* (1961) and *Otherwise than Being* (1974) and notes that the relationship between the father and the son demonstrates the responsibility and ethical dimensions of the subject. However, as Lisa Guenther points out in her critique of Levinas, "The father alone cannot engender the child; this is part of what distinguishes the child from a work of art or the product of a single author. Without the feminine beloved, the transubstantiation of the self in paternal fecundity could not take place" (84). This lack of certainty is quickly changing through scientific development. As Janet Carsten has observed in *After Kinship*, the introduction of "fertility treatments, genetic testing, posthumous conception, cloning, and the mapping of the human genome" (7) will radically change how paternity is imagined. In fact, the evolution of scientific treatments regarding issues around paternity go hand-in-hand with a change in the notion of paternity as a form of power and in the enforcement of gender divisions. That said, the authors studied in this book demonstrate that the father's body is paramount for the self to position itself vis-à-vis the father: The descriptions of the paternal body reveal themselves to be essential points for these four authors in acquiring a consciousness as writers. This could be considered a way of advocating a change with respect to fatherhood – still not the radical change indicated by Carsten but indeed prefiguring the appearance of a more "involved" form of paternity.[14]

Oedipus in Self Writings

The ten primary works of my study – that is, Barral's *Años de penitencia* (1975; Years of Penitence), *Los años sin excusa* (1978; Years without Excuse), and *Cuando las horas veloces* (1988; When Time Is Fleeting); Goytisolo's *Coto vedado* (1985) and *En los reinos de Taifa* (1986); Terenci Moix's *El cine de los sábados* (1990; Saturday's Movies), *El beso de Peter Pan* (1993; Peter Pan's Kiss), and *Extraño en el paraiso* (1998; Stranger in Paradise); and Clara Janés's *Jardín y laberinto* (1990; Garden and Labyrinth) and *La voz de Ofelia* (2005; Ophelia's Voice) – were published as "memorias" or "autobiografías" either when they were printed or reprinted and/or follow Philippe Lejeune's definition of the autobiography, "the retrospective narrative in prose that someone makes of his own existence when he puts the principal accent upon his life" (Smith and Watson 1).[15] In all of them, the protagonists coincide in name, major life trajectory, and personal experiences with the author. That said, in addition to autobiography or memoir,[16] I also use the terms *self-writing* (popularized by Michael Foucault)[17] and *autobiographical text* when referring these texts as well as to others that have a clear autobiographical component – including poetry, novels, essays, articles in the press, and self-fictions.[18] I privilege the theories of what Sidonie Smith calls the second wave of autobiographical studies, particularly the arguments of George Gusdorf, Philippe Lejeune, and Paul de Man, and of the third wave, such as Thomas Couser, as well as works by feminist scholars such as Smith herself, Laura Marcus, and Julia Watson. Smith and Watson differentiate three waves in the history of autobiographical theory: German philologist Georg Misch inaugurated the first wave of modern criticism of the field with his book *Geschichte der Autobiographie* (1907; History of the Autobiography), a wave that understood autobiography as the narratives of "great men" (198) and in which "public figures are the 'representative' and appropriate subjects of what he designates as autobiography" (195). In contrast, "second-wave critics brought a new understanding of the autobiographical subject, involving new understandings of the key concepts of self and truth" (200). Influenced by Marxism, psychoanalysis, and structuralism, second-wave critics such as Gusdorf emphasized "the creative aspect of autobiographical writing. It is for him 'art' rather than 'history'" (202). These critics, accordingly, discussed issues of referentiality, fictionality, and truth telling. In the 1980s and 1990s, feminist scholars of autobiography privileged forms of life narration that do not necessarily conform with or that question the strict definitions of the autobiographical subject and genre described by Gusdorf, Lejeune, or de Man, opening the way for the third wave of autobiographical criticism, which has emerged since the 1990s. This third wave has "relationality"[19] as a privileged term (215) and considers forms of life writing where a model of selfhood that is interdependent is at the centre, contrasting with the autonomous individual privileged in the first and second waves. In addition to terms that are more encompassing of other, non-Western literary traditions, such as *life narrative* and *life writing*, another designation has also appeared in this context: *Auto/biography*, which marks out the difficult and not always clear boundaries between the biographical and the autobiographical.

When looking at father figures in the autobiographical works studied, the distinctions between Franco as a symbolic, authoritarian father and biological fathers in the shadow of the dictator take on a different dimension. Lejeune coined the concept of the "autobiographical pact," one of the most fruitful concepts within autobiographical studies as it involves problematic ideas of truth and referentiality. The "autobiographical pact" complicates a strictly allegorical and metaphorical reading of the family as Spain and of the father as a metaphor for the dictator. According to Lejeune, "the autobiographical pact is a form of contract between author and reader in which the autobiographer explicitly commits himself or herself … to the sincere effort to come to terms with and to understand his or her own life" (in Eakin "Foreword" ix). This "pact" forces us to consider what the implications of writing and reading are when we are aware of the father as a referent who presumably existed and who is distinguished from the dictator. Autobiographies compel us to think on levels other than those on which the intersection of father of the nation and real father operate:[20] Franco and the biological father in all these texts are two different figures, and in fact the biological father is always one of the protagonists of these texts, while Franco, an influential figure for obvious but for very different reasons, rarely appears in them in the complexity with which the real father is described.

Fathers and paternal presences tend to be axial in autobiographical writings: Sidonie Smith links the autobiographical genre to individuality, masculinity, and fatherhood in *A Poetics of Women's Autobiography* (1987) and defines autobiography as a process through which the autobiographer struggles to shape an "identity" out of amorphous subjectivity. Influenced by Lacanian precepts, Smith considers that this identity "does not exist outside language" (5), something that we will see as recurring and present in the works of the authors studied. Coinciding with Laura Marcus and Shari Benstock,[21] Smith points out that traditional autobiographical writing not only "privileges the autonomous or metaphysical self as the agent of its own achievement" and promotes "a conception of the human being that valorizes individual integrity and separateness and devalues personal and communal interdependence" (39) but also inscribes the subject into the phallic realm of power inhabited and valued by men into a linguistic economy and order that, according to Lacan, is ultimately paternal (38–9). To Smith, autobiography has enforced a masculinist image of the self, a masculine tradition, a masculine genealogy, and paternal lines, thus asserting the primacy of patrilineal descent and androcentric discourse. In autobiographical writing, "the boy comes to speak with the authority of the father and all fathers before him, those figures of public power who control the discourse and its economy of self-hood, the male experience is identified as the normative human paradigm" (Smith 12) while at the same time "the father legitimizes the authority of the autobiographer as he gives the name to the child" (40). Indeed, Lejeune's "autobiographical pact" emphasizes ideas of legitimacy, filiation, and origins while also having an "ambition of legality" (Catelli 278) and can be linked to Lacanian ideas of the Name of the Father and the Law of the Father: Through their surnames, the name of the father, autobiographers affirm their commitment to relating the truth in their writings. In addition, autobiography, being the genre that turns the private into the public, reinforces ideas of literary authority (see Benstock 5) and of the writer as an authorial figure. The father's surname gives the subject what

Legendre calls a "genealogic inscription" necessary for taking part in society (see Mékouar 38) and allows what Lejeune calls the "autobiographical pact" to take place. Smith discusses the difficult position of women in autobiographical writing: When women engage in the autobiographical, they do so as interlopers (51). The female autobiographer "raises herself to the symbolic stature of her father" (52)[22] and opts for the scenario of public achievement and authority to write about herself (52); she needs to insert herself into a realm of men, into public space, reproducing the myth of paternal origins and the narratives it underwrites (53). Within this context, she becomes involved in a dynamic dialogue between two stories, two interpretations, and two rhetorical postures (57): The feminine and the masculine, as well as the paternal and the maternal, something that is evident in the case of Janés's *Jardín*, a text that, following Hélène Cixous's term, demonstrates an inseparable relationship between the self and the parents, turning the text into a *biografille*.[23]

In many ways, the autobiographer is an Oedipal subject: Autobiographers revisit their models while positioning themselves in a genealogy and constructing bonds of filiation and affiliation. That said, the autobiographer also tries to overcome the Oedipal and the familial in order to establish the self since, as Gusdorf affirms, autobiography is the mirror in which the individual reflects his own image (32).[24] In *The Ethics of Autobiography*, Ángel Loureiro explores how Juan Goytisolo tries to erect a new superego that competes with the paternal figure, while at the same time the autobiographical self is involved in self-judgment, auto-control, and confessions (120). Loureiro not only speaks of autobiography as an act of self-creation (1), but he also argues that – in Goytiosolo's autobiography – there is a process of "self-fathering" (113). This is visible in the works of Barral and Moix as well: In their autobiographical writings, the (male) autobiographer gives birth to the self and is consequently a father to himself. In the case of Clara Janés writing becomes a somehow contradictory an act of both fathering (assuming the father's place) and mothering (giving birth and creating from as a woman). Autobiographies often enact a stage of the Oedipal drama, but they also rewrite this Oedipal drama through a literary occupying of the place of the father. The autobiographer can then be interpreted as the one who blurs the limits between the Oedipal and the Narcissistic, intercalating both a *superego* and an *ego ideal*. Jessica Benjamin, following Freud, considers that the superego is the heir of the Oedipus complex, while the ego ideal is the heir of our narcissism (*The Bonds* 148). Benjamin points out that it is the father who, according to psychoanalysis, protects the subject from a mother who would pull him back to what Freud called the "limitless narcissism" of infancy (138). Accordingly, while the Oedipal self is subjected to the boundaries and limits of the father, the narcissistic self represents in its plenitude the pre-Oedipal bond with the mother (143). Narcissus represents a self-involvement and denial of reality that is opposed to the Oedipal subject's responsibility and guilt (135),[25] and yet the autobiographer often fluctuates between them, between the paternal and maternal, between Oedipus and Narcissus

The third wave of autobiographical studies also offers compelling ideas of the close links between self-writing and paternity. In a 2005 article entitled "Genre Matters: Form, Force, and Filiation," G. Thomas Couser coined the term "narratives of filiation" when talking about "memoirs of fathers produced during the last twenty years in North America" (148). For Couser, the term filiation is defined as follows: "First, it refers to 'the condition or fact of being the child [not necessarily the son, though the root is the Latin *filius*, son] of a particular parent' (not necessarily a father); second, in law, it refers to 'judical determination of paternity' (*American Heritage Dictionary*)" (151). Couser stresses in his article how, "By calling the texts in question narratives of filiation, rather than merely memoirs of fathers, I seek to highlight their relationality, their rootedness in a sense of entitlement and their intent to enact some kind of engagement with the father, whether living or dead" (151). Couser takes as an object of study a series of texts that certainly differ from the ones I have chosen: While the texts I analyse have the father as an important figure, they cannot be considered to be strictly memoirs of fathers or indeed narratives of filiation following Couser's definition, given that their principal themes are not limited to those to do with the father figure. Yet the notion of narratives of filiation, as Couser understands them, is clearly present in my primary texts: For Couser, this concept signals "the impulse to claim a filial relationship" (151). If "the umbrella term 'memoirs of fathers' accurately names what these narratives are," "the term 'narratives of filiation' gets at what most of them seem to be trying to *do*" (152). Couser does not hide that the genre has obvious roots in patriarchy (152), but he also acknowledges the importance of mothers, who sometimes are more present and prominent than the fathers in the texts (152). In Couser's theory filiation is understood as an impulse that produces the act of writing, a kind of force that destabilizes the unitary subject to evidence instead the subject's relationality. Couser describes this impulse as taking place in two directions, that is, *affiliative* and *disaffiliative* impulses (154). The first, as Rocío G. Davis further explains, could be considered as "the author's awareness of a responsibility to complete their father's unfulfilled dream of literary publication" (229) as well as how "Daughters and sons often write about their fathers in an attempt to discover or learn about a person who was either largely physically or psychologically absent or whose presence was so overwhelming that the autobiographical act becomes an attempt to control the influence of that person on the author's life" (231). In contrast to this impulse, Couser defines the narratives of disaffiliation as "narratives in which the authors accuse their (usually deceased) fathers of wrong-doing against others" (154) and in which "they feel that their testimony has particular authority (significantly, not just in cases in which they were directly victimized)" (154). As I will elaborate throughout the next chapters, in my primary texts these two impulses are not at odds with one another but on the contrary coexist.

The father is a figure that all four authors studied tackle in depth in their autobiographies, but glimpses of him also appear in some of the other literary projects by these authors. There is thus a permeability between autobiographical texts and other texts with certain self-referentiality such as letters, newspaper articles, poems, and self-fictional novels. Autobiographies demonstrate how the father is an ineluctable figure in this genre but by no means exclusive to it. As Xavier Pla, when examining the works of Josep Pla, contends:

> Tot escriptor s'expressa sempre a partir d'ell mateix. Tota escriptura és una escriptura del "jo", construïda sobre el "jo" i a partir del "jo". L'única diferència es troba aleshores en el fet que alguns textos de ficció es presenten com a explícitament autobiogràfics (…). Altres textos de ficció són implícitament autobiogràfics en el sentit que tot escriptor, quan fa la literatura, parla de si mateix. Tot escriptor es basa en el que ha vist, en el que ha llegit, en el que ha sentit, en el que ha pensat, en el que ha desitjat o en el que ha imaginat. (454)

> Every writer expresses himself beginning with himself. All writing is a writing of the "I", built on the "I", and starting from the "I". The only difference then lies in the fact that some fictional texts are presented as explicitly autobiographical (…). Other fictional texts are implicitly autobiographical in the sense that every writer, when he makes literature, speaks of himself. Every writer is formed by what he has seen, what he has read, what he has felt, what he has thought, what he has desired or what he has imagined.

It is then impossible to read the autobiographies of these authors as isolated, as they belong to a family of texts. For instance, in the case of Goytisolo, notions of paternity appear not only in *Coto Vedado* and *En los reinos de Taifa* but also in his trilogy on Álvaro Mendiola (*Señas de identidad*/Marks of Identity, *Don Julián*/Count Julian and *Juan sin Tierra*/ Juan the Landless) and other texts. Furthermore, father figures in Juan Goytisolo's autobiographies also resemble the vision of paternity in some of Luis Goytisolo's writings, such as the novel *Antagonía*. Juan Goytisolo and his family history appear in some self-fictional works by Monique Lange, Juan Goytisolo's wife, such as *Les cabines de bain* (1983, Bathroom Stalls), and he is considered as a father in *Fille de* (2011; Daughter of), a memoir that Monique Lange's daughter, Carole Achache, wrote about her mother. In many ways, the figure of the father in Ana María Moix's book *Julia* (1970) can also be interpreted vis-à-vis Terenci Moix's reflections on the familial and the father in *El dia* or in his *Memorias*. In all three literary projects, we see the traumatic death of a young brother, and in the case of *Julia* the father figure is seen as a weak, hated, and despised character, with some characteristics of the father figure in Terenci Moix's *Memorias*.

These relationships show yet another layer in the connection between reality and literary projects: That the life experience of an author and his or her blood, family, and human ties are often present in his or her writings in different levels, as Xavier Pla points out. Ultimately, the authors studied in this book push the limits of (non)fiction writing in ways that lead their autobiographies often to spill over into their other creative work, while at the same time both their writings and their lives affect other authors' lives and texts, closely interlinking fiction and truth. Even when the texts studied conform for the most part to the definition of the autobiographical genre, these texts also question the genre to different degrees. This subversion is often a way to play with and thus ratify the genre, more than a form of not-belonging. A last consideration is how these texts are part of the boom of autobiographical writing that took place after Francoism, preceded by memoirs and autobiographies of those exiled after the Spanish Civil War but also followed by a growing number of self-fictions (or autofictions) that deliberately play with the autobiographical pact as one of (un)truth.[26]

Linguistic Filiations

The four authors studied here were raised during a period in which Catalan was forbidden in the public sphere, and Spanish was the official language of education and culture. Catalan remained in the household, linked to the familial and the popular: People continued to use it in the streets and at home, and it was sometimes taught, albeit extraofficially. The early years of the regime were the most punitive, and the history of publishing in Catalan is revealing in this regard: Until the first half of the 1940s, it was prohibited to publish in Catalan, and after that the number of books published in Catalan was small, as Heinemann explains, "El 1944 es publicaren 5 llibres en llengua catalana i el 1955 se n'editaren 43, nombre encara molt minso, especialment si es té en compte que el 1933 ja se n'havien publicat 740, i que el nombre de títols en català ascendia l'any 1936 a 865" (31; In 1944, five books in Catalan were published and in 1955, 43 were published, still a very small number especially if we take into account that in 1933, 740 books were published and that the number of titles in Catalan in 1936 reached 865). During the sixties, more books in Catalan were published "El 1960 es publicaren 183 llibres en català, el 1962 en foren 270 i el 1966 el nombre ja ascendia a 548" (21; In 1960, 183 books were published in Catalan, in 1962 there were 270 and in 1966 the number increased to 548).[27] It is not surprising, then, that the four authors studied here, like many others born in Catalonia and educated in an educational system that favoured Spanish – such as Jaime Gil de Biedma (1929–90); the brothers of Juan Goytisolo, José Agustín Goytisolo (1928–99), and Luis Goytisolo (1935); Juan Marsé (1933); Esther Tusquets (1936–2012); Manuel Vázquez Montalbán (1939–2003); Eduardo Mendoza (1943–); Maruja Torres (1943–); Ana María Moix (1947–2014); and Enrique Vila-Matas (1948–)[28] – chose Spanish as their literary language when they started to write. Other writers born in a similar period, such as Josep Maria Castellet (1926–2014), Pere Gimferrer (1945), or Terenci Moix himself, alternated between Spanish and Catalan.[29] These alternations took place in unique ways for each author: For instance, Teresa Pàmies (1919) published mostly in Catalan but also wrote some works in Spanish, and the poet Joan Margarit (1938) wrote first in Spanish to then switch to Catalan in the 1980s. Of course there were authors who had been educated either before the war or during the dictatorship who wrote almost only in Catalan during the dictatorship and afterwards, such as the brothers Gabriel Ferrater (1922–72) and Juan Ferraté (1924–2003), Marta Pessarrodona (1941–), Montserrat Roig (1946–), and Quim Monzó (1952–), but they were not in the majority, particularly during the dictatorship. The presence of Spanish as a main literary language for many raised in Catalonia under the Francoist regime, while indeed not unique to this time period – as Sergio Vila-Sanjuán points out in *Otra Cataluña. Seis siglos de cultura catalana en castellano* (Another Catalonia. Six Centuries of Catalan Culture in Spanish), Spanish as a literary language has always been present in Catalonia – is nonetheless a clear indicator of Franco's linguistic politics, in contrast with the previous generation, who wrote and published in Catalan before the war: Salvador Espriu, Josep Pla,

Josep Vicenç Foix, Mercè Rodoreda, Jacint Verdaguer, Joan Salvat Papasseit, Joan Vinyoli, Pere Calders, Ventura Gassol, Joan Sales, Ramon Xuriguera, Xavier Benguerel, Ramon Palazón, Josep Carner, Francesc Trabal, and Carles Riba.

That said, it is important to note that bilingualism is present in the works of several of these authors educated under Francoist linguistic politics who wrote mostly in Spanish, showing how permanent Catalan was for many of them in their daily lives and in their authorial consciousness. Bilingualism as a theme is palpable in the works of Juan Marsé, such as *El amante bilingüe* (The Bilingual Lover) and in the language of novels such as Luis Goytisolo's *Antagonía*, where a "Catalinized" Spanish is constant. In this regard, I am interested in how several of the authors raised under Francoism mention their family when talking about their linguistic upbringing, weaving a complex tapestry that is influenced by the political but not determined by it. For instance, Kathryn Crameri explains that, for Montserrat Roig, "born in Barcelona in 1946 and educated in the more liberal 1960s, Catalan was clearly the preferred language, although much of her journalistic work was done in Castilian" and then quotes the author's words, "Gràcies al pare, i a la família, la meva llengua sempre ha estat la catalana" (*Language* 159; Thanks to my father and family, my language has always been Catalan). Date of birth and education but also family contribute to the choice of literary language, but the decision to write in one language does not exclude the possibility of writing in the other. It is in this context too that I see the works of these authors studied here as more flexible than the political reading that is sometimes imposed upon them: Not only linguistic politics, although this is certainly key, but also nuances such as class, date of birth, or even place of education or gender models are taken into consideration when explaining their linguistic identity. A good example of this is the writings of Esther Tusquets, an author that could have been included in my study. In *Habíamos ganado la guerra* (2007; We Had Won the War) she explains how Catalan was the language of communication between her parents and her but not the language they used with her younger brother, Oscar Tusquets, an architect and also a writer in Spanish:

> Mis padres, que siempre habían hablado conmigo el catalán, utilizaron con mi hermano, nacido tras la guerra, el castellano (y esto se mantuvo inalterable: cincuenta años después, en las comidas familiares, mis padres y yo seguíamos dirigiéndonos a Oscar en castellano y hablando entre nosotros tres en catalán, casi sin reparar en el cambio de idioma, y sin que nos pareciera raro, a pesar de que para entonces el catalán de él fuera tan bueno,

o tan malo – no dejaba de ser el denostado y degradado catalán de los barceloneses – como el nuestro), que era, por una parte, el idioma de gran parte de la pijería aristocrática y alto burguesa, y, por otra, el que utilizábamos con el servicio, procedente casi siempre de otras partes de España. (24–5)

My parents, who had always spoken to me in Catalan, to my brother who was born after the war, they spoke Spanish (and this never changed, as fifty years later, at family meals, my parents and I would speak to Oscar in Spanish and amongst ourselves in Catalan, barely registering the change of language, and without it seeming strange, even though in that period his Catalan was so good, or so bad – it never stopped being the maligned or degraded Catalan of the people of Barcelona – as ours) that was, on the one hand, the language used by the majority of the upper crust aristocrats and the great bourgeoisie and, on the other hand, the language we used with our servants, who nearly always came from other areas in Spain.

Here we see how the two siblings received different linguistic treatment, as the son was born during the dictatorship, but we also see the extent to which the household fluctuated always between two languages, how Catalan was understood as mostly oral, how there was a consciousness of Catalan not being spoken "correctly," and of Spanish being the language of the Catalan "upper class" as well as the one used with the servants. The works of Esther Tusquets, particularly the most autobiographical ones, published as memories – as many of her works have been interpreted in an autobiographical key – such as *Confesiones de una editora poco mentirosa* (2005; Confessions of an Editor Who Rarely Lies), *Habíamos ganado la guerra* (2007; We Had Won the War), and *Confesiones de una vieja dama indigna* (2009; Confessions of an Indignant Old Lady), as well as *Tiempos que fueron* (2012 written with her brother Oscar Tusquets; Times That Were), but also her letters in *Correspondencia privada* (1991; Private Correspondence) and "Carta a la Madre" in *Madres e hijas* could be part of the corpus of this study – and indeed have multiple affinities with the works of Barral and Janés, particularly because of the importance of publishing houses. Ana María Moix's *Manifiesto Personal* (2011; Personal Manifesto), her letters and interviews, or Juan Marsé's works, which play with the autobiographical, could also have been considered. That said, I have chosen to examine the autobiographical works of Juan Goytisolo, Barral, Moix, and Janés because of how deeply the issue of language is considered and how this issue of language integrates with the father figure. It is not by any means my intention to be exhaustive or to theorize whether ideas of paternity (and maternity), inheritance, and filiation coincide and diverge in the texts written in Catalan as opposed to those written in Spanish. On the contrary, because I see both maternity and paternity as present in Spanish as well as Catalan literary contexts, often with points in common (such as connection to the literary legacy, space, and gender), I am interested in exploring how the family creates multiple commonalities when understanding language choice, often outside of the political.

The autobiographical works of the four authors studied exemplify, through the family and more particularly the father, how Catalan remained present in daily life and how the consciousness of being bilingual affected these four authors' self-conception as writers. Goytisolo, Barral, Moix, and Janés portray the father as either a person who legitimized in the home a culture and language (Spanish) already legitimized by Francoist law – as in the case of Goytisolo – or who, on the contrary, was representative of a language and culture delegitimized by the Francoist government, as in the case of Barral, Janés, and Moix. These four authors related one of the two languages (Catalan or Spanish) to the father, and this connection is paramount when explaining their linguistic affinities, literary alliances, and perception of the authorial figure. I employ the terms of the mother and the father tongue as the language of the mother and the father. Yet these two terms are loaded with gendered assumptions: The idea that one's dominant language is the mother's is a construction that might not be true for many individuals, yet the concept of "mother tongue" is present in numerous cultures, placing an important weight on the mother as the one who transmits linguistic abilities. The concept of the "mother tongue" uses the idea of "motherhood" to enforce a monolingual cultural paradigm tied to a nation-state. As Yasamin Yildiz eloquently explains in *Beyond the Mother Tongue*, monolingualism – and not multilingualism – "is the result of a relatively recent, albeit highly successful, development" (3). The strong weighting of monolingualism as the default reality and multilingualism as an exception was enforced during the construction of nation-states in Europe in the nineteenth century and "rapidly displaced previously unquestioned practices of living and writing in multiple languages" (6). Yildiz identifies the concept of "mother tongue" as fundamental in the rise of nationalistic monolingual expectations: The unique mother tongue is not only an "affectively charged kinship concept" (7) but also "a vital element in the imagination and production of the homogenous nation-state" (9).

Influenced by the language policies of Franco's dictatorship in Catalonia – which became progressively less repressive of the Catalan language and culture from 1939 to 1975 – and by the language politics of the transition to democracy, with an important turning point in the 1980s and 1990s, when Catalan became one of the two official languages of the Autonomous Community of Catalonia, these four authors explain their relationship through their familial contexts to these two languages that have mostly been read as mutually exclusive and as ideologically (and politically) opposed. While Colleen Culleton speaks of a labyrinth when reading the confluence between space and language in the literature of Barcelona, I see the coexistence of Catalan and Spanish as a thread throughout these author's autobiographies: Two languages that keep appearing in and disappearing from their lives in relation to particular family members. Markedly important in this thread is how a double temporality is established in the primary texts: The affections developed towards a language and towards the father in the moment of writing are different and yet merged with the affections of the authors' childhood memories. These four authors, who published their autobiographies between 1975 and 2005, from Barral's *Años de penitencia* in 1975 to Janés's *La voz de Ofelia* in 2005, look at their childhoods and reflect upon how they were linguistically and culturally raised, and their representations of their past and of the father figure aim to portray a reality that is also impacted by the 30-year span during which they are writing. When considering this double temporality, it is important to keep in mind that they were publishing in a linguistically changing politicized environment and that geography also had an impact, even when they were perhaps not living their daily lives in it, as Goytisolo lived in Morocco for much of his life and Clara Janés in Madrid. The time in which they were born matters as well: We note the differences between Moix – an author born after the war – and Goytisolo and Barral, who experienced it as children.

We could consider these books as published roughly during what is known as the normalization period that Josep-Anton Fernàndez dates from 1976 to 1999, "del Congrés de Cultura Catalana fins al final del pujolisme" (*El malestar* 32; from the Congress of Catalan Culture to the end of Pujolism) or in the period that Jaume Subirana considers to extend from the death of Franco (1976) until the Frankfurt Book Fair in 2007, four decades in which Catalan language went from silenced to internationally celebrated (236). Over these years, we find a huge social and affective paradigm shift regarding the place of Catalan in Catalonia, symbolized by the Linguistic Normalization Act (Llei de Normalització Lingüística), which marks how Catalan went from marginalized to coofficial in Catalonia. For some, this normalization period is a time that solidifies Catalan culture as what Fernàndez defines as "una cultura del malestar" (*El malestar* 15; culture of discomfort). Indeed, the linguistic and literary environment in which some of these authors started to publish was a moment with varying connotations for both Catalan and Spanish: During the transition to democracy, Spanish was still seen by some as the language of Francoism and of Spain's (oppressive) state while Catalan was the language of the defeated, a language that was endangered, forbidden, minoritarian, and subordinate, and writing in Catalan was interpreted as a political statement. Authors born or raised and/or who lived in Catalonia writing in Spanish during the late 1970s, 1980s, and 1990s were pointed to as those whose language choice was motivated by a desire for prestige and access to a larger readership and market (Heinemann 23). In this regard, Joan Ramon Resina and Josep-Anton Fernàndez point out that it was those authors writing in Spanish in Catalonia who were better known and who sold better in Spain and in international markets. Following Resina, Fernàndez clarifies: "És en aquest sentit, segons Resina, que es pot dir que la literatura espanyola escrita a Catalunya és hereva del franquisme, perquè l'avantatge de què gaudeix quant a la seva universalització prové objectivament d'una situació creada per la dictadura, és a dir, la imposició (mitjançant l'ús brutal i il.legítim de la violència física i simbòlica) d'un mercat lingüístic unificat dintre les fronteres del regne d'Espanya" (*El malestar* 227; It is in this sense, according to Resina, that it can be said that the Spanish literature written in Catalonia is a legacy of the Franco regime, because the advantage it enjoys in terms of its universality objectively stems from a situation created by the dictatorship, i.e. the imposition (through the brutal and illegitimate use of physical and symbolic violence) of a unified language market within the borders of Spain).

Yet despite the fact that Spanish is certainly a more international language than Catalan, other readings are also possible: Stewart King maintains that "las narrativas escritas en catalán y en castellano son expresiones de la misma cultura" (n.p.; the narratives written in Catalan and in Spanish are expressions of the same culture) and questions through the work of Terenci Moix, Francisco Candel, Ignasi Riera, Montserrat Roig, Juan Marsé, Ramon Pallicé, and Manuel Vázquez Montalbán "la exclusión del castellano como una lengua capaz de expresar la 'catalanidad' (n.p.; the exclusion of Spanish as a language capable of expressing Catalaness). Similarly, Kathryn Crameri considers to what extent it is possible that authors such as Juan Marsé or Eduardo Mendoza are also "part of Catalan culture, in the broadest sense of the term" (*Catalonia* 77–8). It is my intention to add the importance of the family as an explanation to this debate. Interpreting familial dynamics offers us the possibility of reading these authors' works as proof of the sentimental importance of Catalan despite its prohibition. In this context, even when these texts are written in Spanish, I consider them to be essential to understanding the emotional history of Catalan during the dictatorship and after.

Accordingly, I consider bilingualism as opening a door to understanding gender identities and transformations, just as I see sexual desire and gender expectations complicating these linguistic subjectivities: While defending their attraction to men, Goytisolo and Moix each develop in their texts a very strong consciousness of fighting against the homophobia upheld by their biological fathers. In the work of these two writers, the father plays an essential role in establishing how Francoist law is perceived at home, and this also translates into their attachment to languages and their language choice in different ways, as Goytisolo's father was a Spanish speaker and Moix's father was a Catalan speaker. Goytisolo compares writing in Spanish – his father's tongue – with his sexual desire for men, a desire that was forbidden but that emerged forcefully as he grew up, one that silenced his Catalan roots. Terenci Moix similarly connects language choice, sexual desire, and the subversion of a homophobic father figure, but for him there is an alternation and ambiguity: He first wrote in Catalan as a way to subvert and question his Francoist upbringing, but he later wrote in Spanish, subverting the linguistic and cultural legacy of the father. Moix felt the need to resist both a repressive (patriarchal) linguistic system and repressive heteronormativity when writing, and the two forms of resistance were inseparable to him. In the case of Carlos Barral, the Catalan father is idealized as a nonauthoritarian figure whom Barral places outside Francoist ideas of paternity and law. This allows the autobiographer to explain certain linguistic publishing practices both as a publisher and as a writer. A refined vision of the Catalan father figure is indispensable to Barral's exposition of his guilt for believing in his youth that Catalan was a language with no literary tradition and for rejecting Catalan – the father tongue – as his literary language. This linguistic rejection goes hand in hand in Barral's texts with Barral's exclusion of a certain model of masculinity (that of Catalan fishermen) from high culture and of Catalan from his publishing practices. In the case of Clara Janés, the Catalan father is a necessary stronghold for the writer's female subjectivity and for her becoming a woman writer. However, the autobiographer ultimately chooses Spanish as her literary language rather than Catalan, the language of her father, who was an important Catalan publisher and writer – a choice that she presents as nonpolitical and connected to her leaving Barcelona after her father died, and yet one that is full of political as well as gender implications. Joan Ramon Resina explains regarding the Catalan context that there is a direct correlation between the lack of state and masculine imagery, as this lack of state is somehow parallel to castration ("L'imaginari mascle" 75). In fact, as I propose in this book, this correlation affects how authors explain their language inheritance and the literary canon.[30] But what happens with a female author like Clara Janés? How does she place herself within or outside of the masculinity of the state or that of the father? Catalan authors not only play with the concept of multiple fatherlands, as Stewart King has observed (56), but they also propose a system in which the mother and the father have certain sentimental associations (sometimes different) within these authors' views of bilingualism and language choice and in their conception of the canon and their place in it.

Bilingual Legacies demonstrates how the family and particularly the father is primary when coming to terms with one's language choice for these writers and how gender and linguistic identifications established between father and son and father and daughter are displayed; further explored therein are the consequences of these connections for authorial and canon purposes. These four authors' multiple literary alliances – with Spanish, Catalan, Central European, American, or other literary traditions, as presented in their autobiographical works – reveal a masculine perspective on the canon influenced by the father, which illuminates the bonds between paternity and literature. The tropes of fathering a text and of literary fatherhood, present in all four authors' works to varying degrees, are not unique to the Spanish-Catalan context. In their classic, *The Madwoman in the Attic*, Sandra Gilbert and Susan Gubar study how the notion of the (male) writer as the one fathering his text has been a constant in the Western literary tradition. Following the work of Harold Bloom, Gilbert and Gubar point out how poetic influence is often described as "a relationship of 'sonship'" (6) and how, in Western culture, "the text's author is a father, a progenitor, a procreator, an aesthetic patriarch whose pen is an instrument of generative power" (6).[31] This masculinist and patriarchal literary economy is one in which the author is both a father of the text and a son taking up the work of literary models seen as "forefathers" (46). That said, the diglossic upbringings complicate the connection between the father figure, literary paternity, and the construction of literary bonds with a national canon. In this regard, these four authors provide a privileged position from which to understand how literary, linguistic, and gender subjectivity go hand in hand. In each of the four authors' texts, there is an acknowledgment of the biological father as the one transmitting a particular culture, a language, and a canon and of other canonical writers as paternal authority figures, whether they share the father's language or not. These *paternal* presences often compete with the autobiographer's authority over the text, the author's own *paternity* over his (or even *her*, in Janés's case) writings. There is consequently a tension of authorities, to the extent that these authors end up "self-fathering"[32] themselves – sometimes in the language inherited from the father and sometimes in a different language. The Oedipal structure vis-à-vis literary creation highlights the importance of *lacks* for those raised under the dictatorship, both in reference to certain Hispanic models and also in relation to the Catalan literary legacy, which puts into question whether Bloom's "anxiety of influence" always works in the straightforward way the critic describes. In fact, while references to the biological father and other literary paternal models are constructed, there is also a sense of orphanhood or a desire to recover a particular Spanish or Catalan tradition in these authors' works. This is further complicated by both the desire and need to distinguish oneself from previous models, particularly the ones that emerged and were privileged during the dictatorship. Accordingly, the four authors studied here found themselves at a crossroads, where they were not inheriting a *desired* literary canon to refer to but rather experiencing the need to create a literary canon for and by themselves.[33]

Chapter Overview

Despite the similarities between the works of these four authors and the affinities in the ways they perceive the biological father as connected to language, the body, space consciousness, issues of memory, gender identity, the author's engagement with a literary canon, and the development of a self-awareness as writers, the chapters in *Bilingual Legacies* have been organized author by author to contribute to a broader understanding of each one individually. Chapter 2 analyses Juan Goytisolo's *Coto vedado* (1985) and *En los reinos de taifa* (1986). Goytisolo both constructs and breaks with the dyad that fuses the biological father and the dictator, two figures that he relates to law, censorship, repression, and homophobia. The use of a Freudian structure and the overlap between father and dictator are ideas I depart from. I pay particular attention to Goytisolo's description of his father, a Spanish speaker, in relation to the loss and descent into oblivion of Catalan after Goytisolo's mother's death. By looking at Goytisolo's explanation of his linguistic affinities and literary influences and at how he builds similarities and distinctions between the father's and Franco's bodies, I argue that Goytisolo purposively overlaps Franco and the biological father in these two texts. That said, the instances where the biological father differs from the dictator are not only numerous but also telling, demonstrating a double impulse of *filiation* and *disaffiliation*, from judgment to tenderness, towards the biological father, which contrasts with a unidirectional impulse towards Franco, for whom the only feelings are resentment and blame. These fluctuating feelings towards the biological father permeate Goytisolo's passions and interests. In this way the chapter explicates how the subject, in his autobiographical world, negotiates with the biological father's legacy, a man who is ultimately a pillar for the autobiographer in constructing and expressing his desires and in sketching out a proto-paternity that is diluted and antipatriarchal in other of his texts.

Chapter 3 studies Carlos Barral's *Años de penitencia* (1975), *Los años sin excusa* (1978), and *Cuando las horas veloces* (1988), three texts republished under the title *Memorias*, which I consider vis-à-vis some of Barral's most autobiographical poems in *Metropolitano* (1959) as well as the lesser-known books in Catalan, *Catalunya des del mar* (1982; *Catalonia from the Sea*) and *Catalunya a vol d'ocell* (1985; A Bird's Eye View). This chapter tackles how a linguistic, spatial, and material legacy stands in for the father's body and persona and how this legacy places the autobiographical subject as the legitimate (masculine) heir of the family business, configuring the subject's consciousness as a Spanish writer and generational leader. In Barral's autobiographies, the father is a person outside the dictatorship, a vanishing presence linked to Barral's fetishization of Catalan as a loved yet dismissed language. The father provides Barral with a reality from before the dictatorship, linking Barral to the Catalan maritime landscape of the town of Calafell, a space of nature, spontaneity, bodily pleasures, and sensuality, where the sailors are models of manhood – popular, warm, and proximate. As heir to the paternal publishing house, Barral participates in the hegemonic system, and while this participation enables him to resist the dictatorship from within and to oppose Franco's censorship, the publishing house also represents a responsibility as well as the relegitimization of the Spanish language in Catalonia during the Spanish transition to democracy. In this context, writing about the father allows Barral to explain the inherited linguistic values that placed the Catalan language as secondary in his childhood. The chapter highlights how the father is a primary discursive figure in Barral's self-writing in order to explain Barral's linguistic, literary, and professorial subjectivity, which is presented as tinged with an apparent sense of guilt and failure despite all the successes he experienced in his life.

Chapter 4 analyses the autobiographical works by Terenci Moix published under the title *El peso de la paja*, which include *El cine de los sábados* (1990), *El beso de Peter Pan* (1993) and *Extraño en el paraiso* (1998). In *El peso de la paja*, the father is a figure – in the shadow of the mother – who alternates between being a protector of Catalan culture and a *macho ibérico*. On the one hand, the father is admired by the son, as he is the one who introduces Moix to one of the main libraries of Barcelona – the Biblioteca de Catalunya – and thus is responsible for Moix's love of books; on the other hand, Moix also despises his father, as the father surrounded him with a confining model of masculinity. Through a representation of the father's cultural and linguistic legacy, the father's body, and the comparison between the heterosexual, sexist father and Moix's gay godfather, a man who offers a different model of masculinity and sexuality, Moix questions his father's homophobia, heterosexuality, and sexism to the point of making them unacceptable. His relationship with his father highlights the writer's desire to play with expected national literary conventions through the autobiographical project – such as (not) choosing one language and one national canon to belong to – and thus to create a sense of selfhood that is able to overcome what seem to be inflexible rules. Moix's description of his father offers an exaggeration of an incongruent, paradoxical masculinity and reveals how, in fact, normative models of masculinity are performed, alienating, and *alienable*. Moix not only subverts the father but also offers the opportunity to think about both gender and the Catalan/Spanish divide as two elements that work together. In so doing, he demonstrates how the need for transgression of any authoritative paternal model goes hand in hand with the opening up of new models of sexuality, gender identity, and performance, as well as fluid linguistic affinities, in the democratic Spain of the 1990s.

The last chapter considers Clara Janés's *Jardín y laberinto* (1990) and *La voz de Ofelia* (2005) as well as Janés's relationship with her Catalan father as fundamental in positioning her as a woman writer. Janés finds a way to establish a feminine voice in what she perceives as a masculine and patriarchal domain, the world of writing and literature. This is a tense and contradictory yet necessary negotiation that takes place in a dramatic way. The father shapes this process as both a real and a symbolic figure: Mourning her father's death is essential for Janés to be part of the male-centred realm of literary production. Through an exploration of the death of the father and of how the recovery of this figure is presented in relation to language and by considering Janés's encounter with the poet Vladimír Holan vis-à-vis her positioning of herself as a woman writer, I argue that in Janés's self-writings her father and later Holan are placed in the foreground in the construction of a heterosexual and female subjectivity as a writer. Despite the seemingly apolitical nature of Janés's texts, her writings also offer a telling example not only of how a woman writer navigates the autobiographical genre in Spain in the 1990s and 2000s, but also of the place of the Catalan language in the subjectivity of some authors born and raised in the Barcelona of the dictatorship and publishing at the end of the twentieth and beginning of the twenty-first centuries and their need to overcome a sexist legacy in which family and society did not always correspond but still influenced each other.

2 Juan Goytisolo: Oedipal Dissolutions

The work of Juan Goytisolo Gay (Barcelona 1931–Marrakech 2017) was marked by his desire for moral integrity and by a torturous relationship with Spain, which was evident in his production under Franco's dictatorship, where the intellectual's moral duty is conceived as the responsibility to denounce the regime. His death in June 2017 reanimated public interest in his private life,[1] making clear the close relationship between the writer and his work, as well as the equivocal relationship he had with Spain.[2] *Coto vedado* and *En los reinos de taifa* are Goytisolo's two autobiographies, published in 1985 and 1986 respectively, where Goytisolo revaluates his childhood under Francoism and his adult life in self-exile. These two volumes have been considered "la autobiografia española contemporánea de mayor éxito tanto entre el público en general como entre los críticos" (Pope "Juan Goytisolo" 26; the most successful contemporary Spanish autobiography not only with the general public but also with the critics) and are particularly innovative due to the ways in which Goytisolo came to terms with his homosexuality – something "unprecedented" in the Spanish context, according to Anna Caballé ("La sinceridad").[3] Yet, as Manuel Alberca points out, *Coto* and *En los reinos* continue to be puzzling texts: On the one hand, they are a cornerstone to understanding Goytisolo as an author, "un instrumento hermenéutico y crítico imprescindible" (229; an indispensable hermeneutic and critical tool), but on the other hand the two texts are – something considered by Goytisolo himself – "anachronistic" (229).

Coto and *En los reinos* were preceded and followed by a series of works with strong autobiographical content, including Goytisolo's journalistic contributions and literary criticism, travelogues, letters, and many of his novels, such as *Señas de identidad* (1966; Marks of Identity), *Reivindicación del conde don Julián* (1970; Count Julian), and *Juan sin Tierra* (1975; Juan the Landless), known as the "Álvaro Mendiola trilogy" or

Telón de boca (2003; The Blind Rider), which Goytisolo wrote after the death of his wife, Monique Lange.[4] His works can be considered in this regard as autofictions in gradations, that is, texts that come closer to or move farther away from his experiences, creating a certain elasticity with his life and between them as well. Linda Gould Levine explains, following José Manuel Martín Morán, "los textos de Goytisolo parecen 'guardar memoria' de sí mismos'" ("Resonancias" 817; Goytisolo's texts seem to 'retain memory' of themselves) in a constant tension between what he has already written and what is being written for the first time. Furthermore, the borders between Goytisolo's life and writings and between his life and the writings of those who influenced him and/or who knew him personally are in many ways blurred: He was partner to the French publisher Monique Lange, who also wrote about her relationship with Goytisolo in *Les cabines de bain* (1983); he had two brothers who were also recognized writers, José Agustín and Luis Goytisolo, and his stepdaughter with Lange also published a book of memoirs about her mother in which Goytisolo appears, *Fille de* (2011). Goytisolo took from life to create his literature, took from literature to create his life, and let others take from his life to create their own literature.

Fatherhood is crucial in this dissolution of borders between self and writing and in his creation of an authorial self. Influenced by psychoanalysis,[5] *Coto* and *En los reinos* present the Spanish dictator Francisco Franco and the biological father, chemist, and businessman José María Goytisolo Taltavull (1886–1964) as two interlinked figures that situate the autobiographer's self. The superimposing of father and dictator is created though their bodies, both being described as sick and convalescent – and through the similarities between the space of the familial house and the borders of Spain – but also by considering a series of common precepts that the father and Franco shared, such as their right-wing ideals, anticommunism, and homophobia. By looking at Juan Goytisolo's explanation of, first, the bodies of the father and of Franco as ones that are both in the process of decay and, second, at his linguistic affinities and literary influences as also impacted by the father and Franco, I argue that Goytisolo purposively overlaps these two figures to create the self as an author. That said, the instances where the biological father differs from the dictator are not only numerous but also telling; Goytisolo offers a complicated fusion of pro-Francoist but weak father, showing that the father is under Francoist precepts but inspires both contempt and tenderness in the son. Portraying himself as father of his texts, the autobiographer competes with Franco and the biological father in order to express his truth, while he blurs the limits between the creator and what is created and establishes and breaks a hierarchy of competing paternal characters: The figure of Franco as a castrating father, the ambivalent figure of the biological father, the admired paternal figures of other writers he saw as his models, and himself, the author, as father of the text.

Bodies in Decay

At the beginning of *Coto*, Goytisolo's biological father is evoked as a diminished, sunken, and fallen man: After explaining the father's ascendency, the most striking element in Goytisolo's description is how, in order to disclose how the father suddenly stopped being an admirable figure and became the disappointing man, he presents his biological father as an infectious and convalescent body. Demonstrating a clear desire to have a father capable of being a guardian, Goytisolo portrays the father as unable to protect his children. Goytisolo starts his narration at the beginning of the Spanish Civil War, when his father was briefly imprisoned by the Republicans. The father returned home severely sick with pleurisy and was transformed into a vulnerable man, which caused a drastic change in the son's admiration for this figure:

> Durante años, mi padre permaneció en cama semiinmovilizado, sujeto por aquella horrible cánula incrustada en su pecho al tarro de vidrio en el que se vertían sus humores. Esta nueva imagen paterna no se imprimió en mi memoria sino en Viladrau; pero, de modo imperceptible, se extendió entonces sobre la forjada de mis primeros años – la de un hombre si bien maduro, activo, y cuya diferencia de edad con mi madre no resultaba chocante – hasta anularla del todo. La admiración y respeto que probablemente sentía por él sufrieron así un daño irreparable. La figura abatida, yacente, unida hipostáticamente a la cánula y el tarro de pus, comenzó a inspirarme una injusta, pero real, repugnancia. Aquel hombre mísero, recluido entre algodones, medicinas, vendas, inyecciones, drenajes en una habitación que olía a hospital no se conformaba en absoluto a mi expectativa del papel que correspondía a un padre ni a su supuesto valor de refugio. Sin incurrir en ninguna hipérbole ni manipulación retrospectiva de los hechos, he llegado desde hace tiempo a la conclusión de que, meses antes del mutis de mi madre, la cúpula familiar protectora había empezado a derrumbarse sobre mí. (67–8)

> For years, my father half paralysed stayed in bed, subject to that horrible tube incrusted in his chest attached to a glass jar in which his humours were emptied. This new paternal image didn't impress itself upon my memory until Viladrau: but, in an imperceptible way, it then spread out

> onto the formation of my early years – that of a man while being old, still active, and whose age difference with that of my mother's wasn't striking – until completely invalidating it. The dejected person lying, merged hypostatically to the tube and jar of pus, began to inspire in me an unjust but real, repugnance. That miserable man, imprisoned among cotton wool, medicines, bandages, injections, drains in a room that smelled like a hospital definitely did not conform to the role I expected of a father nor to his supposed value as a place of refuge. Without incurring in any hyperbole, I had arrived for some time at the conclusion that, months before my mother's departure, the protective family dome had begun to collapse around me.

The sick father is crucial in the transformation of the son's attitude towards him. This image appears just at the beginning of the Spanish Civil War, is placed in parallel with the death of his mother, and is metaphorized as the failure of the father's protective dome. The father's sickness and what it means for the son – that strong feeling of lack of protection – is strengthened by the incipient material poverty as well as by the sense of abandonment, both of which were exacerbated after the death of Goytisolo's mother. The text returns later to the repulsion felt for the father's body, linking uncomfortable feelings to the father's religious rituals: "El olor acre de la pieza, la cánula y algodones manchados, la escupidera, el orinal, el tarro de pus creaban en cambio para mí, alrededor del enfermo, un círculo difícil de franquear … Los rosarios y Padrenuestros que rezábamos en común en su cuarto constituían el momento más fastidioso de la jornada" (81; The sour smell of the room, the tube and the stained clothes, the spittoon, the urinal, the jar of pus created a change in me, around the sick man, a circle difficult to negotiate … The rosaries and the Our Fathers that we prayed together in his room compromised the most annoying part of the day). The autobiographer adds that it was in this context that he "formulé por primera vez mi desafecto hacia él, no sé si a solas o en conversación con alguno de mis hermanos" (82; I developed for the first time my disaffection towards him, I don't know if alone or in conversation with one of my brothers), thus sharing his feelings with that of his brothers.

While the former are images that affect the consciousness of a six- or seven-year-old child, their voluntary inclusion in the autobiography accompanies the crumbling of the father figure on other levels. The physical disappointment is directly linked to a moral one: Goytisolo's mother died in 1938 during a bombing in downtown Barcelona by the Nationalists while Goytisolo's father was sick at home in Viladrau – approximately 100 kilometers from Barcelona, where the family spent part of the war. Profoundly imbued with right-wing ideas, the father told his children their mother had died in a Republican bombing, and thus put the dictatorship's ideals before the ethical right of his children to know the truth. Goytisolo's father followed the dictatorship's precepts blindly, in what Juan Goytisolo terms a "operación de blanqueo" (*Coto* 75; white-washing). Juan Goytisolo believed that a Republican bomb had killed his mother until he went to university and discovered that "las bombas de Franco – no la maldad ingénita de los republicanos – eran las responsables directas de la quiebra de tu familia" (75; Franco's bombs – not the innate evil of the Republicans – were directly responsible for the collapse of your family). When Juan Goytisolo and his siblings found out the truth, they felt betrayed by their father's lies, and, in fact, Goytisolo affirms that the lies Franco used to rule Spain were the same ones his father used to rule his home. This extreme loyalty to Franco presents Goytisolo's father as someone whose political convictions were undiscerning and who, perhaps also moved by a desire to protect his children, ended up doing the contrary.

The descriptions of the father's body are pivotal to establish the subject's affections. Even when the autobiographical texts I study in this book are not narratives of filiation strictly following G. Thomas Couser's definition – given that they also have central themes other than the father – both affiliative and disaffiliative impulses (154) are present in Goytisolo's autobiographies, and the father's body is key in the son's resentment. After the death of Goytisolo's mother, the father was depressed, defeated both physically and morally, but he inspired neither love nor pity in the third of his children, Juan, who sees him as an embittered man and feels profoundly embarrassed by him. In this context, the father's body illustrates the destruction of an ideal father figure, projecting instead the image of an unsatisfying father who could have been comforting during the war and upon the mother's death but who wasn't. The father's physical decay is a metaphor not only for the father's inability to protect his children but also for his inability to fulfil certain ideals of masculinity (strength, virility) from the son's perspective. Goytisolo has explained his own and his brother Luis's literary productivity as coming from the same source; that is, the images of a helpless father along with the void of a missing mother created the need to reimagine and overcome what he called a familial myth, although this led to different literary projects on the part of each son: "Que un mismo estímulo y situación inicial – declive paulatino del estatus social de la familia, rechazo de la figura paterna, desaparición temprana de la madre – operen o hayan operado de forma tan dispar en mi caso y el de mi hermano" ("Lectura familiar de *Antagonía*" 43; That the same stimulus and initial position – a gradual decline of the family's social status, rejection of the father figure, early disappearance of the mother – operate or have operated in such a disparate way in my case and that of my brother). In Juan Goytisolo's reading of his brother Luis Goytisolo's novel *Antagonía,* he talks about the "la desaparición, tan brutal como súbita, de nuestra madre; el descubrimiento prematura de un padre viejo y enfermo, a quien resultaba imposible admirar, la realidad de una familia venida a menos" (40; the disappearance, as brutal as it was unexpected, of our mother; the premature discovery of an old and sick father, who it was impossible to admire, the reality of a family in social decline) and how it shook him to read his brother's "retrato conmovedor de este padre 'débil y enfermo y deprimido y acabado' de la noche en que 'al llegar a casa, se lo había encontrado vomitando en su orinal, anguloso y endeble sobre la cama como un aguilucho en su nido'" (4; moving portrait of this father "weak, sick, depressed and finished" from the night when "upon arriving home, he'd found him vomiting in his urinal, angular and feeble on the bed like an eaglet in his nest"), indicating exactly how emotional it was for him to read about this paternal decayed body.

Goytisolo's portrayal of his father's body could be read alongside the Francoist imagery and discourse around sickness, health, and manliness as well. In this context, the image of the ailing father can be seen as an allegory for the destruction caused by the Spanish Civil War or vis-à-vis the pro-fascist narrative that troped the Republic to disease and the dictatorship to the recovery of the nation through the "amputation" of "feminine" traces in both men and the country. In *The Seduction of Modern Spain,* Aurora Morcillo explains how, in the work and research of doctors such as Antonio Vallejo Nájera, the Spanish Republic was linked to illness and infection. Spain's political tribulations were seen as a result of the degenerative decline of the once "virile Hispanic race" (25–6). The Francoist discourses of sacrifice (as well as those of the Monarchists, Falangists, and Carlists and the Catholic Church) became more present, and "blood constituted precisely the life-giving foundation of the restored Spanish organic nation" (Morcillo 44). Morcillo points out that "in order to be an active member of the new body politic a blood offering was required. Those who died in the front for the Nationalist cause were declared martyrs who spilled their blood for the mother country" (44). Morcillo continues to explain that "blood as a means to gain membership in the national community goes back to the Catholic Monarchs' forging of Spain as a nation and the promulgation of the *estatutos de limpieza de sangre*" (44; statutes governing racial purity). The body of Goytisolo's father could be considered as fitting into this discourse of sacrifice for the nation. Yet Goytisolo's images also point to the problematic concept of sacrifice imposed by the dictatorship, one that contradicts, in his family's case, the desired image of the father as a strong, protective man. As Tatjiana Pavlovic explores, the exhibition of a mutilated body was questionable during the postwar period and was in fact strictly prohibited during the Francoist regime, "está terminantemente prohibido – y esto lo pone en conocimiento de todos – que los Caballeros Mutilados de la categoría que sean, absolutos, permanentes y útiles; los privados de la vista o de sus miembros, hagan jamás y en parte alguna, pública ostentación de sus mutilaciones, moviendo a excesiva compasión o solicitando dádivas y otros obsequios" (44; it's strictly forbidden – and this is known to all – that the Caballeros Mutilados (Disabled Knights) no matter what category, complete, permanent and useful; those deprived of sight or their limbs, would never anywhere, parade their mutilations (disabilities) eliciting undue compassion or soliciting gifts or any other form of charity). To the son, the father is an inconvenient body that does not conform to ideas of virility and is not a "winning" figure at all. As Elizabeth Grosz explains in *Volatile Bodies*, masculine bodies are traditionally perceived as solid and as offering clear boundaries (195–205). In Goytisolo's text, the father's body is infectious, and his borders are blurred by medical tubes and bandages; even his tears are seen as proof of his physical and moral weakness. Beyond the Francoist context, these descriptions are important, as they portray an image of the father that does not fit the standard noncorporeal figure of the father present in Western thought: In Western philosophy, the father is often imagined as a disembodied and absent person. The father, as Kelly Oliver explains in *Family Values*, "legislates from some abstract position" (3). Oliver points to the contradiction that, even when the father represents the authority of culture against nature, his authority comes from nature (2). Yet his body seems to be somehow unnecessary to transmit his will: His abstract presence, the idea of punishment is enough. An example of this can be found in Freudian theory, from which Goytisolo draws heavily when establishing a sense of the subject's idea of limits. Similarly, in Lacanian theory, in which the father is identified with a "No" or Name, his abstract power to legislate and enforce social precepts makes possible the separation between the child and the mother's (abject) body, not through his body but precisely because he is an abstract image.

If the first images of the father in *Coto* are the those of a broken man, in *En los reinos* Goytisolo presents the figure of the dictator in a similar way, expressing his reprobation of what on November 20, 1975 became the corrupted and defeated body of the dictator. The images of the dictator coincide with the descriptions Goytisolo offers in his article "In memoriam," one that he considers in *En los reinos* to be the seed of his autobiographical project and where he claims that he internalized Franco as a continuous presence that was impossible to get rid of and that provoked endless "auto-censorship" in him. The link between the two decaying bodies is evident and coincides with Goytisolo's acknowledgment, at the beginning of *En los reinos*, that he saw his father as a figure who followed the precepts of the dictator in a game of eclipses and shadows:

> Su recurso a ese otro Padre castrador y tiránico, cuya presencia ubicua y omnímoda se extendía sobre nosotros eclipsando la suya, revela de forma cruda y escueta la correlación de fuerzas de ambos y el carácter débil, vicario de su autoridad parental: impotencia, senectud, frustración de un progenitor nominal sumiso al que en realidad, desde las cimas del poder absoluto, regía y modelaba nuestras vidas. Mi odio al Otro, al destinatario de la humillante misiva, se transmutaría a partir de entonces en una verdadera manía. (271)

> This recourse to that other castrating and tyrannical Father, whose ubiquitous and ominous presence spread out over us eclipsing his own, reveals in a crude and succinct way the correlation of both of their forces and the weak, vicarious nature of his paternal authority: impotency, old age, frustration of being a father in name only submissive to the one who actually, from the peaks of absolute power, ruled and shaped our lives. My hatred for the Other, to the target of my humiliating missive, would from then on become a true mania.

The paternal law, promulgated by Franco, is seconded by the father. The references to the dictator's dying body just after calling him "father" are part of this fusion between the personal father and the collective one. In "In memoriam," as well as in *En los reinos*, Goytisolo refers to Franco's drawn-out and painful death. In the former, he uses images of the dictator's sick body in bed, surrounded by an increasingly spectacular medical apparatus, to request that this body not reign after its demise. The writer depicts Franco's sinister end as "digno del pincel de Goya o la pluma de Valle Inclán" (worthy of Goya's brush or Valle Inclán's pen) to highlight the deformed appearance of the scene and portrays his feelings towards Franco in the following way: "¿Cómo explicar entonces, tratándose de él, la tenacidad de mi aborrecimiento? En la larga, irreal agonía de estas últimas semanas – mientras era torturado cruelmente por una especie de justicia médica compensatoria de la injusticia histórico-moral que le permitía morir de vejez, en la cama – dicho sentimiento no me ha abandonado nunca: ningún afecto de piedad ha acompañado la lectura – objetivamente monstruosa – de las nuevas y más rigurosas dolencias que día tras día divulgaba el parte oficial de un equipo médico que parecía crecer en razón directa al número de sus enfermedades" ("In Memoriam" 160–1; How to explain then, when it came to him, the perseverance of my hatred? During the long, unreal agony of those last weeks – while he was cruelly tortured by a kind of compensatory medical justice from the historical-moral injustice that would allow him to die of old age, in his bed – that sentiment has never left me: no feeling of pity has followed on reading – objectively speaking monstruous – of the new and more severe ailments that day after day were disclosed by the official part of his medical team which seemed to grown in direct proportion to the number of his diseases).

Tatjiana Pavlovic interprets the breakdown of Franco's body as a breakdown of Francoism (73). She points out how Franco's death was particularly public and how the press reported vivid details of his sicknesses. Franco's dying body turned into the vital signs of the regime. According to Pavlovic, the end of Franco's reign was marked by an abjection that was also anticipated by Franco's loss of *le trait unaire* (the unary feature, that is, the most important component of the dictatorship) and by the regime's inability to accommodate change (4). Franco's death was, according to this scholar, surreal (74) and tragicomic (81). The way this death was made public, in fact, strengthened the feeling of symbiosis between Franco's body and the Spanish nation, as "not respecting borders from the very beginning of his reign, Franco was like some alien, horrific creature that entered the entrails of Spain" (121). Pavlovic highlights how the boundaries between Franco's body and the body politic of the entire country were unclear, quoting Martín Gaite's words in *Usos amorosos*, "¿Quién se ha metido en las entrañas de España como Franco hasta el punto de no saber ya si Franco es España o España es Franco?" (6; Who has entered into the bowels of Spain like Franco to the point of no longer knowing if Franco is Spain or if Spain is Franco?) and Giménez Caballero's description of Franco as someone who "nadie conoce bien de cerca pero que todo un pueblo presiente" (20; nobody knows very well but everybody has a premonition). Pavlovic also studies how Franco's despotic body, besides exhibiting traits coded as masculine (cruelty, coldness, a propensity for killing) was also marked by a rarely mentioned femininity (such as a tenuous, feminine voice), which, according to her, continuously challenged and negated the dictator as a powerful figure (see page 104).

The images of the old dictator in "In Memoriam" and in *En los reinos* provoke a deep sense of disdain. The description of the grotesque elder somehow destabilizes the dictator's power, anchoring him in his most human nature, and, as in the case of the biological father, is used by Goytisolo as a form of moral judgment. In "Juan Goytisolo, F.F.B. y la fundación fantasmal del proyecto autobiográfico contemporáneo español," Cristina Moreiras Menor points out that Franco's death constitutes the event upon which Goytisolo's biographical project is constructed (332). In this context, Moreiras Menor argues that "la desaparición del padre da origen al nacimiento de un texto cuyo objetivo fundamental será enterrar definitivamente a partir de la revisión de la Historia una presencia que ha formado, dirigido y limitado la vida de un hijo resistente" (333; the disappearance of the father gives birth to a work whose fundamental objective will be to definitively bury by means of historical revision a presence that has shaped, directed and limited the life of a resilient son). Following Moreiras Menor's reading, the death of the dictator, as well as the parallels between father and dictator and those between Spain's and the familial narrative, all strengthen the link between the self and the collective and place the autobiographer – and thus the person with authority to explain the true facts of his life – in a privileged position regarding the telling of Spanish history. Ángel Loureiro has a different interpretation of Franco's presence in Goytisolo's autobiographies, arguing that Franco does not play a particularly important explanatory role in them (*Ethics* 134). Loureiro points out how "Franco's death is dealt with on one page of *En los reinos de taifa*" (134). Loureiro does, however, highlight the importance of fatherhood and notes the centrality of passages such as the ones in *Coto* in which the author narrates several dreams where, once the father is dead, the autobiographical subject dreams about the father's phantasmal presence and experiences "un ramalazo insospechado de ternura" (112; an unsuspected rash of tenderness). Despite their different interpretations, Moreiras Menor and Loureiro both point out how paternity and sonship are significant to the autobiographical construction but follow two different lines of criticism seeking to determine the most important paternal presence in the text, a reading that fails to acknowledge the multiple and continuous overlaps between the two figures. In these overlaps, the father is linked to the dictator in both explicit and implicit ways, evidencing that the strength of the dictator is only possible because of the presence of a Francoist father and that the Francoist father is always seconded by the dictator. In this superimposing of the two figures, the differences are nonetheless telling: The first image, that of the ravaged father, is the one experienced by Goytisolo as a child, an image that lies behind his desire to have a strong father and turns out to be essential in creating his desire for a particular type of men, while Franco's senility, experienced by Goytisolo as an adult, arrives after a long and conscious fight against this figure. In a way, it seems that Francoism had the impact it did on Goytisolo's early literary consciousness because the father did not offer any form of resistance to the regime, a resistance that ends up coming instead from the son's writings. The position of heir, as Teresa Vilarós explains, is part of a patriarchal economy (45), and in this context masculinity, lineage, and inheritance are organizing principles central to the projection of the self.

Homosexuality is fundamental in this negotiation with the father and with Franco and the regime. In *Coto* the decline of the paternal body, concurrent with the lessening of admiration for his persona, is placed in parallel with the rise of sexual desire: Just after the passages describing the sick father, Goytisolo explains "por estas fechas – verano y otoño del 1938 – experimenté mis primeras emociones sexuales" (82; at that time – the summer and fall of 1938 – I experienced my first sexual feelings). The father's decline coincides with a sexual awakening in which, as the masculine model of the father fails, at the same time another model of man arises. The autobiographer acknowledges an affinity to an inherited paradigm of masculinity, as Ryan Prout points out (11). This paradigm in fact mixes the model of the physically strong and virile man praised by patriarchal Francoist society with a model rejected by Francoism: The autobiographer is fascinated by men who are rude and uneducated and who resemble the rejected or forbidden Other, that is, the "Moor," who is associated in the medieval imagination with an unbridled and aberrant sexuality. We cannot forget the importance of medieval Spain to Francoist Spain: Jessamy Harvey documents how Francoist Spain was depicted "as a glorious National-Catholic empire with roots in the mythicized past of the fifteenth century: the era of the Catholic kings, the expulsion of Arabs and Jews (seen as positive 'racial cleansing'), and the conquest of America was central for the nationalism of the dictatorship" (110). To this, we could add the importance of Morocco in the Spanish Civil War: Morocco is a central location in the Francoist political imagination, as the rebellion against the government of the Second Republic started in Melilla in July 1936. Accordingly, the North African coast carries a strong symbolic meaning, but Goytisolo does not mention Morocco in the context of its important role in the start of the war, instead alluding to the medieval imagination. He seems to see Morocco rather as an escape from Francoism, a kind of blind spot, where Morocco is perceived as somehow utopian.

Further, the exotic and strong model of desired manhood is opposed to the father's abject, weak, and sick body, and, in this way, Goytisolo's relationship with the male body does not escape the paternal shadow but rather is invoked by it. Even more so if we consider, as Alberto

Villamados comments, that "Un gran número de escritores homosexuales, según señala Arturo Arnalte – que podríamos extender a los intelectuales en general – ha sentido atracción hacia sujetos ajenos a su grupo social, sobre los cuales reproducirían el esquema de explotador y explotado como una respuesta a la vergüenza que sienten por su sexualidad" (174; A large number of homosexual writers, according to Arturo Arnalte – that we could extend to include intellectuals in general – have been attracted to subjects outside of their social group, on who they will replay the scheme of exploiter and exploited as a response to the shame they feel because of their sexuality). The paternal body is phantasmal because it seems to delimit the object of desire while at the same time having been forbidden as an object of love. Indeed, Ángel Loureiro analyses the final episode of *En los reinos*, which takes place in Tangiers, in which Goytisolo is beaten in a sadomasochistic sexual encounter by an Arab man. Portraying it as a purgative act, Loureiro relates this experience to Deleuze's theory of masochism. Loureiro explains that, for Deleuze, the masochist feels guilty for his resemblance to the father and instructs a disciplinary agent to dispense punishment, but in reality this punishment is for the father (*The Ethics* 115). According to Loureiro, the scene in which Goytisolo is beaten and abused by his lover responds in fact to the necessity of punishing his father as "a weak and morally unacceptable model" (115–16). The author's guilt, aggression, and self-reproach during this last scene in Tangiers, the narcissism so vital to the autobiographical project, and finally Goytisolo's obsession with those familial deaths – the mother's, the father's, and their caretaker Eulalia's – provoke a narration in which solitude, independence, and certain refusal or separation from the feminine are necessary in order to come to terms with one's own desires. In this purgative, violent sexual encounter, Goytisolo's role seems to be not only passive but also enmeshed in the tension of being feminine and weak. Thus, the impossibility of admiring the father, of taking him as a model, turns the father into a figure that ultimately forces the subject to find a model of man that is anything but the father, a man whose hypermasculinity is in complete opposition to the father's weakness. *Coto* and *En los reinos* are example of what Thomas Couser calls an act of disaffiliation through the autobiographical writing (154), in which the son does not pay tribute to the father but, on the contrary, accuses him. Thus, what predominates in the former descriptions of the father's body is a disaffiliative impulse in which we find an accusation (154) and a strong and perhaps even overly exaggerated moral judgment of the father that places Goytisolo as an authority over the father but also over himself. In fact, as an adult the subject sees the child's disaffection towards the suffering of the father as somehow unfair: The autobiographer feels an ambivalence towards the biological father too, as Goytisolo says he felt for his father once he died, "un ramalazo insospechado de ternura" (112; an unexpected wave of tenderness). The fluctuating feelings that go from judgment to tenderness clearly differentiate the subject's relationship with his biological father from his relationship with the dictator. A double impulse of filiation and disaffiliation towards the father contrasts with a unidirectional pulsion towards Franco, for whom the only feelings are resentment and blame. The shifting feelings towards his biological father allow for forgiveness to appear as part of the autobiographical project and also establish a sentimental path for the subject that allows him to shift between negation and acceptance of the Spanish language – the language of the father – the Spanish canon, and his desire for men.

A Masculine Language

In Sidonie Smith's 1987 work *A Poetics of Women's Autobiography*, the scholar theorizes how traditional autobiographies enforce not only a masculinist image of the self – an image based on ideas of autonomy (39) – but also a masculine tradition, a masculine genealogy, and paternal lines (39, 40). According to Smith, autobiography is an assertion of arrival in the "phallic order" (40): It sustains the myth of origins and "asserts the primacy of patrilineal descent and androcentric discourse" (40). Published not long before Smith's assertions, Goytisolo's *Coto* and *En los reinos* show this effort to align the self with a masculine (and dissident) genealogy and tradition and to construct a masculine and autonomous self that, in Goytisolo's case, is entangled with the Spanish language and literary canon. We note all of this in his work despite a number of "fractures" that come in the process but that the self uses as a turning point to reevaluate and reconstruct its core values. *Coto* starts by following a quintessential autobiographical structure: It revisits, first, the father's and then the mother's genealogical lines, even before relating the subject's first memories of infancy. In this way, it follows the literary convention of the autobiographical genre, in which the subject pays tribute to previous family members and influences. The two lines, the paternal and the maternal, are presented as opposite: At the beginning of *Coto*, Goytisolo describes himself as the fruit of two opposing genealogies, and the union of these paternal and maternal lines triggers a divided self in a series of linguistic and sexual tensions: "El conflicto familiar entre dos culturas fue el primer indicativo, pienso ahora, de un proceso futuro de rupturas y tensiones dinámicas" (46–7; The family conflict between two cultures was the first indication,

I now believe, of a future process of ruptures and dynamic tensions). The Goytisolos, of Basque origin, are described first: They had lived in Cuba, where they accumulated a considerable fortune through their participation in the plantation economy. Catholic, right-wing, authoritarian, and, according to Goytisolo's father, of noble descent, they are "ultimately linked to the political figure of Franco, whose politics Goytisolo's father supports" (Ribeiro de Menezes 21). Conversely, the history of the maternal line, surnamed Gay, is a history of "sombras" (*Memorias* 38; shadows).[6] The Gay belong to the Catalan bourgeoisie, with interests in the world of literature and culture. Goytisolo's mother is described as impressively cultured, and Juan Goytisolo had access to the books of her library, mostly French and European classics (167). The mother's library reveals to the son the mother's hidden passion, which influenced Goytisolo's own devotion to literature (61). Goytisolo's maternal great-grandmother wrote a novel entitled *Las barras de plata* (38; The Silver Bars), and she could be, according to him, "esa posible y lejana transmisora genética de la vocación literaria que marcaría mi vida y la de mis hermanos" (38; that possible and distant genetic transmitter of the literary vocation that would mark my life and that of my brothers). Goytisolo's maternal aunt, who lived part of her life in a mental hospital, also published some poems in *Mirador* (42; Viewpoint), and his mother, Julia Gay, in addition to being an avid reader (of Proust, Gide, Ibsen, Anouilh), wrote a text entitled "El muro y la locura" (61; The Wall and the Madness).

At the beginning of *Coto*, Goytisolo also makes reference to a great-great-uncle from the maternal line: Ramon Vives Pastor, a Catalan nationalist, bohemian, and liberal who was also a writer. He translated some Persian poems into Catalan (39), "que dedica en catalán a su amante irlandesa Bertha St. George 'filia tristoia i dolça d'aquella verda Erin, esclava, com ma terra, d'una llei opressora'" (39; who he dedicated to his Irish lover Berthe St. George "the sad and sweet daughter of that green Erin, a slave, like my land, of an oppressive law") and wrote a book of poetry in Catalan entitled *Notes poètiques,* subtitled *Poesia és llibertat* (41; Poetic Notes. Poetry Is Freedom). Juan Goytisolo recalls in *Coto* that this uncle's books and manuscripts arrived at his house in Pablo Alcover Street in Barcelona but that he destroyed them as a child by painting and writing in them (40); an act of annihilation of which Goytisolo is ashamed. Nonetheless, no one in the family condemned the child's act, because Ramon Vives's name was surrounded by silence: He was guilty, according to Juan Goytisolo's father, of giving meningitis to Juan's older brother, which led to the boy's death. Juan Goytisolo affirms that he shares with Ramon Vives a moral affinity beyond the blood connection, "afinidad teñida, en su caso, de remordimiento y melancolía" (41; affinity tinged, in his case, with remorse and melancholy). Goytisolo talks about his own contribution to his uncle's second death (41), as he destroyed his uncle's writings, and he concludes by affirming the existence of a genetic line between Ramon Vives's and his own works: "La palabra anulada y hecha trizas por mí siendo niño me ha contaminado tal vez sin saberlo para brotar insidiosa en cuanto he escrito y escribo. Sea cierta o no, la idea de esa posible transmigración me consuela de mi acto irreparable, transmutándolo sutilmente si no en una palingenesia, en una forma discreta de sobrevida" (41; The writing that I nullified and shattered as a child has since contaminated me, perhaps without knowing it, and my later writing emerge insidious. Whether true or not, the idea of this possible transmigration consoles me in the irreparable damage, subtly transforming it, if not into a rebirth, into a discreet form of survival). Thus, writing in *Coto* is presented as a genetic heritage, a legacy that comes from the mother's line – mostly a domain of women – and of one uncle, a figure tinged with sickness, purposely forgotten, whose works disappeared. In *En los reinos*, Goytisolo asserts that to him writing is an unchangeable destiny "si eres escritor es porque no puedes ser otra cosa, la escritura es un elemento esencial de tu vida, como pueden serlo, por ejemplo, tu origen familiar, tu lengua nativa, tu orientación sexual" (408; if you are a writer it's because you can't be anything else, writing is an essential element of your life, as for example, your familial origin, your native language, your sexual orientation), yet the maternal genes of literature do not align with his embracing the language of the mother – Catalan – but rather the language of the father, Spanish, a language whose canon Goytisolo feels passionate about. In fact the very same concept of canon as Goytisolo envisions it, that is, as a dissident masculine genealogy in which he participates as son and heir, positions him doubly as son of the father's language and as heir of mostly male writers.[7]

The organized account of family members and the hierarchy of languages in which Spanish is prioritized (versus Catalan, French, or Arab) is fundamental in the creation of an autobiographical self in control, something that gives us a sense of Goytisolo's authorial disposition as a narrator distant from the text, who builds it with purpose and structure. As James Phelan explains in *Living to Tell about It*, "the extent to which the narrative act is doubled in this way will depend on the extent to which the author signals her difference from or similarity to the 'I' who tells the story" (18), and Goytisolo's distance as narrator is evident in his double writing as well, as his autobiographies are divided between fragments in normal typography and sections in italics that break with the temporal line and offer a "subconscious" account of his experiences. In this manner, Goytisolo's autobiography offers a strong sense of *aesthetic control*, defined by Phelan as the "narrator's ability to achieve the effects he seeks and to have those effects endorsed by the implied author" (104). In this ordering, the maternal, the feminine, the effeminate, shadows and silences, and Catalan are all placed in a secondary position and interconnected among each other.

Bilingualism and language choice are among the first issues tackled in *Coto*: They are presented even before his own birth, as if a subject's language precedes the subject's existence. While describing the mother's line, Goytisolo talks about the gradual eclipse of his mother's language after her death on 17 March 1938, when he was seven years old, directly linking the death of the mother with linguistic oblivion: "el eclipse gradual y definitivo de la rama materna tuvo una importancia especial para mí y mis hermanos a causa de nuestra futura condición de escritores. A la pregunta tantas veces repetida de unos años acá de por qué no escribimos en catalán me veo obligado a sacar a luz las circunstancias en que se desenvolvió la vida de mi familia" (44; the slow and definitive eclipse of the maternal line was essentially important for me and my brothers, because of our future status as writers. To the question so often repeated in the last few years of why we don't write in Catalan, I find myself obliged to point out the circumstances in which the life of our family unfolded). Yet Catalan is not only the language of his late mother and the mother's family but also a language forbidden by Goytisolo's father. While the maternal grandparents spoke Catalan, Goytisolo's father required the family to speak Spanish at home: "mientras los abuelos Marta y Ricardo hablaban entre sí en aquel idioma, se dirigían a nosotros en castellano por expresa indicación paterna" (44; while our grandparents Marta and Ricardo spoke to each other in that language, they would talk to us in Spanish under direct paternal orders). Catalan was, in fact, condemned by the father, who, in his anti-Catalan diatribes, would make fun of the sounds and words of the Catalan language, contrasting them with what he perceived as the beauty and sonority of Spanish:

> Papá, en el nirvana de su fobia anticatalanista, se complacía en contrastar la prosapia, distinción y eufonía de la lengua de Castilla – sonoridad rotunda de su toponimia: Madrigal de las Altas Torres, Herrera del Duque, Montilla de Palancar – con la zafiedad y plebeyez de unos Terrassa, Mollet u Hostafrancs grotescamente pronunciados para rematar su singular cursillo de etimología y fonética comparadas con la obligada referencia a la belleza misteriosa del término «luciérnaga» frente a lo grosería y miseria del «cuca de llum» local. Por una razón u otra, lo cierto es que la lengua

> materna – desvanecida para siempre con mi madre – me resultó con su muerte profundamente extraña: una lengua en cuyo espacio me movería con incomodidad y apenas sabría leer de corrido hasta que, instalado ya en Francia, me tomé la molestia de estudiarla a ratos libres para acceder al conocimiento de sus obras sin ayuda del diccionario. (45)
>
> My father, in the nirvana of anti-Catalan phobia, took pleasure in contrasting the origin, distinction and euphony of the Castilian language – the resounding sound of its toponymy: Madrigal de las Altas Torres, Herrera del Duque, Montilla de Palancar – with the uncouthness and roughness of a grotesquely pronounced Terrassa, Mollet or Hostafrancs to finish off his lecture on comparative etymology and phonetics with the obligatory reference to the mysterious beauty of the term "luciérnaga" (firefly in Spanish) compared to the rudeness and misery of the local "cuca de llum" (firefly in Catalan). For one reason or another, the truth is that the mother tongue – vanished forever with my mother – was profoundly strange to me after her death: A language in whose space I navigated with discomfort and a language I could barely read until, already living in France, I took the trouble to study it for a while in my free time to gain access to the knowledge of Catalan works without the help of the dictionary.

The father's prohibition of Catalan at home takes place simultaneously with Franco's prohibition of the language in the public sphere, while at the same time the Spanish language is also reduced: "tanto en casa – con mi padre y Eulalia – como en el colegio – en las aulas y entre compañeros – se empleaba exclusivamente el castellano – un castellano empobrecido y adulterado según descubriría más tarde, al extender el ámbito de mis frecuentaciones y amistades más allá de la insulsa y convencional burguesía barcelonesa. Bajo la fuerte presión de unos años en que debía cultivarse por decreto la «lengua del Imperio», el catalán subsistía a duras penas en la intimidad de las casas" (44–5; both at home – with my father and Eulalia – and at school – in the classrooms and among classmates – we used Spanish exclusively – an impoverished and adulterated Spanish as I would later discover when I extended the scope of my friendships beyond the bland and conventional Barcelona bourgeoisie. Under the strong pressure of the years in which the "language of the Empire" had to be cultivated by decree, Catalan barely survived in the intimacy of the home). Goytisolo places himself consciously as unable to use in his writing the oppressed language: "La desaparición temprana de mi madre y el medio conservador, religioso y franquista en que me criara fueron sin duda elementos primordiales de mi inserción en una cultura que, cincuenta años atrás, el tío Ramon

Vives había motejado de 'opresora'" (46; The early disappearance of my mother as well as the conservative, religious and Francoist environment in which I grew up were undoubtedly essential elements of my insertion in a culture that, fifty years ago, Uncle Ramon Vives had nicknamed "oppressive").

Goytisolo explains his choice of writing in Spanish in several ways, one of them being that the inclination towards a language in a bilingual context is the result of a familial and social conjuncture that needs to be passively accepted: "la inclinación a una u otra lengua por parte del escritor potencialmente bífido no es producto exclusivo de una libre elección personal sino resultado más bien de una serie de coyunturas familiares y sociales posteriormente asumidas" (46; the bilingual author's preference for one language or another is not only the product of a personal choice but rather the result of a series of family and social situations that emerged around him). Spanish is presented as an unchangeable destiny but also as a language that evokes great fascination, particularly when Goytisolo moved to France. In this context, Goytisolo talks about an ardour for Spanish, a language that he identifies in his self-exile in France as his "patria auténtica" (46; genuine fatherland) and with which he is infatuated: "Pero, más significativo que ese determinismo histórico en favor de una de las lenguas en liza es, en mi caso, la relación apasionada con ella a partir del día en que, lejos de Cataluña y España, descubrí que era mi patria auténtica y objeto simultáneo de odio y amor" (46; More significant than that historical determinism to the benefit of one of the languages in dispute is, in my case, the passionate relationship with it from the day when, far from Catalonia and Spain, I discovered that [the Spanish language] was my authentic homeland and simultaneously the object of both my hatred and love). And while in *Coto* he writes about "la victoria de un castellano vuelto bumerán de sí mismo" (47; the victory of Castilian turned into boomerang of itself) and there is a sense that Spanish invades him (that he is somehow colonized by the language), in *En los reinos* he also talks about writing as a form of conquest: "La empresa novelesca, tal como la concibes, es una aventura: decir lo aún no dicho, explorar las virtualidades del lenguaje, lanzarse a la conquista de nuevos ámbitos expresivos" (418; The novelistic project, as you conceive it, is an adventure: saying what has not yet been said, exploring the realities of language, setting out to conquer new expressive areas) as if he was the one colonizing the linguistic system. The term *conquest* seems to be used in both of its meanings: According to the Real Academia Española, *conquistar* means "Ganar, mediante operación de guerra, un territorio, población, posición" (to win, through battle, a territory, population, or position) as well as "Lograr el amor de alguien, cautivar su ánimo" (win somebody's love, capture their attraction).

Thus, that writing is a form of "conquest" suggests both an erotic capture in which there are active (the self) and passive (the language, the written text) elements and also a military imagery that seems to allude to Spain's history of colonialism. Spanish is the language both of writing and of the paternal ancestors, connecting Goytisolo directly to his family's exploitation of slaves in Cuba. The writer, in this case, takes up an ambiguous position of both heir to and censurer of his familial colonial injustices, as he is astonished by his past reality but also uses it to write his story and to construct intertexts between his own writings, both in *Coto* and elsewhere: "La impresión que me causó la lectura de las cartas de los esclavos cuidadosamente conservados por el abuelo Antonio las expuse en las primeras páginas de *Coto Vedado*. Desconocía en cambio el Reglamento de la Esclavitud del que extraigo este párrafo del libro de Martín Rodrigo: 'Los esclavos están obligados a obedecer y respetar como a padres de familia a sus dueños, mayordomos, mayorales y demás superiores'" (Goytisolo "Prólogo" in Rodrigo y Alharilla 16; I shared my feelings about those letters written by slaves and carefully saved by my grandfather Antonio in the first pages of *Coto Vedado*. However, I was unaware of the Regulations of Slavery that appeared in Martín Rodrigo's book and that I borrowed: "Slaves are obliged to obey and respect their owners, masters, overseers and other superiors as parents").

In *Coto*, Goytisolo compares his embrace of and desire for Spanish to an erotic orientation that in fact corresponds to his desire for a virile man:

> Decir que no elegí la lengua sino que fui elegido por ella sería el modo más simple y correcto de ajustarme a la verdad. La oscilación entre dos culturas e idiomas se asemeja bastante a la indecisión afectiva y sensual del niño o adolescente: unas fuerzas oscuras, subyacentes, encauzarán un día, sin su consentimiento, su futura orientación erótica. El impulso ciego a una forma corporal masculina será así tan misterioso como el que le conducirá a enamorarse para siempre de una lengua a la escucha de Quevedo o de Góngora. (46)

> To say that I did not choose the language but that I was chosen by it would be the simplest and most accurate thing to say. Alternating between two cultures and languages is quite similar to the affective and sensual indecision of the child or adolescent: some dark, underlying forces will one day channel, without his consent, his future erotic orientation. The blind impulse to a masculine body will thus be as mysterious as the one that will lead him to fall in love forever with a language listened to by Quevedo or Góngora.

This *jouissance* towards Spanish – and the admiration for the male writers who form the Spanish canon – correlates with his erotic disposition towards men and is described as violent and uncontrollable, a relationship based on the ideas of struggle and conflict. Goytisolo's relationship to Spanish and the Hispanic canon also seems to coincide with his desire for men in that, after a period of repression, his passion for both the Spanish canon and men came back forcibly. Goytisolo explains in *Coto* that he was lured to the "goce del castellano en virtud de la misma lógica misteriosa por la que hallaría en el sexo la afirmación agresiva de mi identidad" (215; the enjoyment of Spanish by virtue of the same mysterious logic by which I would find in sex the aggressive affirmation of my identity). Spanish, the paternal and masculine language, is therefore associated with desire, power, survival, and fighting, as well as a masculine form of love and fertility. Spanish is seen as a body, an enemy and a lover, and an instrument of work, against which he battles on a daily basis: "reducido casi exclusivamente a instrumento de trabajo literario, el castellano conquistaría a la inversa un estatus único al ser el enemigo con quien brego en un implacable cuerpo a cuerpo cuya rijosa ferocidad me otorgó la gracia del enamoramiento" (231; reduced almost exclusively to an instrument of literary work, Castilian would conversely conquer a unique status by being the enemy with whom I grapple in a relentless struggle, whose lusty ferocity gave me the grace of falling in love), and indeed it was his embracing of Spanish that made Goytisolo into a prolific writer.

The writer's inclination towards Spanish rather than Catalan – and a certain feminization of the latter – confirm what Alison Ribeiro de Menezes describes: "writing, unlike its original formulation at the beginning of *Coto vedado*, where it was associated with Goytisolo's lost mother, is not ultimately, a feminine principle, but an aggressively gay, masculine one" (27). At the beginning of *Coto*, Goytisolo's words echo not only Lacanian ideas around language being a paternal domain but also the impossibility of separating one own's linguistic subjectivity from one's sexual identity. The notion of the mother tongue – or better, the initial passive disappearance of Catalan, in Goytisolo's case, in favour of the father's language, Spanish – is central when taking on a literary canon. The marginalization of the maternal language implies the inheritance of certain linguistic practices that are not only linked to Francoism but that also have defined Spain's negation of peripheral cultures and languages within Spain and of indigenous languages in the Americas for centuries. If, as Jacqueline Amati-Mehler notes, there are "intellectual and affective pathways" (quoted in Yildiz 13) for any language, in Goytisolo's case these primary attachments to the father's tongue are charged with passionate feelings of ambivalence that are also heavily impacted by linguistic historical politics. These feelings are constructed in a very particular pattern defined by destruction and reconstruction (a set identified in Labanyi's "The Construction/ Destruction of the Self"): First there is a negation and refusal of the father's language, the Spanish nation, and its canon, but following this there is an enforcement and embracing of these elements by the subject.

Goytisolo's statements need to be read in the context of Catalonia's linguistic politics during the late seventies and eighties. As explained in the introduction, in this period of "normalization" Catalan stopped being forbidden and became the Catalan Autonomous Community's official language. Goytisolo's autobiographies offer an explanation about his choice of Spanish, an explanation in which he correlates the death of Catalan with the death of his mother and equates his inclination to write in Spanish with the final acceptance of his desire for men, all of which are personal, untransferable, and impossible to judge. He also recalls being brushed aside because he wrote in Spanish. At the beginning of *Coto*, similarly to Carlos Barral, Goytisolo affirms that his situation as a writer from Catalonia who writes in Spanish put him in a marginalized, ambiguous, and contradictory space in relation to literary classifications: "Castellano en Cataluña, afrancesado en España, español en Francia, latino en Norteamérica, nesrani en Marruecos y moro en todas partes, no tardaría en volverme a consecuencia de mi nomadeo y viajes en ese raro espécimen de escritor no reivindicado por nadie, ajeno y reacio a agrupaciones y categorías" (46–7; Spanish in Catalonia, Frenchified in Spain, Spanish in France, Latin in North America, Nesrani[8] in Morocco and Moorish everywhere, I would soon return as a result of my nomadic ways and travel in that rare specimen of a writer not claimed by anyone, alien and resistant to labels and categories). Goytisolo acknowledges that his marginalization was probably due more to his physical nomadism and open criticism of Spain than it was to his being a Catalan writing in Spanish, but writing in Spanish was essential for Goytisolo (as it is for any author born in Catalonia) in order to have an international reputation, particularly since he lived in Paris, worked for Gallimard, and was translated into French and English, [9] thus putting into question to what extent someone who chooses a privileged language can say that he or she is oppressed by this choice.

A Familial Canon

In "La novela familiar del autobiógrafo," James Fernández, building on Edward Said, explains that the modern writer in the autobiographical genre tends to replace filiation – the biological, hereditary, and familial bond – with connections of "affiliation": intellectual, moral, and spiritual ties (55). Fernández talks about a new genealogy or, better yet, in the case of Goytisolo, an antigenealogical tree that involves the abandonment of the familial surroundings and the questioning of familial values (56). According to Fernández, Goytisolo does this by taking on the literary tribe as a familial substitute (56). However, one can see that there is a direct correlation between filiation and affiliation and that the father and the mother impact Goytisolo's relationship with writing and culture. Accordingly, blood and literary families are interconnected: The paternal and Francoist cultural heritages establish a sense of sonship with a male literary canon, and while the self recognizes feminine or femininized elements as influential in his works – Catalan language, Catalan authors, female authors, and the impact of his wife, Monique Lange – these are almost always placed in a secondary position or acknowledged as absences.

In *Coto*, the familial influences on the mother's side contrast with the exterior, dry literary and cultural landscape of Spain. Both the figure of the father (at home) and that of the dictator (through education and censorship) controlled reading and knowledge, but they also reaffirmed and strengthened the importance of literature in Goytisolo's life. Goytisolo received a biased and incomplete education in which literature and history were narrated following the precepts of the dictatorship, without acknowledgment, for instance, of left-wing or exiled Republican authors. Similarly, the father, as opposed to the disappeared members on the mother's side, was not especially interested in culture. Indeed in *Coto* the biological father's perception of language and literature is doubly entangled with the Francoist cultural legacy: First, literature is described as unattainable, stagnant, and dry while Goytisolo was living in Barcelona in his father's house and under Franco's jurisdiction. In this context, both the paternal/Francoist language and the canon behind this language are first studied following dry pedagogies and later discovered with passion when Goytisolo self-exiles to France in 1956. Second, the father's and Franco's literary censorship and homophobia go hand in hand in connecting Goytisolo's self-censored sexuality to his writings. Goytisolo explains that censorship was crucial in his relationship to the canon, something that he shared with other writers of his generation: The difficulties of acquiring certain prohibited and inaccessible books made literature more desired and prestigious (163), and he was forced to read and write in secret: "Encerrado en mi habitación de Pablo Alcover, permanecía a menudo en vela hasta la madrugada recorriendo escrupulosamente los libros franceses de la biblioteca de mi madre o devorando centenares de páginas de

Dostoievski, Poe, Conrad, Pirandello o Bernard Shaw" (167; Locked up in my room in the house on Pablo Alcover, I often stayed up until dawn scrupulously browsing through the French books of my mother's library or devouring hundreds of pages by Dostoevsky, Poe, Conrad, Pirandello or Bernard Shaw) and converted the act of reading into a transgressive pleasure that took place clandestinely (168). Similarly, he would hide from his father the fact that he was writing:

> Escribía por las tardes, en mi habitación, ocultando dolorosamente los manuscritos tras una pila de libros de Derecho: mi padre asomaba de vez en cuando por la puerta su perfil de aguilucho a fin de cerciorarse de mi aplicación en los estudios y la concentración y entusiasmo que descubría disipaban sus dudas y reconfortaban su ánimo. El Derecho Civil debe de ser muy interesante, ¿verdad, hijo?, musitaba antes de eclipsarse; y yo, fingiendo salir de un profundo ensimismamiento en los minuciosos requisitos del dominio enfitéutico, afirmaba que sí, que efectivamente lo era. Mi novela avanzaba a buen paso. (177)

> I wrote in the afternoons, in my room, painfully hiding the manuscripts behind a pile of law books: my father would occasionally poke his hawk-nosed profile out of the door in order to make sure I was studying; the concentration and enthusiasm that he discovered dispelled his doubts and soothed his spirits. Civil Law must be very interesting, right, son? He whispered before disappearing; and I, pretending to come out of a deep absorption in the meticulous requirements of civil law, affirmed that yes, it was indeed. My novel was progressing at a good pace.

He explains that censorship incited in him and his generation of writers a different approach to reading and writing. As an example, after the publication of his novel *Juegos de manos* (Hand Tricks) was delayed in the process of censorship, he wrote *Campos de Níjar* (Nijar Fields) with an extreme awareness of how the censors would react to his words. He constructed a book completely conditioned by censorship, where ellipses, associations, and implicit deductions are important. This experience made him realize that, in order to avoid censorship, he had converted himself into the censor, which he describes as a "penosa automutilación" (325; painful self-mutilation). The Freudian imaginary of castration is used to establish a parallel between body and text, but the same experience of self-censorship also connects the text with sexual desire. Goytisolo also explains that censorship gave Spanish writers the possibility of measuring themselves against a power that would consider them important, given that, in the end, being forbidden meant to have ideas that annoyed and subverted the regime ("Discurso" 46). In this context, the figure of the father is essential to enforce prohibition at home: Not only does Juan Goytisolo describe the father as watching closely and with suspicion to see whether his children wrote, but he is also described as heavily impacted by the fact that Juan Goytisolo and his brother Luis Goytisolo were considered personae non grata by the dictatorship because of their writings and political involvement.

Father and dictator also converge in their homophobia. As we will see in Terenci Moix as well, Goytisolo repeatedly speaks about his father's homophobia, a hate that is uncomfortable for Goytisolo because of his suspicion of his own desire for men even when he had established a long-lasting relationship with the French publisher and writer Monique Lange. His fear of being gay is exacerbated because of the relationship between the father and Goytisolo's maternal grandfather, who abused Goytisolo as a child. The scenes of the grandfather molesting Juan Goytisolo are depicted with clarity at the beginning of *Coto* and are tangible by the distance in the grandson's and grandfather's relationship from then on. The reaction of the father (who asked the maternal grandfather and grandmother to leave the family home and go live elsewhere after the abuse) is lived by Juan Goytisolo with a sense of relief and justice but is also seen as a form of punishment of a form of desire that is unacceptable. This punishment of the grandfather by the father is later prolonged by the torturous relationship between them when the grandparents came back to live with the family once Goytisolo and his siblings were grown up. As with literature, homosexuality is at some point described by Goytisolo as a genetic inheritance using the internalized deprecation that the father expressed towards gay men. In *En los reinos*, Goytisolo speaks of the "monstruosa semilla de desorden, aberración y desvío de la rama materna" (295; monstrous seed of disorder, aberration and deviation from the maternal branch) to illustrate his father's homophobic words about the grandfather but also to describe how the paternal reaction would result in self-censorship. Goytisolo also recalls that his brother told him of their father explaining that Mussolini would execute all homosexuals (118), merging the law at home with the authoritarian law.

In many ways, Goytisolo's father corresponds to Freud's depiction of the father in *The Ego and the Id* and in *Civilization and its Discontents*, where the father is the one who establishes the superego, which creates a punitive internal structure that simultaneously sets limits and controls the instinctual drive of the subject. The father, an authoritarian presence, has a direct impact on the repression of the subject's desires. Goytisolo's father has the semblance of a punitive figure, the one who is responsible for the creation of the superego and the control of instincts, but at the same time he is not a figure who is strong enough to enforce his precepts on his own and therefore needs the shadow of the dictator. Indeed, in Goytisolo's use of explicit Freudian terminology and imagery, the laws – both familial and external – coincide, and the biological father and Franco overlap in a game of mirrors in which the father is in the shadow of the dictator and the dictator in the shadow of the father: They both awaken the subject's urgency to write and to escape Spain.[10] Goytisolo describes in his autobiographies the cultural situation of Spain as an "orfandad intelectual y yermo cultural" (213; intellectual orphan and in a cultural wasteland), an idea that, as James Fernández observes, strengthens the myth of the self-made man (56). As an autodidact, Goytisolo inherited a disorganized cultural legacy. This led him to ignore the Spanish literary canon until he was in his late twenties, when he was living in Paris. When in France, he revised the values and norms that had earlier regulated his ideology (158–9). Goytisolo describes his culture as "forjada a tientas y aun a contracorriente" (134; forged by trial and against the current), with the prejudices, gaps, and insufficiencies of this "España asolada y yerma, sometida a la censura y rigores de un régimen sofocante" (134; Spain devastated and barren, subjected to the censorship and rigors of a suffocating regime). For instance, of all the novels he devoured from the age of 18 to 25, none were written by a Spanish author (134). He affirms that he denied the importance of *El Quijote* and knew nothing about the Spanish Golden Age (135) until at age 26, in Paris (135), he discovered Cervantes and authors such as Arcipreste de Hita or Blanco White. This discovery disturbed him: "comprobaba que me había privado por mi culpa de mis más enjundiosos gozos" (135; I found that I had deprived myself of my deepest joys) and turned into a fascination with the Spanish canon.

This idea of rediscovery is crucial to his becoming an autonomous canon builder, and his immeasurable fascination for the Hispanic canon also helps construct authorial figure. In *Coto* and *En los reinos*, we find an enumeration of those writers who influenced him, and, in this sense, Goytisolo's autobiography is quite traditional, listing the numerous male writers he met who became models for him. *Coto* and *En los reinos* offer exhaustive lists of those authors whom Goytisolo tried to emulate, or in whose shadow he wrote, for instance the works of foreign authors such as James Joyce, Montaigne, Wilde, Bergson, Kierkegaard, Proust, Kafka, Malraux, Gide, Camus, Sartre, Baudelaire, Hermann Hesse, Dos Passos, Hemingway, Faulkner, Lukács, Pavese, and Vittorini. For him, these international writers demonstrate the lack of culture of those from Spain as well as the culturally inferior position of Franco's Spain in comparison to France, Italy, or the United States. This list of foreign writers is important to Goytisolo's portrayal of silence and then the return of the Spanish canon as a movement that is unavoidable and that unfolds with enormous power. Once he is in France, rediscovery takes place: Goytisolo flags and privileges Spanish writers central to the national canon from medieval times to his contemporaries, including Juan Ruiz, Miguel de Unamuno, Federico García Lorca, Pío Baroja, Rafael Alberti, Luis de Góngora, and Blanco White as his primary literary interlocutors. He also quotes the Hispano-Arab and Catalan traditions by mentioning Ibn Hazm, Palau y Fabre, and Mercè Rododera, although Catalan, Arab, and Hispano-Arab names appear in smaller numbers. Goytisolo also professes great admiration for the French author Jean Genet, probably the most privileged of all the authors he names, as Genet and Goytisolo established a close friendship, and Goytisolo admires Genet not only for his texts but also because of his open homosexuality and his behaviour counter to the rules and social norms. In this way, he claims the existence of literary fathers for whom he develops an Oedipal devotion, which allocates Goytisolo as a faithful follower of the autobiographical tradition. Goytisolo constructs a mostly male genealogy, and the real father and the dictator lie beneath this list of influential writers. In many ways, Goytisolo's canon consists of heterodox writers: It includes exiles and peripheral authors, but this is a canon that grants him a privileged position and generational acceptance as well. Goytisolo affiliates himself with Spanish writers such as Rafael Sánchez Ferlosio, Carmen Martín Gaite, Gil de Biedma, Salinas, Barral, Ferrater, or Ana María Matute as authors he knew from Spain. We may note that women are underrepresented, but this is not because Goytisolo's inclusion of them is tokenistic but more probably because this canon is a result of the historical circumstances inherited by the autobiographer.

Through his participation in the homage to Machado in Colliure (327) and later in the literary conversations in Formentor, he also considers himself to be a member of something similar to a literary generation. He explains how in Paris he met the Spanish exiles Jorge Semprún, Teresa de Azcárate, and Tuñón de Lara as well as the leaders (some of them exiled) of the Spanish Communist Party. During the project of creating the intellectual journal *Libre*, he worked with the Latin American writers Carlos Fuentes, Julio Cortázar, Gabriel García Márquez, Mario Vargas Llosa, and José Donoso. Thus, in his autobiographies, he gradually strengthens the place of the Spanish-language tradition over other "external" literary and cultural influences by signaling how he was late to discover Spanish authors, and therefore, with a sense of guilt and indebtedness, places himself as a central author within the Hispanic tradition. As Bradley Epps comments, while Goytisolo "increasingly reasserts the importance of Spanish literary tradition … he continues to engage issues of sexual identity, cultural conflict, and political oppression that do not admit to national containment" (19). Contrastingly, Alison Ribeiro de Menezes uses the idea of "canonizing dissidence" (29) to argue that Goytisolo's essays "reflect a cultivation of marginality and dissidence that finds expression in the adoption of a series of literary doubles and in a discursive act of ventriloquism" (30). Even when Goytisolo claims an affiliation with dissidents, Ribeiro de Menezes comments on how surprising it is that a writer who is constantly at odds with "official" culture could simultaneously express such loyalty to the idea of the canon (32). Goytisolo's essays are, according to Ribeiro de Menezes, unexpectedly traditional and essentialist: While he proposes an alternative literary tradition, he never questions the notion of the canon. The same happens in Goytisolo's autobiographies, where we find unmistakable attention to and insistence upon the need to create a literary persona by signaling literary genealogies, influences, and confluences. It is because of this reinforcement of a literary genealogy that *Coto* and *En los reinos* can be taken as examples of Laura Marcus's assertion that autobiographical texts not only follow, in their order and structure, other exemplary texts – sacrificing originality so as to be included in the canon – but also reinforce the importance of mentors and models (2). Through an amalgamation of the father's and Franco's censorship and literary legacy, family and canon go hand in hand.

Literary genealogies are impacted by family relationships in Goytisolo's autobiographies, and along both lines (the literary and the familial) there is an internalization of inherited elements. The place of Goytisolo's partner, Monique Lange, is telling in this regard. Goytisolo solidified his relationship with Monique Lange when he moved to Paris and to her home in 1956, and they were married from 1978 until Lange died in 1996; that is, as Jo Labanyi explains, Goytisolo married Lange fourteen years after "coming out" ("The Construction" 213) and after 22 years of being together, evidencing that their relationship went beyond traditional ideas of the heterosexual monogamous couple, something that he expressed in a letter to her that is published as part of *En los reinos*. During their marriage and until Lange's death, Goytisolo travelled back and forth from Morocco to France, without repressing his love for Arab men, and once Lange died Goytisolo moved definitively to Morocco. It was through Lange, who was also a writer and an employee at the publishing house Gallimard, that Goytisolo established contact with an impressive series of international writers and philosophers when he arrived in Paris.[11] Thanks to her, Goytisolo met international and French writers and philosophers such as William Faulkner, André Malraux, Marguerite Duras, and Roland Barthes as well as Jean Genet, who, according to Goytisolo "ha sido en verdad mi única influencia adulta en el plano estrictamente moral" (461; has been in fact my only adult influence on a strictly moral level). Goytisolo was granted a privileged position, that of Gallimard's literary adviser, which invested him with power in relation to those writers from Spain and Latin America who wanted to be part of the French literary landscape. In this context, the French writer and political activist Jean Genet is presented as a model of life and work for the autobiographer. Goytisolo felt inspired by Genet's relationship with young men, and Genet not only "anticipate[s] Goytisolo's own sexual commitments" (Smith 36) but is also a figure who offers an image of paternity that contrasts with the ideas of paternity Goytisolo had formulated around his father. Genet adopts younger sexual partners as a kind of family (452) in what Goytisolo describes as similar to a father–son relationship. In this paternal–filial bond, Genet protects and guides the lives of his young lovers in a bond in which paternity, desire, and affection play important roles. Goytisolo observes with admiration this paternal–filial experience, as he does Genet's values and the fact that Genet always does the unexpected and never depends on the applause of critics and other writers, thus acknowledging Genet as an example. In parallel, Goytisolo decisively refuses the possibility of having children, alleging that the only legacy he wants to leave behind are his books. In this regard, Goytisolo conceives of writing as a form of dominated fecundity (47, 132). At the beginning of *Coto*, he compares himself with a mother who, after a miscarriage, desires to be pregnant again, in order to explain his irrational necessity to continue writing: "Como la madre frustrada después de un aborto involuntario busca con impaciencia, a fin de superar el trauma, la forma y ocasión apropiadas de lograr un nuevo embarazo, sentir aflorar bruscamente, en el dormitorio de la habitación en donde os reponéis del percance, la violenta pulsión de la escritura tras largos meses de esterilidad" (36; Like the mother who frustrated after a spontaneous abortion impatiently looks for, in order to overcome the trauma, the appropriate way and the occasion to get pregnant again, to feel suddenly emerge, in the bedroom of the suite where you happen to be resting, the violent desire to write after long months of sterility). In *En los reinos*, he affirms that for him writing is an alternative form of paternity and that the book is a controlled form of procreation: "la procreación de un libro gestado a salvo de las contingencias de una ley genética aleatoria" (512; the procreation of a gestated book safe from the contingencies of a random genetic law). This is something that he reformulates in *Telón de boca* speaking about himself using the third person: "Buenos o malos, los libros serían sus hijos" (58; Good or bad, the books would be his children).

Goytisolo's admiration for Genet and Goytisolo's words somehow resonate with a masculinist, patriarchal, ideal of literary production: "in patriarchal Western culture ... the text's author is a father, a progenitor, a procreator, an aesthetic patriarch, whose pen is an instrument of generative power like his penis" (Gilbert and Gubar 6). Alison Ribeiro de Menezes considers the experience of writing to be self-centred and phallic in Goytisolo's texts (27), and in effect Goytisolo comes to the father's language and to a male canon in order to accomplish an act of masculine rebirth. That said, Goytisolo's idea of paternity is often complicated by the presence of the feminine, which is always existent although present as an absence, a void that is yet constant in his literary production, such as the death of the mother and the relationship with Monique Lange. Indeed, the relationship with Lange, particularly once they married, appears as a void, a silence, as Linda Gould Levine explains:

> [*En los reinos*] termina con un gran salto cronológico ... lo que no se narra es la historia de los dos entre 1965 y 1978 y los obstáculos que superaron para llegar al matrimonio veintitrés años después de conocerse. Precisamente porque la historia de Goytisolo y Lange sufre de esta laguna cronológica, es difícil terminar la lectura de estas memorias apasionantes y en particular *En los reinos de taifa* sin preguntarse por los sentimientos y reacciones de la receptora de las confesiones desgarradoras de Juan Goytisolo, sin querer saber cómo responde Monique Lange al reto que le propone su compañero en 1965.

> [*En los reinos*] ends with a large chronological leap ... what it narrates is the history of the two of them from 1965 to 1978 and the obstacles they overcame in order to get married twenty-three years after they first met. Precisely because the story of Goytisolo and Lange suffers from this chronological gap, it's difficult to finish reading these passionate memoirs and, in particular, *En los reinos de taifa* without inquiring about the feelings and reactions of the receptor of these heartbreaking confessions of Juan Goytisolo, without wanting to know how Monique Lange responds to the challenge her companion proposed to her in 1965.

Lange did offer a certain account of her relationship with Goytisolo in *Les cabines de bain / Casetas de baño* (1983), where the female protagonist explains what it meant for her to have a relationship with a man who loves other men. The narrator explains how her partner felt "poseído, embrujado. Como si hubiera recibido una maldición" (43; possessed, bewitched. As if he'd been cursed) when he traveled to Arab countries and the difficulties she had opening up their relationship and accepting that he was also with men: "Creyó que podría volver a los países árabes con él. Muchas mujeres viajan alegremente con la querida de su marido. Muchos hombres pasean con el amante de su mujer. Sin embargo, la pasión por el mundo árabe era tan fuerte en él, tan invasora" (42; I thought I could go back to the Arab countries with him. Many women happily travel with their husband's lover. Many men travel with their wife's lover. Nevertheless, his passion for the Arab world was so strong in him, so invasive). The protagonist of *Les cabines de bain* feels these male lovers as a threat "ellos le roban su marido. No quiere tener malos pensamientos" (55; they steal her husband from her. She doesn't want to have evil thoughts), and she acknowledges that there is an element of perversion in her partner's form of loving: "era consciente del margen de perversión que podía existir en un escritor que sólo amaba analfabetos" (51; she was conscious of the margin of perversion that could exist for a writer who only loved men who were illiterate). It is hard to tell whether her voice as a partner and wife is silenced in Goytisolo's autobiographies or whether Goytisolo is on the contrary acknowledging that she is the one who needs to formulate a voice of her own, but what is obvious is that, surrounded by literature, the canon is something deeply personal and intimate to him.

Conclusion

In Goytisolo's autobiographies, the biological father is presented as the one responsible for bringing the social machinery of control to the home, for enforcing the dictatorship's precepts in the household. The biological father is discursively essential when positioning the subject: The self is unable to escape the legacy of Francoism because this is a personal heritage too. The similarities between father and dictator are evident and are marked by the superimposing of the father's beliefs and of Francoist ideology, as the father supports the regime's homophobia, anti-Catalanism, right-wing ideals, and Catholicism. These parallelisms are constructed by establishing a series of correspondences between Franco's and the father's linguistic and literary precepts and by an amalgamation between the father's and Franco's bodies. Father and dictator both are castrating entities that control reading and knowledge; they reaffirm and strengthen the importance of literature and culture, as well as the subject's need to embrace a Spanish canon. The father is essential for the subject to embrace the autobiographical canon, not only because autobiographical texts are traditionally permeated with paternal presences but also because Goytisolo's writing is understood as a form of paternity in which the authority of the autobiographer is placed, first, vis-à-vis the father's authority and, second, vis-à-vis the dictator's.

Coto and *En los reinos* demonstrate the complexity of fatherhood beyond the figure of the dictator. The "foundational" lie about the mother's death, the father's inability to protect and sustain the family in the way Juan Goytisolo would have hoped, the father's irrational homophobia, and the particular way his father dealt with the sexual abuse Goytisolo experienced on the part of his maternal grandfather turn the autobiographical subject into a judge of the biological father and the autobiographical text into a denunciation. *Coto* and *En los reinos* show what Thomas Couser calls an act of disaffiliation through the autobiographical writing (154), in which the son does not pay tribute to the father but judges him. Yet, in contrast to his relationship with the figure of the dictator, the autobiographer is marked by an ambivalence towards the biological father, as Goytisolo says he also felt tenderness for him (112) and acknowledges that perhaps his judgment of his father was at times exaggerated. These fluctuating feelings that go from judgment to tenderness differentiate the subject's relationship with his biological father from his feelings towards the dictator. At the same time, these shifting emotions regarding his father permeate Juan Goytisolo's passions and interests, as he also establishes a sentimental path that fluctuates between negation and acceptance of the Spanish language, the language of his father; the Spanish canon; and his desire for men, a path on which the self is unable to free himself completely from the paternal (colonization, the language of the father, and the absence of the feminine). Despite his unwillingness to have biological children and his considering books to be his offspring, Goytisolo was the stepfather of Carole Achache, Monique Lange's daughter, and became the de facto father to the son of his male partner and to the two children of his partner's brother, something he speaks about in *Telón de boca* "aquellos niños adoptados por él a fin de paliar el vacío eran su última defensa frente a la inminencia de la caducidad" (25; those children he adopted in order to alleviate the void were his last defence before the imminence of his expiry date). He lived with these three children in Marrakesh and accepted the Spanish Cervantes Prize in order to pay for their education. Thus, perhaps ironically, Goytisolo accepted being canonized in Spain as a form of responsibility towards his children, evidencing not only that he was an author marked by complexities, paradoxes, and a desire for moral integrity but also that paternity structured his works and life in multiple ways.

3 Carlos Barral: Masculine Subjectivity and the Catalan Father

Born Carlos Barral Agesta in Barcelona in 1928, Barral was an influential publisher in twentieth-century Spain as well as a prolific writer. He left an important legacy of poetry placed within what is known as the Escuela de Barcelona, a group of authors from Barcelona who were part of the Spanish Generation of 50 movement.[1] As a publisher, from 1955[2] to 1968, Barral turned Seix Barral into one of the biggest publishing houses in Spain, reestablished Barcelona as a centre of the country's publishing industry, and was key in the creation of the Latin American Boom. However, a sense of failure surrounds his publishing endeavours and is fundamental in his autobiographies. The two publishing houses he was involved in (Seix Barral and Barral Editores) ended up insolvent, and, though Barral was well known as one of the central figures of the Latin American Boom for publishing novelists such as Mario Vargas Llosa and José Donoso, he missed the publishing coup of a lifetime when he did not publish *Cien años de soledad* (One Hundred Years of Solitude), and García Márquez decided to send it instead to Editorial Sudamericana in Buenos Aires.[3] Politically involved during the beginning of the Spanish democracy, Barral served as senator in Tarragona for the Partit dels Socialistes de Catalunya (Socialist Party of Catalonia) from 1982 to 1986 and later as Eurodeputy (1986–7) for the same party. In these roles, he advocated for the law of intellectual property and the "Ley de Costas" (Coast Law), which aimed to control the unrestrained construction taking place in the littoral zone during the '80s. Despite these achievements, both the publishing business and his political involvement were to him impediments to his writing and are often described as frustrations in his *Memorias*.

In Barral's *Memorias*, fetishization, guilt, and a certain dissatisfaction tinge his language choices both as poet and publisher. He belonged to a generation that was educated under Franco's dictatorship and was not schooled in Catalan, and he wrote the majority of his texts in Spanish. The family constellation as well as Francoist linguistic politics are crucial in Barral's explanation of his choice to write and publish in Spanish during his youth and adulthood: Barral was the son of a Uruguayan-Argentine mother and a Catalan father, and his bilingualism was affected by his father's death in 1936. In addition to the language politics of the dictatorship, his father's absence contributed to the fading of Catalan in Barral's day-to-day life during his childhood and youth. The father's absence meant that Catalan became a language around which Barral had a sense of heritage and indebtedness, a language that he saw as capable of literary expression but that he did not take on as a language to write in until late in his career. It was only after Franco's death that Barral decided to portray a very specific world, the sea landscape of the Mediterranean, in Catalan.

The memory of his father, Carlos Barral Nualart, who died when Barral was eight years old and whom Barral associates with a nebulous time before the dictatorship, is a recurring presence in Barral's autobiographies. Barral's father died of a heart attack in August 1936, just one month before the Spanish Civil War started. Even though this death took place in circumstances unrelated to the Civil War, his father's loss foreshadows the sense of disaffection and lack of protection of those who experienced the war as children and who had to grow up in post-war Spain. At the same time, the father's absence creates an aura of idealization around the father's memory, linking him to the time of the Republic. Barral credits his father with introducing him to the world of writing and publishing. The father's material and cultural inheritance and the effort to recover it are also basic in developing Barral's bourgeois and masculine consciousness. In addition, in Barral's autobiographies, his father is a person outside the dictatorship, a vanishing presence linked to Barral's fetishization of Catalan as a loved yet dismissed language that is linked to his desire to paint in words his childhood in Calafell. This fetishization goes hand in hand with the shadowing presence of very precise models of masculinity: The father is a physically strong, protective figure that fades away, just as the sailors of the Catalan coastal village of Calafell progressively vanish during Barral's adulthood. These men slowly disappeared while a different form of masculinity emerged in the city – the authoritarian presence of the priests – and their disappearance was later reinforced when Barral became friends with other writers from his generation, intellectuals who conformed to an urban model of men. The coastal versus the urban forms of masculinity impacted the creation of a distinct but divided self in Barral: He was at once a poet attached to the sea, to the popular, and to bodily pleasures and a publisher linked to the city, his bourgeois intellectual friends, and his unending professional struggles and responsibilities.

This chapter casts light on the importance of the father as a longed-for presence that Carlos Barral uses to construct and explain his masculine, linguistic, poetic, and professional subjectivity in his autobiographies. I argue that the father colours the sentimental place that Catalan language and culture occupy in Barral's *Memorias* and that his father is essential to Barral in delineating his linguistic practices. In his memoirs, Barral explains his role as a publisher and generational leader and also explores the importance that literature and languages had in his life. His first autobiography, *Años de penitencia* (Years of Penitence), centred on his childhood under the dictatorship and, published in 1975, months before Franco's death, pioneered the rise of the autobiographical genre in Spain that aimed to reevaluate the recent history of the country.[4] *Años de penitencia* was followed by two more autobiographical texts: *Los años sin excusa* (Years without Excuse) in 1978 and *Cuando las horas veloces* (When Time Is Fleeting), in 1988. In these two books, Barral wrote about his work as a publisher and writer during Franco's regime and during the transition and about not being able fully to embrace his passion as a poet. All three books were republished together by Península in 2001 and by Lumen in 2015 as *Memorias,* which included the posthumous text "Memorias de infancia," in which Barral presents in the third person his earliest memories.[5] The various reprintings of these works signal the importance of the autobiographical project as part of Barral's persona as writer, publisher, and public intellectual. Barral's autobiographies are in dialogue with his poetry, newspaper articles,[6] poetry diaries, and autofictional novel *Penúltimos castigos* (1983; Last Punishments), as well as with two less well-known texts in Catalan, *Catalunya des del mar* (1982; Catalonia from the Sea) and *Catalunya a vol d'ocell* (1985; Catalonia: A Bird's Eye View). These last are rarely considered part of his self-writings but can help us understand the imprint of his father and the author's sense of responsibility towards his father's linguistic and cultural legacy.

The Space of the Father

In 1928, the year in which Barral was born, Barral's father rented a house in Calafell, a small seaside town in the province of Tarragona. A few years later, he bought another house some metres away, and this second house served as Barral's second residence for the rest of his life. Distinguished by its colonial balcony, the house today is a museum that reveals details of Barral's life and preserves a past reality of the town of Calafell through maritime objects, photographs, and books from the Barral family. The seascape that surrounds this house and the town of Calafell are of foremost importance in Barral's poetry and autobiographies, and Barral often closely connects that landscape to his memories of his father.

In Barral's *Memorias*, particularly in the third chapter of *Años de penitencia* entitled "Calafell y la cuestión del lenguaje" (Calafell and the Issue of Language) and in the posthumous text "Memorias de infancia" (Memories of Childhood), Barral presents Calafell as a place of freedom and plenitude, linked to a happy childhood and to the discovery of the Catalan language through the father and the Catalan-speaking fishermen. Barral describes the familial house and its history in detail (77) and explains how as a child he spent the majority of his time in the open space of the beach (79), surrounded by sailors and their boats, a landscape that he describes "de una armonía cromática perfecta" (86; as forming a perfect chromatic harmony). In this context, this town constitutes a totality: It is a closed system, sustained for years in an indestructible equilibrium (99). The author links it to life before the Civil War, asserting that Calafell gave him a sense of identity and differentiation from the rest of the world: "De cuanto recordaba de antes de la guerra civil, eran las largas temporadas en Calafell las que contenían todo lo exaltante y todos los pequeños acontecimientos que, me parecía a mí, me identificaban como una persona totalmente distinta a las demás" (76; What I remember of the years before the civil war were those long stays in Calafell, which contained all that was exciting and all the seemingly insignificant events that, I believe, distinguish me as a person completely different from everyone else). Because Barral's father died when he was a child, Calafell is also a place of mourning and recovery, where the boundaries between the subject and others are diffuse and unstable. Calafell is described as a space of conjunction and as "el lugar litúrgico del culto al padre desaparecido" (76; the liturgical space of the cult to the missing father).[7]

Calafell is "un mundo primitivo, presuntamente original y estrictamente marinero" (907; a primitive world, seemingly authentic and exclusively nautical), a sacred space where Barral developed a liturgical devotion to his father. In this maritime setting, Barral's father emerges as an idealized figure. Barral describes his father as "el maestro escultor y un personaje altísimo y barbudo" (913; the master sculptor and a very tall, bearded character) and as "el hombre que, con tanta fascinación y tantas veces, había visto arribar a la playa a primeras horas de la tarde al timón del primer y esbelto [barco] Capitán Argüello, con hermosos peces sobre los corredores de cubitera; el paseante extrañamente vestido por la playa solitaria del invierno; el personaje de quien me hablaban con admiración" (76; the man who, so many times and with such fascination, I'd seen arrive first at the beach in the early hours of the afternoon at the helm of the graceful [boat] Captain Argüello, with beautiful fish lining the sides of the deck; the eccentrically dressed figure walking on the solitary winter beach; the person of whom they spoke to me in admiration). The mythical, admired father has an aura of strength and physical presence. Barral's father is described as a distant figure that the self aims to reclaim through the memory of his body, gestures, and heirlooms such as boats, photographs, and video recordings. The father embodies a nurturing image that Barral associates with his "hambrienta memoria" (76; hungry memory) and that will feed the writer's imagination over the years.

In some ways, in Barral's childhood memories, the father is an "imaginary father," a concept coined by Julia Kristeva in opposition to the Lacanian father as a figure of seizure and law. Instead of relating paternity with control and punishment, Kristeva conceives of this "imaginary father" as an intermediary, a loving figure who enables the child to negotiate a nontraumatic separation from the mother.[8] Following her revision of Lacanian theory, Kristeva also coins the concept *semiotic chora*,[9] understood as a liquid space of fluctuation between the Freudian and Lacanian pre-Oedipal and the Oedipal world of language that alludes to a womb-like environment. In effect, while Barral describes Calafell as a space tightly linked to his father, he also calls it a "uterine landscape" (*Almanaque* 54), thereby invoking the idea that this coast is a maternal womb. At a talk Barral gave entitled "Privilegio de la galera," he also inferred "en cuanto a la mar, lo principal es hacerse a la idea de que venimos de ella" (142; as for the sea, the main thing is to accept that we come from her). This repeated reference to the maternal element of the sea has been noted by Carme Riera, who considers the seascape in Barral's life in these words: "Tal vez debamos relacionar ese interés por el paisaje marítimo con el ansia de volver al útero materno, el húmedo espacio primigenio en el que el medio acuoso es fundamental" ("Carlos Barral, entre vida y literatura" 26; Perhaps we must relate this interest in the seascape with the desire to return to the womb, that damp primordial space in which the watery medium is everything). In Calafell, surrounded by the sea and sailors' boats, Barral's father is an idealized man not only placed outside the paternal law and the Francoist repressive state but also occupying a space that seems to combine both maternal and paternal elements. The father's surroundings produce this "oceanic feeling" that Freud associated at the beginning of

Civilization and Its Discontents with the sensation of absolute conjunction between subject and world, with a religious energy (2), and with the restoration of limitless narcissism (7).

Nonetheless, as in Freud, there is a problematic representation of the feminine behind Barral's descriptions. In fact, Freud's "oceanic feeling" is closely linked to the fear of being engulfed by the mother, as this sensation is understood as a vestige of the infant consciousness while still breastfeeding, that is, of a subject unable to differentiate himself or herself from the mother. Similarly, in Barral's autobiographies, the sea apparently has the potential to erase class and gender boundaries or to situate the autobiographer as preexistent to them. It evokes an image of the father as a protective, loving figure in a womb-like place of the imagination, while Calafell constitutes a place where the bourgeois father, the publisher from Barcelona, as well as his son become friends of the sailors, men without a formal education. Yet, in many ways, the sea is also the space where these boundaries start to be tenuously yet consistently perceived by the child, and the construction of these boundaries is something that the adult recovers in an obsessive way, to the extent of helping him acknowledge a divided self. Indeed, Barral's descriptions of Calafell present a value system in which, even when gender, class, and space limits seem to be questioned, traditional notions of class, of gender, and of urban versus natural landscape are reinforced. Calafell is essential for Barral as he identifies with the bourgeoisie and with the educated class of Barcelona in contrast to the fishermen, and, while certain feminine attributes are given to the father and the maritime landscape of Calafell, it is mostly men who are evoked in this landscape, and these men are the ones who carry out the active roles of fishing and sailing, who serve as models and teach Barral how to swim and sail (98).

Important in this regard is the correlation established between the sea and the poetic, following a determinate literary tradition that includes writers such as Herman Melville and Ernest Hemingway in the Anglo-Saxon tradition or Rafael Alberti in the Hispanic tradition. The sea is a recurring element in Barral's writings beyond his autobiographies, as we can see in the books of poetry from *Las aguas reiteradas* (1952; The Ebbing Tide) to *Lecciones de cosas* and *Veinte poemas para el nieto Malcolm* (1986; Lessons of Things and Twenty Poems for My Grandson Malcom), as well as in *Diecinueve figuras de mi historia civil* (1960; Nineteen Figures of My Personal History) and in the novel *El azul del infierno* (2009; Hell's Blue). The liquidity of the maritime landscape, often a central source of inspiration, is also often evoked in gendered ways: In Barral's writings, the sea recalls the traditional female muse that aids or gives voice to the male author. Indeed, as Pierre Thiollière posits, the speaker in many of Barral's poems enters the feminine space of the sea as a way to occupy the paternal space (119). Thiollière argues that the paternal figure in this context is an androgynous figure (127). There is no doubt that there is a questioning of the maternal and paternal borders through idealization in several of Barral's images of the father in the Mediterranean. Barral uses the sea, which is linked to his own origins and to the father figure, to evoke a *Weltanschauung* in which uncertainty is primary by placing the father in a maternal, feminine domain and also by presenting a father who ambiguously melts into a fluctuating figure that neither invokes law nor confers punishment.

Yet the landscape of Calafell imparts a sense of physical and intellectual freedom from which women and particularly the mother are excluded or eclipsed by the fascination that men instil. In addition, the sea is a space of sensual pleasures, "porque Calafell era la libertad corporal, el espacio salutífero y, sobre todo, un campo de experiencias que, por cuanto incompletas, conducían, a veces, a la masturbación ocasional" (141; because Calafell was bodily freedom, a salubrious space and, above all, a world of experiences that, being incomplete, would lead to, at times, the occasional masturbation),[10] where some women are desired but absent of this desire as subjects. Thus, Barral's descriptions of Calafell invoke a masculine space of the father, the male sailors, and the self in which physical and later literary pleasure are experienced through homosocial experiences of learning coastal traditions, sailing and fishing. The use of the feminine article when referring to "la mar" is telling in this regard. While both the feminine and the masculine articles are allowed in Spanish, the use of the feminine indicates the desire to use the article not only traditionally considered more poetic but also the one used by sailors.[11] What is more, Barral often speaks about "la mar doméstica" (the domestic sea): The Mediterranean is "domestic," given its dimension and its connection to his childhood. It has a homey atmosphere and is a small sea that always remains recognizable. However, "domestic" also implies a second meaning closer to domestication. Jorge Edwards mentions, "ese mar que él había reinventado, que había domesticado en la imaginación" (84; this sea that he had reinvented, that he had domesticated in his imagination), making reference to the sailor's control of his boat on the sea, which could be read as male control over women or the writer's control over his writings and language.

In Barral's texts, certain feminine traits of the sea contrast with the masculinity that surrounds this landscape, particularly through the description of father and sailors. These men, depicted in contrast to the men of the city, are described as natural and spontaneous, and Calafell is described as an uncorrupted world that contrasts with the urban landscape of Barcelona. Barral speaks of the fishermen as models of easy imitation and explains that, as a child, he would try to mimic their ambiguous and mistrusting gestures. The fishermen, he affirms, were exotic and proximate, and had a different attitude towards the surrounding space from the one he observed in adults from the city. Their gestures are a body language that Barral learns alongside their words. This corporeal language is affected by the rhythms of sailing and fishing, by the rolling boats, and by the ongoing movement of the sea. The fight with the indomitable language, comparable to sailing on the unconquerable sea, could be interpreted in Barral's work as an impulse or desire to return to the paternal-feminine in his poetry but also as a desire to control this paternal-feminine and domestic coast. The division between the small maritime town and the urban landscape of Barcelona is important in constructing a boundary between the city as a space of the Spanish culture and prestige and the Catalan coastal and interior landscape as one of popular culture, intimately connected to differentiated models of masculinity and differentiated linguistic realities. Both the father – idealized in the eyes of the child – and the sailors faded in importance as Barral grew up and were ultimately eclipsed by the urban and intellectual model of men that included his generation of writers, who mostly chose Spanish as their literary language. That said, Calafell, "una patria adoptiva, pueblo más que natal" (754; an adoptive country, a town that felt like the birthplace), is the place where the self identifies the self, while at the same time it is the place of the father, as well as that of "los orígenes del lenguaje personal" (100; the origins of his personal language).

A Linguistic Subjectivity

Surrounded by his father and the fishermen, Barral attributes his discovery of a private language (Catalan) to the sea landscape of Calafell. The idea that Catalan is a private, unique language likely reflects a mixture between the sociolinguistic reality and the personal experience in which Barral was raised as a child: At the time Barral was growing up, just before the Spanish War, Catalan was quite certainly the primary language spoken by the inhabitants of Calafell, yet it coexisted for Barral with Spanish in his experience in the city of Barcelona, where Barral's Argentine-Uruguayan family were present. Here there are no repressive or punitive feelings towards the Catalan language, but Barral does signal how Catalan was perceived as private and as marking the distinctness of the self.

The distinction between languages and how they form the subject and literary consciousness are a central part of Barral's *Memorias*. Catalan and Spanish are placed in opposition to each other, as two languages associated with different spaces: "La lengua de la casa de la ciudad era el castellano" (884) "Pero el catalán era la lengua del mar y de la playa ... En el fondo la lengua habitual de las vacaciones y de sus muchos regalos" (884; The language of our house in the city was Spanish (Castilian)) (884; But Catalan was the language of the sea and of the beach ... And ultimately the everyday language of the summer vacation and its many gifts). Spanish, considered by Barral to be his first language, is the language of the city and the school. This Spanish as taught in school is described as poor, a language with a limited vocabulary, almost as poor as the French he would learn, which had only twenty verbs and a short list of some of the objects of everyday life (73). Spanish is also somehow "divided" in its dialectal, class, and spatial diversity for Barral, as the Argentinian Spanish of the mother and the mother's family, *los Medina*, is perceived as distinct from the peninsular Spanish of the street, the school, and classmates. In the chapter "Retrato de familia" in *Años de penitencia*, Barral explains: "Por la nómina de los personajes se adivinará que en mi casa se hablaba castellano ... La lengua de los Medina y la de mi madre era básicamente el argentino, un argentino en ocasiones teñido de un color local que lo diferencia del que luego he oído en boca de los cosmopolitas literatos rioplatenses" (69; From the list of characters one could guess that at my house we spoke Spanish. The language of the Medinas and of my mother was basically Argentinian, an Argentinian sometimes shaded by a regional colour that differentiated it from what I've since heard from the mouths of the cosmopolitan literary denizens of the Rio de la Plata region). Barral emphasizes the differentiated phonetic system and the *voseo*, to conclude: "La fonética de mi madre ha tenido en mí gran influencia, y en estado de fatiga pronuncio yerba (que me repugnaría escribir con h) o caballo, en argentino" (70; My mother's way of saying things has had an enormous influence on me and when I'm tired I say "yerba" "grass" (which I would find it repugnant to spell with an "h") or "caballo" "horse" in Argentinian). Barral talks of "mi sudamericano uterino" (74; my South American womb), reflecting his need to embed the concept of the "mother tongue" in his own linguistic reality. That said, this maternal dialect has surprisingly rarely been connected to Barral's interest in and work with Latin American authors. Indeed, it is surprising how absent Barral's Argentinian-speaking mother – and Barral's

Argentinian uncle, the gaucho Medina, who is presented as also an influential figure – are in the interpretation of the literary canon Barral forged as publisher.

While Catalan is seen as a rich language in the context of Calafell, full of specific words about the sea, navigation, and fishing, the Catalan Barral remembers from Barcelona was the Catalan of maids, chauffeurs, and *porteras* (doorwomen), a rude language that he related to unpleasant people and situations and to the low class, except for "las criadas, que como mas adelante las putas, eran de lengua castellana sin excepción" (73–4; the maids, who, as the whores later on, without exception, all spoke Spanish). Barral also comments on a potential Catalan girlfriend and concludes: "Tal vez el catalán no me resultaba en aquel tiempo un buen vehículo de comunicación erótica" (267; Maybe at that time I didn't think of Catalan as a very good means to communicate erotically). In many ways, Catalan has a mixed status in Barral's autobiographies, as it is presented as the subject's childhood language, the language that raises the subject's linguistic consciousness, but it is also deemed, particularly in the urban context, uncomfortable or foreign, "[el catalán] era la primera de mis lenguas extranjeras" (73; Catalan was the first of my foreign languages). Catalan, in this context, produces a sense of estrangement and is opposed to Spanish, the language of the mother, the language of the urban and of culture as he becomes an adult. In his memoirs, Barral explains that bilingualism is something much more complicated than just being able to speak two languages (73). Language acquisition is portrayed as a blurred and somehow contradictory process, deeply related to differentiated spaces and charged with emotions.

The Catalan from Calafell is described in "Memorias de infancia" as a language in a pure state, alive, ungoverned, and natural. As a child, he explains, he started inhabiting this language of others just as he inhabited the space of the coast: "La mar litoral y sus gentes comenzaban a ser, antes de que tú despertaras al arte de la memoria, un mundo y un lenguaje privados en los que empezabas a moverte con la misma habilidad que todos los adultos, imitados y distantes" (908; The seacoast and its people would become, before you awoke to the art of memory, a private world and language in which you started to move with the same ease as the adults, who were distant and who you imitated). The process that transforms him from an infant lacking speech into a differentiated subject originated in the linguistic and gestural imitation of the fishermen, in which language is perceived as something quasi-physical – thus placing Catalan, the father tongue, as a first language of consciousness.[12] This status of Catalan and Barral's mixed feelings about it speak to the inadequacy of the concept of the "mother tongue" for those raised in bilingual and multilingual societies and families, particularly if the "mother tongue," understood literally as the language of the mother, is only one of the languages one is raised in. Catalan, a language that nonetheless falls away because of the father's death and the political reality after the Civil War, is conceived as "Una lengua llena de locuciones especialísimas, que eran imágenes concretas y directas de las cosas de la mar, y de pintoresquismo, al que, en la adolescencia, me parecía estar muy lejos de una lengua de cultura" (73; A language full of idiosyncratic expressions, consisting of direct and concrete images for things pertaining to the sea and of picturesqueness that, as an adolescent, I thought of as being far removed from the language of culture).

For Barral, Calafell is a dominant space for the construction of the self, as well as the place where he learned Catalan, a language that is full of direct expressions about the sea, oral and spontaneous but that Barral rarely experienced as a language of literature and high culture (*Memorias* 105). Spanish, by contrast, is the language of the maternal family, the language of the city, and the language imposed by Francoism, one supported by the state that holds a position of legitimacy as the language for writing and publishing. Barral affirms that it took him years to understand that Catalan could also be a literary language. He blames this on the Francoist administration but also on the Catalan bourgeoisie, to which he belonged, who were willing to sacrifice their own language in order to maintain social status:

> Mis relaciones con el catalán eran, pues, como las que se tienen con el *patois* de la región, y lo siguieron siendo aun después de que cobré plena conciencia de que era, para otros, una lengua literaria y culta totalmente equivalente a la mía. Posiblemente sea éste uno de los mayores crímenes de la administración franquista contra mi generación: haber conseguido, con la colaboración de una burguesía obsecuente y dispuesta a todos los sacrificios, degradar una lengua nobilísima ante los ojos de los que estaban naturalmente destinados a expresarse en ella … Con a literatura catalana y con el catalán vivo como lengua de cultura no tuve familiaridad, y aún menos intimidad, hasta mucho más tarde. Y ya lo era demasiado para pensar y escribir en él como una lengua propia. (74)
>
> My relationship with Catalan was, then, similar to the one I had with the patois of the region, and it continued to be even after I became fully conscious that it was, for others, a literary and cultured language fully equal to my own. Possibly one of the Franco regime's worst crimes against my generation was to have successfully, with the collaboration of the ever-obsequious bourgeoisie always willing to make any sacrifice, denigrated

> a noble language in the eyes of those who were naturally destined to express themselves in it. I had no familiarity and even less intimacy, until very much later, with Catalan literature and actual Catalan as a language of culture. And it was already too late to think and to write in Catalan as if it were my own language.

Barral also comments on his layered relationship with words and the landscape, expressing anxiety about languages and seeing them as systems that he needs to dominate, given that words are in perpetual tension with one another. For instance, Barral considers that it was impossible to translate this very particular environment of Calafell from Catalan into Spanish, as translating his impressions of the coast and of sailing would have been a kind of annihilation: "el caso es que las equivalencias castellanas, especies de una lengua no vivida en aquellos casos determinados, resultaban cadavéricas, léxico de disección, y totalmente inútiles e inasimilables" (101; the point is that the Spanish equivalents, variations of a language that didn't exist in those specific circumstances, were cadaverous, a lexicon of dissection, and completely useless and unassimilable).

The linguistic divide between Catalan and Spanish relates to poetry and questions the borders between the literary genres Barral wrote in, as his obsession towards languages materialized in several ways in a diversity of his writings. Barral was an author who respected borders regarding literary genres, yet several of his texts are intimately connected between them: In his diaries, poetry books, autobiographies, or journal articles, he often expressed similar concerns. Furthermore, in Barral's autobiographies and in the literary criticism around his works there is the acknowledgment that Barral was conscious of words as being almost objects, and this consciousness of the material aspect of language is deeply linked to his bilingual upbringing. According to Tomás Sánchez Santiago, words in Barral's texts are "unidades físicas, como piezas no sólo portadoras de energía fónica sino también de una presencia espacial" (66; physical units, like pieces which are bearers not only of a phonetic energy but also of spatial presence).[13] The estrangement produced in the child's awareness when being raised bilingual (or better, the memory of the adult about this childhood awareness) gives birth to a consciousness in which languages are systems that the subject has not fully mastered but needs to master, a system linked to the paternal absence and portrayed as significant to Barral's development as a poet. Riera contends that the "abundante en la poesía es la jerga marinera que se relaciona con el mundo mítico de la infancia del poeta, igual que el léxico del mundo arcaizante de las armas antiguas tiene que ver con el culto al padre muerto" ("Prólogo" in Barral's *Poesía Completa* 31; extensive in the poetry is the seafaring slang associated with the mythical world of the poet's childhood, just as the lexicon of the archaic world of antique weapons has to do with the cult of the dead father). Thus, the alienating yet attractive vocabulary of the sea in Barral's poetry, fostering a sort of cult of the dead father, is presented as seminal in his development of a poetic and literary voice in which words are carefully selected. This unique consciousness towards vocabulary, translated into his poetry, is linked to being raised bilingual; to the maritime vocabulary of Calafell, originally in Catalan; and to the father, thus giving great importance to his experience as a bilingual self and to the father figure when forging a poetic project.

The decline of Catalan in Barral's life is placed alongside the death of the father and the shadowing of a particular model of masculinity, a decline parallel to the prohibition of Catalan during dictatorship. In Barral's *Años de penitencia* and *Los años sin excusa*, Catalan is associated with the Catalan fishermen of Calafell, men whose way of life gradually disappeared over the course of the century. Barral states, "y los viejos eran los últimos viejos, últimos viejos de la mar que no habrían de ser sustituidos" (609; and the old men were the last old men, the last old men of the sea, who would not be replaced). Catalan and the noble fishermen vanish simultaneously. Calafell is a dying world, a system in the process of extinction because of the invasion of tourists who radically changed the landscape of the Spanish Mediterranean coast during the 1960s, turning the fishing village into a city of tall hotels and high-rise apartments. The ageing and disappearance of the fishermen is the theme not only of Barral's autobiographical writings but also of some of the poems in his book *Diecinueve figuras de mi historia civil* (1961; Nineteen Figures of My Personal History), a poetry collection that is closely related to his memoirs.[14] The poem "Hombre en la mar" (Man in the Sea) alludes to the fishermen's solidarity, bodily strength, and simple cosmology. In the poem, the fishermen accept the speaker as one of them: "Porque entendía de nudos y de velas / y del modo de armar los aparejos, / me llevaban con ellos muchas veces; me regalaban el quehacer de un hombre" (*Poesía completa* 162; Because I understood about knots and sheets / and how to rig the sails, / many times they took me out with them, and they gave me the work of a man). The disappearance of these men and their boats is a salient topic in the second part of the poem: "Lo sé. Desaparecerán los últimos, / sus barcas demasiado pesadas envejecen" (166; I know. The last ones will vanish, / their too heavy boats grow old). This poem reflects a transition similar to the one we find in Barral's *Memorias* regarding both the fishermen and their

Catalan linguistic and cultural surroundings: There is a movement of identification towards the fishermen that then leads towards alienation – when the speaker slowly moves away to differentiate himself from these men. Scholar and poet Jordi Jové highlights the feeling of pain in this poem, which, according to him, is associated with decadence and disenchantment (136). Carme Riera highlights the guilt of the poetic subject (*La obra poética* 83) and explains that "sensación de fraternidad, de amistad, que está por encima de las distintas clases sociales a las que pertenecen los pescadores y el sujeto poético, se quiebra en la sección II del poema" (83; the feeling of brotherhood, of friendship, that goes above and beyond the distinct social classes to which the fishermen and the poetic subject belong, breaks apart in section II of the poem).

In another poem in *Diecinueve figuras* entitled "Sol de invierno" (Winter Sun), the speaker describes the fishermen and the estrangement he has felt when looking at them, expressing this through the fishermen's hands, a symbol of their manual work that certainly contrasts with the speaker's upper-class consciousness: "Yo miraba / sus manos casi grises, con las uñas / de pájaro, liando un cigarrillo, / y luego hacia la playa" (125; I looked first at / their almost grey hands, with nails / like those of birds, rolling a cigarette, / and then toward the beach). The poem highlights the exotic and close character of these men: "Eran nuestros amigos. El cariño que les tenían les hacía reír, / los ayudaba en su papel de pintorescos" (125; They were our friends. The love we felt for them made them laugh / adding to their picturesque role). This sense of belonging, later transformed into a feeling of alienation tinged with a clear sense of superiority, is present in both Barral's poetry and in his autobiographical texts. As José Vicente Saval explains, fishermen appear in this poem as "others" (*Carlos Barral, entre el esteticismo* 50). Saval reads the bird's grasping claws as a metaphor for the fishermen's economic struggles (52). Carme Riera similarly affirms, "la relación que se establece entre los pescadores y la familia del sujeto poético, relación que, según el propio Barral, tenía mucho de colonial, pese a que la palabra 'amigos' se reitera en el poema" (*La obra poética* 80; the relationship established between the fishermen and the poetic subject's family, a relationship that, according to Barral himself, despite the reiteration of the word "friends" in the poem, had elements of colonialism). There is indeed an obsession with the construction of boundaries between the subject and the fishermen, an obsession with differentiation that is both fundamental in Barral's poetic and autobiographical projects and that translates into the differentiation between the two languages, Catalan and Spanish, as two languages that imply a choice in creating the subject's position.

Catalan is invoked as a language essential to understanding the self, but this discursive centrality is followed by an excusatory tone when Barral explains his linguistic choices. When his father passed away, Catalan disappeared from the familial sphere, while Spanish (particularly at home, a Spanish with Argentinian traits) became more predominant. This personal linguistic reality coincided with the prohibition of Catalan in public domains during Franco's dictatorship. In this sense, in the autobiographical project we find a parallel marginality of the mother and Catalan, in which Catalan, despite being the language of the father, is evoked somehow as secondary, as the mother is also a blurred figure in Barral's *Memorias* who is seemingly not granted the same influence as the father and other men such as the sailors from Calafell or the paternal uncle, the gaucho Medina.

The diglossic relationship between the two languages from the 1940s to the 1970s had an impact on Barral's internalized hierarchical understanding of Spanish and Catalan as well as on his writing and publishing business. Barral's descriptions need to be considered as a projection from adulthood in which the adult recalls his childhood and, in so doing, somehow feminizes elements such as the sea, the father, and the figures of these protective men, the sailors of Calafell and their language. This is further complicated by the fact that Barral was writing and publishing his autobiographies after 1975, at a time when the language politics and linguistic perceptions around Catalan were changing drastically from those of his childhood and youth. In fact, there is an evident desire to recover a Catalan linguistic subjectivity in Barral's autobiographies at a very particular historical moment, that is, the years of "linguistic normalization," when Catalan became coofficial with Spanish, as *Años de penitencia* was published in 1975, *Los años sin excusa* in 1978, and *Cuando las horas veloces* in 1988. The death of the father goes hand in hand with the delegitimization of Catalan: In the absence of an idealized father, Catalan lacks the social and historical context to resist discrimination. The vanishing presence of the father leads to Barral's fetishization of Catalan as a loved yet dismissed language and to the possibility of constructing a discourse, after 1975, in which the subject expresses indebtedness towards this paternal linguistic and cultural legacy.

An Industrial Surname

In Barral's autobiographies, Calafell contrasts with Barcelona, a city linked to the postwar experience: Barral describes the inhabitants of Barcelona as defeated people (34), families who have lost their sense of authority and their energy (34). The city, grey, dusty, and sordid (35), represents Spain itself, a country doing penance (37), something that the descriptions by Juan Goytisolo, Terenci Moix, or Esther Tusquets concur in. Barral explains how, over a short period of time, Barcelona suffered an unimaginable transformation and was converted from a liberal European city into a place of repression and hunger. Barral describes Barcelona as a suffering body, "aquella Barcelona escarnecida, con los tendones al aire, como un reo de la Edad Media" (247; that scorned Barcelona, with its tendons exposed, like a convict from the Middle Ages). In the urban context, Barral also refers to the appearance of another form of masculinity, one that differs from the natural gestures of the fishermen: After the war, the city was invaded by Falangists and priests. The clergymen "se me impusieron como un mundo autónomo y devorante desde que entré en el colegio" (36; when I started school, they assumed complete control over me like an autonomous and devouring world). They took power and were invested with a limitless authority, through which they desired to reestablish "el quebrado orden de las cosas" (36; the broken order of things). This seizure of control included taking over schools. Barral recalls his teachers in the Jesuit school with irony, all of them with "gestos artificiosos y solemnes, ligeramente orientales, hombres altos, fornidos, como gente de guerra, que movian las manos como marionetas" (40; solemn and artificial gestures, slightly oriental; tall, strong men, like men of war, who moved their hands like marionettes). The use of the adjective "orientales" shows the distance between the child and these new men and their behaviours. The clergymen spoke Spanish and "parecían impregnados de guerra civil, como hechos a propósito para las ceremonias de izar y arrar las banderas y dirigir los cantos patrióticos cotidianos" (40; they seemed steeped in the civil war, as if they had been made specifically for flag-raising ceremonies or for leading the daily patriotic songs). It was in this priestly, disciplinary environment that Barral learned about literature. He remembers how the educational system was based on competition and hierarchy (106–7, 109), a culture that was immobile, and a code that young students had to believe rather than experience. These religious men contrast with the exotic yet warm sailors of Calafell, who appear in Barral's "Memorias de infancia" as "modelos de fácil imitación" (907; easily imitable models); "[a]quellos otros adultos exóticos eran más próximos" (907; those other exotic adults were closer).

In post-war Barcelona, Barral became aware of his professional surname, which carried the responsibility of being heir to the publishing house Seix Barral. As we will see in the autobiographical texts by Clara Janés, in *Los años sin excusa* the mother is essential for the child to acknowledge the death of the father: "y de pronto mi madre, ya al anochecer, descompuesta, dejándose caer en un cojín o un colchón, no recuerdo, en la habitación donde acampábamos: «Ya no tenéis padre», y el llanto que abre paso a un desamparo que ya no tendría fin" (*Memorias* 469; and all of a sudden my mother, in the evening, broken, collapsing onto a cushion or mattress, I don't remember which, in the room where we had set up camp: "You don't have a father now," and the tears giving way to a desolation that would now have no end). Yet, in contrast with Janés, in Barral's text, the son surfaces as the legitimate heir to his father's publishing house. In his twenties, Barral started to become involved with his father's printing and lithography business. This inheritance entails a strong sense of moral obligation, in contrast with the sea, which remains a yearned-for place of recovery of the paternal. The professional legacy puts Barral in line with the values of the Catalan bourgeoisie and establishes his place as heir to the family industry started by Barral's father and uncle. Barral describes it as a "sociedad fraternal" (888; fraternal society), "socidedad de varones," "con una legalidad masculina" (889) and "sociedad viril" (890; society of men; with a masculine legality; a virile society). The insistence on the masculine aspect of the family and the business is striking, and it was probably determinative in Barral's feelings of obligation as the legitimate son, given that he was the only male descendant.[15] Barral also talks about his entrance into this paternal space, Seix Barral, as "sumergirme en las aguas de la industria familiar" (218; my submersion into the waters of the family business), mirroring his relationship with the paternal in Calafell but also reinforcing the sense that the maritime landscape was in opposition to the urban space.

Barral's entrance into the family business is ambivalent: While it allows him to regain a space of his father, at the same time his father's legacy turns him into a part of the hegemonic system. In the city, the memory of Barral's father remains remote and obscure, and the physical space of the father at Seix Barral, in contrast with the seaside of Calafell, connotes certain suffocation: "el rincón del padre en aquel edificio" (885; the father's corner in that building). Furthermore, Barral's acceptance of his status as heir meant repressing his desire to become a poet, and coming to terms with that tension is a recurring theme in Barral's self-writing. The title of one poem, "Apellido industrial," (Industrial Surname) in *Diecinueve figuras de mi historia civil* (1961), acknowledges the importance of the surname in this patriarchal system and the sense of responsibility the surname entails, something that is also evident in his autobiographies. In *Años de penitencia*, Barral conflates the paternal legacy of the publishing house with Franco's Spain and affirms that, by inheriting Seix Barral, "aceptaba decididamente una situación histórica, un país en cuyo presente no me había sentido hasta entonces incluido y cuyo pasado oficial me resultaba particularmente antipático y totalmente extraño" (314; I decidedly adopted a historical situation, a country in whose present time, up to now I hadn't felt included, and whose official past was particularly repugnant and totally foreign to me). Barral describes the repugnant feeling that the inheritance aroused in him, and how he felt like a coward: "me asumía, tiritante, indefenso, infantilmente impresionado por una augurio" (315; I took on the responsibility, shivering, defenceless, childishly impressed by an omen).[16] In the publishing house itself, depicted as dark, narrow, and suffocating, Barral felt as though he were sacrificing his moral freedom and his desire to become a writer (327–8). Yet in Seix Barral, Barral also starts imagining a new business, "una editorial distinta a la que configuraban el fondo escolar de la anteguerra y los torpes intentos de diversificación de los últimos años" (329; a publishing company different from the prewar one which had mainly published educational texts and its clumsy attempts to diversify in recent years). As a result, he begins the extensive task of publishing old classics, international writers, and Spanish authors who did not always toe the line of Francoist ideals. Later, he included the authors of the Latin American boom.[17]

In many ways, the publishing house became a place of resistance, where Barral fought against the dictatorship and censorship on a daily basis.[18] Despite being associated with inherited values and hegemony, Seix Barral turned out to be a command centre for a battle against the system from within and also bound to Calafell: Calafell ends up being the site of the workshop to which Barral enthusiastically brings his writer-friends.[19] Despite presenting them as opposite realities, Barral established bonds between the two worlds, and the publishing house was aligned in many ways with the somehow freer and more authentic sense of self of Calafell. He presents these two realities as giving birth to two different personae: The writer and his desire to find time to write versus the publisher immersed in economic concerns. In Barral's discourse, Seix Barral somehow stands in opposition to Calafell, which is depicted in the following terms: "Calafell era una ventana hacia fuera desde el ghetto intelectual que mi nueva profesión de editor no hacía más que extender" (415; From the intellectual ghetto that my new profession as an editor did nothing but extend, Calafell was a window to the outside).[20] On a day-to-day level, however, it seems that these two different personae were more of a needed construction than a reality and that the two spaces of Calafell and the publishing house were closely interconnected. In the end, both Seix Barral and Calafell were paternal legacies through which Barral fulfilled a filial duty, but the publishing house is tinged with a sense of obligation while Calafell is tinged with a sense of desired recovery.

In Barral's texts, these two spaces (the maritime and the urban) and two personalities related to them are fundamental to the excusatory tone that shows Barral's self-consciousness as someone who inherited a privileged situation and who also positions himself on the margins as a poet. For instance, Barral describes his literary generation as being outside of the official groups and as lacking tradition and filiation. As such, Barral's decision to offer a tribute to Antonio Machado – a canonical Spanish poet whose poetry has been placed between Spanish modernism, the Generation of 1898, and the Generation of 1927 and who died in exile – could be read as a way to question the literary legacy of the dictatorship. According to Laureano Bonet, this "juego de 'paternidades' estimuladoras para nuestros autores retrocede considerablemente en la búsqueda de nombres, textos, ricos en inspiraciones y experiencias, no manchados por el evento de la guerra. Los *hijos*, así, se enfrentas a los *padres*, negándolos con aspereza, para por el contrario descubrir – es su propio vuelo reconstructor – nombres más antiguos y, a la vez, más puros que anidan en la tradición cultural hispánica, entendiendo aquí 'lo tradicional' en un sentido ante todo vivificador y, dato paradójico, colmado de 'futurización'" (113; stimulating "game of paternities" for our authors recedes considerably in the search for names and texts, rich in inspiration and experiences, and not tarnished by the fact of the war. The sons, in this way, confront the fathers, acrimoniously denying them, to discover, on the contrary – through their own restorative voyage – names that are older and, at the same time, more authentic residing in the Hispanic cultural tradition. "The traditional" is to be understood here as meaning above all invigorating and, paradoxically, brimming with a sense of the future). In Barral as well as in Bonet, literary affiliation and canon construction are presented using metaphors that belong to the familial domain and are understood as a bridge linking past and future. It is important to remember that the Francoist discourse emphasized medieval works such as *The Poem of the Cid* as well as Spain's expulsion of Jews and Muslims during Isabella's reign – but not poets in exile, like Machado. When talking about his university group, Barral notes their lack of admiration for Catalan literature and concludes "no sabría cómo explicarlo" (242; I wouldn't know how to explain it). Barral later explains that the rejection of Catalan language and literature by his generation was a consequence of their schooling: "La resaca de la guerra civil nos había hecho a todos de lengua castellana" (243;

The hangover from the civil war had made us all Spanish speakers). This was despite the fact that he was in contact with and knew of both Catalan writers such as Eduardo Cirlot and Catalan publishers such as Josep Janés and the Ferraté(r) brothers. Yet the war and the dictatorship made it somehow impossible for him to connect fully with this Catalan literary landscape that had previously existed. Barral also defines his generation as "elementos de privincialismo decimonónico" (247; constituents of nineteenth-century provincialism), contemporary to their grandparents and older than their parents (250). He affirms that the eternity of the dictatorship had hypnotized them and had kept them out of combat, which he observed through the themes and topics of their conversations and their different attitudes towards culture and the world. Barral asserts that the Francoist state had humiliated them and turned them into cowards, both culturally obedient and docile.

Later on, Barral delves into the difficulties of his generation, of those writing in Spanish while being located in the peripheral geography of Catalonia. In Madrid, he explains, they were seen as "the Catalan exception" because they grew up at a crossroads of languages and influences. Nonetheless, inside Catalonia, they were seen as imperialists:

> Éramos ... una especie de negritos confinados en lejanas islas a los que se dispensa por educación el favor de un rincón de página, para no caer en las apariencias de la discriminación. Escribíamos en una situación incómoda desde dentro y hacia fuera. Éramos extraños y a lo sumo tolerables desde el punto de vista de una literatura nacional, la catalana, a la que nuestro medio de expresión traicionaba. Escribir en castellano nos hacía cómplices de la Guardia Civil, de las fuerzas represoras de una cultura cuyo destino histórico y cuya condición política compartíamos, pero que no era la nuestra, a la que éramos inmediatamente extranjeros. (504)

> We were ... like Black subjects confined to distant islands and to whom education was doled out in the form of a corner of the page, so it wouldn't look like discrimination. We wrote in an uncomfortable situation from both within and outside. We were foreigners and only barely tolerable from the point of view of a national literature, Catalan; the manner in which we expressed ourselves betrayed us. To write in Spanish made us accomplices of the Guardia Civil, of the repressive forces of a culture whose historical destiny and whose political status we shared but which was not our own, and in which we were immediately considered foreigners.

Barral's analogy between Spanish-language writers in Catalonia and Black colonial subjects is a dangerous exaggeration, particularly since authors born or living in Catalonia and writing in Spanish during this time period have often been integrated into the Spanish canon (Carmen Laforet or Juan Goytisolo, for instance), though perhaps not in the same way as authors from Madrid or Castille. Moreover, the feeling of belonging neither to the Catalan canon nor to the Spanish one and the self-excusatory tone are surprising for someone who, writing in the mid-1970s, had already achieved a notable career as writer and publisher. Indeed, as Kathryn Crameri explains, writers from Catalonia, at the end of the dictatorship and during the post-Franco era, lived in an environment in which language choice was a political issue (6). In this context, the Catalan language was very often associated with freedom, while Spanish was known as the language of authority (37) and thus Barral's apologetic tone is taken further towards a sense of victimization and marginalization.

It is not a coincidence that Barral's desire to write in Catalan emerged just when Catalan was experiencing a process of revitalization towards the end of Barral's life in the 1980s. During this decade, Barral published two books in Catalan related to the maritime world of Calafell: *Catalunya desde el mar* (Catalonia from the Sea; 1982) and *Catalunya a vol d'ocell* (Catalonia: A Bird's Eye View; 1985). In both books, he recovered the fishermen's knowledge and linguistic expressions in a sort of ecolinguism. These two books try to portray his father's intangible legacy by describing, in Catalan, a Catalan world that is dying because of tourism and urbanization, two elements that Barral describes as two of Spain's fevers (103). Barral acknowledges that the changes Calafell is going through with suburbanization and the building of apartments are both urbanistic as well as social (609). This obsession to keep alive a decaying world appears repeatedly in Barral's *Memorias* too, particularly in *Cuando las horas veloces* (1988), where the autobiographical self denounces "la degradación del mar litoral" (631; the degradation of the coast) and "la catástrofe urbanística" (631; the urban catastrophe). This changing landscape is also a theme in the autofictional text *Penúltimos castigos* and in some of Barral's press articles.

Barral refers to *Catalunya des del mar* as "un més dels meus texts autobiogràfics" (8; "one more of my autobiographical texts"). It is nonetheless an unusual autobiography. The book dedicates much attention to documenting and preserving a specific Catalan vocabulary associated with the Catalan Mediterranean coast, a language that Barral defines as "una llengua sense precedents literaris" (8; "a language with no literary precedents"). In saying that maritime Catalan has no literary precedents, he means that this Catalan is popular and oral. *Catalunya des del mar* was probably for Barral a way of overcoming his class and linguistic remorse by stressing his knowledge of and keeping alive a type of Catalan that belongs to a very specific area and activity. A reference book combining photography, drawings, and text to illustrate the traditions, objects, and areas of navigation of the Catalan coast, this book narrates an imaginary trip along that coast. The book has an encyclopedic and educational character, while it also denounces the ecological abuses of the dictatorship on the coast and attempts to recover a Catalan lexicon.[21] Barral explains his linguistic choice for the book, writing, "[n]o podria traduir aquestes pàgines a cap altra de les llengües que conec, parlo i escric, sense trair-lo" (8; "I could not translate these pages to any of the other languages I know, speak and write, without betraying it"). By invoking the trope of the translator as traitor – the well-known Italian saying *traduttore traditore* – and assuming that translating the Catalan into Spanish would mean to betray the Catalan, Barral confers a sense of uniqueness upon Catalan and in relation to his persona.

The use of Catalan in this case is exceptional if one looks at the rest of Barral's oeuvre, and there is little need to comment on how these two peculiar autobiographical texts in Catalan compete with Barral's memoirs in Spanish. While the *Memorias* had a wide reception in Spain, with multiple reeditions, *Catalunya des del mar* and *Catalunya a vol d'ocell* were books with short print runs. Barral was someone who knew the publishing world well, and it was evident to him that *Catalunya desde el mar* would not have the success of *Memorias*. That said, the place of *Catalunya des del mar* late in the chronology of Barral's works can lead us to different conclusions: We can read this book as an example of how Catalan was not at the same level as Spanish in Barral's literary project, but we can also read it as a demonstration that Catalan, despite prohibitions, remained alive and, indeed, as he explains in his *Memorias*, continuously present. We can see in it an intention to exorcise a feeling of guilt, an attempt at reconciliation and recovery of his father's language, which, for historical and personal reasons, Barral was unable to use as his literary language. Ultimately, the question here is, in a diglossic reality in which Catalan was not taught in school, can a writer *choose* their language of expression, and are writers to blame for the language chosen to use? Of course, Barral's work as a publisher during the transition certainly continued to give prestige to the Spanish language in Catalonia: Seix Barral and Barral Editores ended up becoming an important institution for the legitimization of Spanish literature in this bilingual Autonomous Community of Spain, and this could be interpreted as undermining Catalan. From a nationalist Catalanist perspective, taking into account Pierre Bourdieu's notion of symbolic power, we can question to what extent Barral consciously continued to present Spanish as more prestigious than Catalan during the transition and how his own writing correlated with a linguistic ideology, but we can also understand that, in the end, this was a generation of authors who chose Spanish over Catalan because their cultural, historical, and personal realities directed them towards it. For any writer who lived this context, language choice in the literary scene of Catalonia was impacted by Franco's linguistic politics, and language politics also developed in parallel to each one's familial situation, in this case coinciding with the death of the Catalan father.

Paternal Objects

To create a distinct subjectivity that is close to an absent father and to purposely manufacture a bourgeois self, Barral found his father's material inheritance essential. In Calafell, he recovered his father's painting tools, navigational maps, maritime objects, clothing, and boats, his collections of maps and swords, and his drawings; they all breathe life into the dead father and grant the son access to the father's life.[22] Some of these belongings were kept in the house in Calafell after Barral's father died and can still be seen at the Museu Casa Barral, where they are mixed with Barral's own objects, intensifying the union between the two. Sailing, collecting, film, and photography are all interests his father shared with his brother, uniting them in their "aventuras científico-deportivas" (877; scientific-athletic adventures), and that ultimately brought together Barral's father; his uncle, Luis; and the sailors of Calafell. Barral imagines his father's personality through his interest in collecting, inventing devices, painting, or sculpting. In *Años de penitencia*, these objects are referred to as "imágenes enfáticas del padre muerto y tan dolorosamente necesario" (76; forceful images of the dead father, and so painfully necessary). Barral practised the father's hobbies as a way of imitating his father: "mi afición a pintar formaba parte del culto a mi padre muerto prematuramente … Pintar era vengar a mi padre de su dimisión industrial, sustituir su historia frustrada por la mía" (119; my love of painting was part of the cult to my father, who had died prematurely … Painting was a way of avenging my father's business side, replacing his troubled history, with my own).

The subject's obsession with the father's objects and the father's material inheritance is a way of recovering not only a lost figure but also part of a masculine and class consciousness; as with language, it is cardinal in his creation of a distinct masculine and in this case bourgeois subjectivity. The self feels "aferrado a un mundo objetual en muchos aspectos raro y sumamente diferenciado" (885; wedded to a rare and distinct world of objects). Barral explains that, as a child, he lived his father's hobbies with fervour, calling them "costumbres con apellido" (885; customs with a last name) and tracing a parallel between these maritime objects and the material world of the publishing house:

> La familiaridad con las armas antiguas y sus infinitas sugestiones, con el arsenal de instrumentos fotográficos y cinematográficos que individualizaban la presencia del padre, o con los numerosos objetos relacionados con la pesca, la mar y la exploración de la naturaleza que mantenían el vigor de un sistema de costumbres con apellido. También, quizá, pero mucho más lejos, todo lo relacionado con las artes de imprimir y la industria de las imágenes. (885)

> The familiarity with antique weapons and their infinite implications, with the arsenal of photographic and cinematic equipment that individualized the father's presence, or with the many objects related to fishing, the sea, and the exploration of nature which ensured the robustness of a system of customs with a surname. Also, perhaps, but more distant, everything related to the art of printing and the industry of images.

Self-creation is in this case rooted in the acceptance of genealogy and filiation. Barral contemplates the father's objects as a masculine inheritance that he accepts as heir, but this obsession with the father's material legacy also betrays a strong desire for a sense of agency: Barral related to objects through control and appropriation. Barral admits that his relationship with familial objects was obsessive (457) and connects objects with a very specific sense of authenticity. In *Family Values*, Kelly Oliver affirms that "the virile subject relates to itself and its world as its property; virility is defined in terms of ownership and ownness" (119). We cannot forget that Barral himself also describes words as "objetos litúrgicos, piezas de devoción" (101; liturgical objects, devotional pieces) and that, when talking about Calafell, he affirms that "referir a aquel lugar las palabras es como usar de ellas con una especie de garantía de propiedad" (102; to refer to that place (with) words is to make use of them with a kind of guarantee of ownership).

Objects are primary to demonstrating a bourgeois identity, an identity that in Barral's case implied guilt but also pleasure, pride, and the development of an affinity for the physical world of publishing.[23] Barral explains that he used to divide objects and materials into two large categories – mass-produced versus handmade objects – and the materials that were more refined versus the more primitive (62). He affirms that he felt "orientaciones primarias como el desmedido amor a las materias nobles y tradicionales y la antipatía a los materiales propios de la industria y más aptos a la serialización, o la atracción por las cosas viejas si no antiguas" (457; primary orientations like an inordinate love for honest traditional materials and an aversion to materials characteristic of industry and better suited to serialization, or an attraction to things that were old, if not antique). The consciousness of the uniqueness of certain products as opposed to mass-produced materials has an important impact on his publishing strategy. Barral was not only, as Andreu Jaume considers, someone who took care of "la general vertebración e implantación de su catálogo, defendiendo la razón del criterio frente a las tiranías varias, entre ellas la del mercado" (24; the overall organization and introduction of his catalogue, defending the selection criteria when faced with assorted tyrannies, including that of the market), but he also considered each book he published not as a mass product but as a unique commodity.[24] In the context of a legacy of production, manufacturing, and industry, the printing and publishing environment is especially relevant, as it stokes Barral's future interests. In a radio interview in 1981, Barral affirmed that he was born with "genes tipográficos" ("Entrevista" minute 1:57; typographic genes). In his *Memorias*, he affirms that his literary culture was influenced by his father's job, as the first books he read were children's books produced by his father's publishing house. Barral highlights the beauty of the illustrations in these books and the care that was taken during the process of design. This perception made him very aware of and careful concerning the form and ways of producing books: He developed a strong interest in materials and forms in order to give every book a personal character. This interest can be seen in direct relation to the book as a paternal object and the literary canon as a canon that also reinforces ideas of masculinity and prestige.

The father's swords are also significant objects for the self, have phallic resonances, and inspire feelings of religiosity and fetishism. From his first impressions of the familial residence on Pau Claris in Barcelona, Barral remembers how his father's swords were hung and how he watched the workers and technicians cleaning them, taking in the smells of oil and wax. Barral describes how, during the war, the National Service confiscated the swords, which were relics from the sixteenth and seventeenth centuries; later on, a friend of the family saw the swords in the palace of Pedralbes, and the family recovered them (50). The swords were then plundered by the Francoist regime, and taking them back represented a personal recovery for Barral. Swords appear intermittently in Barral's memoirs and are always linked to a cult of the father. They become an obsession and a fetish for Barral, who feels eroticized when he names and possesses them:

> Esas espadas han tenido en mi vida una curiosa función como de instrumentos de culto, y se ligan tanto a mi primera mística erótica como a una liturgia lustral, de redención de la espesa vulgaridad cotidiana. Una de ellas, cuya taza cincelada reproduce con abundancia de desnudos rafalianos una batalla en los fosos de una ciudad asediada, fue, durante años, el fetiche central de mi primera religión erótica. Le puse incluso un nombre: Dannina. Curiosamente ridículo. Se trata en realidad de una hermosa pieza de cincel florentino de finales del siglo XVI. (50)
>
> (In my life, those swords have played an odd role as cult objects, and they are as linked to my first erotic mysticism as to a purificatory liturgy, of redemption from the dense vulgarity of daily life. One of them, on whose chiselled guard is reproduced a battle with an abundance of naked cherubim in the trenches of a besieged city, remained, for many years, the principle fetish of my first erotic religion. I even gave it a name: Dannina. Strangely ridiculous. In reality, it's a beautiful piece of Florentine workmanship from the end of the fifteenth century.)

Although collecting is not necessarily a masculine hobby, what we collect, as James Clifford points out, is indeed ruled by gender, history, and fashion (218). The father's swords reflect this world of masculine possession and recall an interest in phallic symbols. This fascination continued into Barral's adult life: Swords were objects he mostly observed and contemplated and that evoked an eroticism of sight and beauty as well as of knowledge and tradition. The fact that he gives one of the swords a woman's name highlights this position of the (male) subject as the possessor in relation to objects. Through his father's swords, Barral escapes an often-unappealing reality, something we will later see repeated in his relationship with boats. Swords hold a bizarre power over the subject, as if they could fortify the self, which understands these swords as a sign of distinction and uniqueness. The religious terminology surrounding the explanation of the swords is striking as well: The use of words such as "liturgy," "redemption," and "religion" indicates how Barral has substituted the Catholic adoration of God, encouraged by the Franco regime, for an idealization of the lost father as a worshiped image.

Philosophical Western theory related to objects and material culture has also highlighted the importance of objects in destabilizing the human world. In his seminal "Thing Theory," Bill Brown contends that objects are meaningful because they organize our private and public affection; they *perform* a meaning in a particular temporal and spatial context, in relation to certain subjects (7). For Barral, objects intensify a sense of selfhood and an Oedipal identification with the absent father. While objects enforce ideas of a distinct subjectivity, they also reveal the subject's feelings of instability: "las sensaciones profundas de desarraigo y de inestabilidad, como en algunos casos concretos, ya lo dije, el de las armas antiguas y los barcos – de un tipo que implica también la antigüedad de la forma y la rusticidad de la materia – con el culto edípico y la perpetuación de la conciencia de desamparo" (533; the deep feelings of eradication and instability, as in some concrete cases, as I've already said, of antique weapons and boats – of a kind that also involves the age of the form and the rusticity of the material – with oedipal worship and the perpetuation of an awareness of abandonment).

The paternal library is telling in this regard. It contains not books produced by the father but the ones the father read. Whereas all the other objects of the father are accessible – photographs, films, and maps – the father's books gradually disappeared after his death and were never retrieved.[25] Repeatedly, Barral expresses his frustration about this loss. These books become a symbol of the father's absence, as Barral's father gave the majority of his collection away. Barral remembers having played with and read many of these books, which all had blue dust jackets, and he explains that he considered them "la verdadera puerta por la que me asomé a la literatura" (137; the true door through which I was able to approach literature). Barral insisted on acquiring his father's library, led by the desire to know more about his father's intellectual interests and culture. This was, however, a frustrated ambition. His inability to retrieve a part of his father becomes a curse over Barral's life. In addition, as publisher of Seix Barral, his house was constantly inundated with books. The description of Barral's house, overflowing with books, feels like a nightmare – and is in fact similar to Janés's nightmare in the paternal library. Barral explains in his *Memorias* how books "comenzaron a amontonarse en las cresterías de los armarios, a apilarse en los sitios más inapropiados, a estorbar por todas partes" (531; they began to stack up behind the cornices of the wardrobes, to pile up in the most inappropriate places, and to constantly get in the way). He refers to books as living objects, doomed to fall ill because of oblivion. He explains that it was impossible for him to keep the books he received from friends and unknown writers in order, as new books constantly appeared, and he was unable to throw them away because of his superstitions.

These books are helpful in understanding the ways in which objects become material representations of the father, but they are also in tension with the subject's desires, as if they had a life of their own. In *Vibrant Matter*, Jane Bennett – in a similar vein to Bill Brown – defends the power of *things*, arguing that *things* are "vital players in the world" (2, 3). While objects are often considered passive and as not possessing subjective agency, Bennett highlights the existence of a "Thing-Power," "the curious ability of inanimate things to animate, to act, to produce effects dramatic and subtle" (6). This vital materialism contends that "nonhuman materialities have power, a power that the 'bourgeois self,' with its pretensions of autonomy, denies" (16). In Barral's text, we see that it is precisely this bourgeois self that is devoted to the power that objects have, but also that it is precisely this "apellido industrial," meaning the inheritance of the publishing house and the strong identification with the father, that condemns him to have to throw away books and to feel overwhelmed by their materiality.

The last item I will analyse is his father's boats, which are foremost in Barral's memoirs and reformulate the stability of the subject and its boundaries. Essential to the search for personal memory, the boats are a patrimonial legacy, a mark of distinction, and proof of belonging to the maritime reality of Calafell. They are a kind of heterotopia, following Foucault's terminology: A sacralized space, a privileged place reserved for a certain individual who, in this case, is in a state of crisis because he is in search of his own authenticity and where there is a break with traditional time ("Of Other Spaces" 26). Boats, as in Foucault's definition of heterotopias, "presuppose a system of opening and closing that both isolates them and makes them penetrable" (26). The search for authenticity is an ever-present theme in Barral's works and is closely related to the two personae I have been exploring in the previous sections: The more public his life was, the stronger the necessity for him of finding authentic values, which, in his case, he tried to recover through poetry and sailing, thus intensifying the role of the father.[26]

The relationship established between the sailors and the boats is described in gendered terms for Barral. According to Barral, men build boats as if they are giving birth to new creatures. Men are, in this regard, considered a sort of demigod: "construir barcas era como armar en madera animales vivos o cosas únicas prometidas a una historia estrictamente singular" (213–14; building boats was not unlike making from wood living animals or unusual objects, objects destined to live their own unique history). The possibility of physical creation goes hand in hand with ideas of paternity, relates to the creation of books, and obliges us to come back to the extent to which the space of the sea and Calafell invokes a masculine self and both blurs and constructs boundaries of femininity and masculinity. Boats are living bodies in

Barral's descriptions; he refers to them as beasts, and their production permits the wood to come alive. These boats are also given human characteristics. A good example was Barral's boat *Francisca. La Francisca* not only has a woman's name but also seems to resemble a woman's body: Francisca had been the model of one of the painters who lived in Calafell, and Barral characterizes *her* as "era esbelta, deliciosamente femenina" (84; she was slender, deliciously feminine). As Bruno Latour explains, we need to question to what extent "the human is not a constitutional pole to be opposed to that of the nonhuman" (137). Another example is how certain boats were painted with moustaches, "casi todas las barcas lucían «bigotes». Así se llamaban en aquella parte de la costa los grandes triángulos, generalmente de color claro, que dibujaban ambas bandas de la proa" (85; nearly all of the boats proudly displayed their «moustaches». That's what, on that part of the coast, they called the large triangles, usually light in colour, painted on either side of the bow). Barral highlights the strong unity between the boats and their owners. He stresses that sailors chose their boats' colours as a way to give expression to their aesthetic ideals. All of these things, unified by this chromatic unity, become an extension of the sailors themselves, identifying them through their objects and occupation.

The boat "Capitán Argüello" is probably the object that most clearly shows Barral's identification with his father. "Capitán Argüello" was not only the name of one of his father's boats; it was also the name his father used to sign his works, writings, and paintings: "el meu pare firmava els seus treballs amb el pseudònim de «Capitán Argüello», nom de les seves i de les meves barques i títol que usurpa alguna de les meves autofiguracions" (*La mar domèstica* 9; my father signed his works with the pseudonym «Captain Argüello» the name of his and my boat and the title that I appropriated for some of my self-creations). Barral also used this pseudonym to sign some of his works. Through the name "Capitán Argüello," Barral reinforces the unity of man and boat, as well as the continuity between father and son. Yet, like Barral's relationship to the rest of his father's objects, this unity and continuity end up being frustrated and fragmented. If to give a boat a person's name is an accepted tradition on the coast, to give the sailor's name to a boat is perhaps not as common, though it certainly establishes a close relationship between the two. Barral feels close to his father's boat, the "Capitán Argüello." He recalls his desire to recover his father's boat as having started during adolescence and how eager he was to possess it. When his father died, his mother had sold the boat for a very low price (213). Barral considers the selling of the father's boat "una estúpida desposesión que me afectaba hasta lo indecible y que no perdoné nunca, ni perdonaré" (428; a stupid loss that affected me indescribably and that I never forgave, nor will ever forgive). Recovering the father's boat implies recovering the father's spirit but also indicates resentment towards the mother, a figure that, as I have shown, remains in the background, particularly in comparison to the centrality of the father.

The father's objects are relics: They are charged with the power of the owner's body and shape the lives of those who come into contact with them. Barral grants a sacred, divine power to the father via these objects-relics. In this context, the "Capitán Argüello" is considered "una vieja reivindicación," (427) and Barral's desire to restore it is associated with a liturgical, religious desire. The boat's first construction is related to the biblical story of Noah and therefore to the beginning of the world and a certain salvation: "Se trataba, evidentemente, de un deseo religioso, de un gesto litúrgico principal en *el culto del padre muerto* ... Mi padre nos llevaba a menudo, los domingos, a aquel lugar insólito en el que, en mitad de un pinar, en lo alto de la colina, iba creciendo, como el arca de Noé, un recio esqueleto de baos y de cuadernas" (*Memorias* 427; It was a matter, evidently, of a religious desire, of a fundamental liturgical gesture belonging to the cult of the dead father ... My father often took us, on Sundays, to that unlikely place in the middle of a pine forest, at the top of a hill, where growing, like Noah's Ark, was a resilient frame of beams and the ribs of a hull). As one of the most well-known patriarchal texts in Western culture and with Noah's being one of the first narrations in which man saves the world through his determination, these biblical passages cannot be underestimated. It is also important to stress Carme Riera's point about the importance of the religious tone and Catholic morality present in the titles of Barral's autobiographical works (for instance the use of "penitencia," "excusa," and "castigos" in his titles; Riera, "Prólogo" in Barral's *Los diarios* 17).

The people of Calafell came to refer to Barral as "Capitán Argüello," an idea that Barral promoted by dressing up as a ship's captain.[27] "Capitán Argüello" becomes thus a theatrical characterization that connects Barral's own body with his father's body, both outfitted to sail in the boat with the very same name. As he became more involved in politics, Barral's sense of theatre and his eccentricity increased. His relationship with the "Capitán Argüello," both boat and paternal figure, exemplifies his existence as a divided subject: On the one hand, his outfit is just a costume, a piece of clothing that allows him to represent a certain personality, but it also brings him closer to an authentic self, separate from intellectual life. The costume is associated with "una vocación a la sencillez y al primitivismo compensadores de una estructuración difícil de la vida intelectual y de su práctica y en una necesidad de huida de la cotidianidad tensa y opresiva" (*Memorias* 534; a calling to simplicity and primitivism compensating for the challenging structure of the intellectual life and its practice not to mention the need to escape the dense and oppressive nature of everyday life). Barral's relationship with the "Capitán Argüello" shows his strong identification with the father but also complements the Oedipal through the creation of a distinct personality within the autobiographical project. Like books, the boat is also a frustrating object; it becomes an unattainable salvation, a fragmented inheritance. The theatrical and literary recovery of the father through his objects speaks to a situation of tension and impossibility.

Conclusion

In Barral's self-writing, the father is a central figure to explain Barral's linguistic, literary, and professional subjectivity. The father provides Barral with a reality from before the dictatorship, linking Barral to the Catalan maritime landscape of the town of Calafell, to a space of nature, spontaneity, bodily pleasures, and sensuality, where the sailors are models of manhood – popular, warm, and proximate. Being his father's heir and inheriting the paternal publishing house, Barral also participates in the hegemonic system: This participation enables him to resist the dictatorship from within and to oppose Franco's censorship, but the publishing house represents a responsibility as well as the relegitimization of Spanish language and culture in Catalonia during the end of the dictatorship and the beginning of the transition to democracy. The business turns into a sort of betrayal of the father's linguistic legacy and publishing enterprise, as Seix Barral and Barral Editores became failed projects for Barral – the first one was transferred to him in 1968, and soon after, in 1969, Barral founded the second one. In many ways, in line with Sidonie Smith's assertions about autobiographical writing, we can read Barral's autobiographies as an explanation of the subject's arrival in the phallic and paternal order – an order that he embraces as a generational leader of a literary group, a publisher, and an elected representative of the Socialist Party of Catalonia – but a role, the role of the son, that in Barral's case also implies a defeat.

The identification with the father is deeply tied to the split autobiographical persona, as the father is fundamental in granting the son access to a series of identity traits felt as somehow divided: Barral's fervour for objects and his sense of responsibility for the family business, as well as his love for the sea and Calafell. In this way, Barral's *Memorias* prove that filiation, the acknowledgment of the place of the son, is essential to the autobiographical project and in constructing the figure of the author and its literary affiliation. Furthermore, in Barral's autobiographies, the death of the father is fundamental to the apologetic tone towards the Catalan language and culture. The father's loss offers an explanation that allows Barral to excuse linguistic acts that put the Catalan language in a secondary place in a process that is perceived as irrevocable, unchangeable, and nontransferable. If in psychoanalytical theory, the father figure, as the source of authority, instils guilt and threatens punishment – as we see in Freud's theory of the Primal Horde – Barral offers a nonauthoritarian version of this primal father yet one where guilt for not having been able to be fair to the paternal, cultural, and linguistic legacy is fundamental. As in the case of Goytisolo, the self exorcises this paternal ghost through the autobiographical project as well as in several of his other writings. Essential to this process for Barral is explaining why he chose Spanish and not Catalan as the language of the publishing business and of his literary project. Most of these explanations appeared when Catalan became the legal language of Catalonia along with Spanish during the democracy, probably because this explanation was then allowed as well as expected. Despite the desire to place his father outside the dictatorship, Barral's image of the vanishing Catalan father and the disappearance of the father's language responds to an institutional image cultivated by Francoism in which peripheral cultures and languages – Catalan, Euskera, and Galician – were seen as secondary and anecdotal, a consideration that Barral himself acknowledged to have inherited. The rivalry between languages (Catalan and Spanish) correlates with a rivalry between masculine models (the coastal versus the urban) in Barral's autobiographies, and both rivalries are necessary for the subject to emerge. In Barral's Oedipal narrative, the fading of the Catalan father pervades the text vis-à-vis the creation of the self: Paternity, inheritance, and filiation are presented as interlinked in a complexity and multiplicity of layers essential for the author to give birth to his literary persona.

4 Terenci Moix: Linguistic and Sexual Disaffiliations

Although not strictly a "narrative of filiation" as Thomas Couser defines it, Moix's *Memorias* display a double impulse that is both a tribute to the father and a sharp criticism of the same figure. Terenci Moix's *Memorias,* the culmination of his self-writing projects, were gathered together under the title of *El Peso de la Paja* (The Weight of Straw) and include three volumes published during the 1990s: *El cine de los sábados* (1990; Saturday's Movies), based on his childhood; *El beso de Peter Pan* (1993; Peter Pan's Kiss), centred on his adolescence; and *Extraño en el paraíso* (1998; Stranger in Paradise), set during his adulthood. In these works, the father – often in the shadow of the mother – is a man who fluctuates between being a protector of Catalan culture and a *donjuán* and *macho ibérico.* On the one hand, the father is admired by the son and is the one who inspires Terenci Moix's love of books. On the other, the self despises the father, his homophobia, and his confining model of masculinity. Consequently, the autobiographical project intercalates the affiliative impulse with a disaffiliative one, both acknowledging the father's cultural heritage and condemning his heteronormativity and sexism.

Born Ramón Moix i Meseguer in Barcelona in 1942 and self-renamed Terenci, Terenci Moix has been considered "one of the most important contemporary Catalan novelists, and the first ever openly gay Catalan author" (Fernàndez *Another* 5). Best-selling, self-educated, popular[1], and prolific, Moix published more than thirty books, which include a large variety of genres and themes, from novels set in Egypt to essays about the cinema. With his younger sister and openly lesbian writer, Ana María Moix, Terenci Moix was part of Barcelona's *gauche divine,* a group of bourgeois left-wing intellectuals in Barcelona, even though the Moix siblings did not belong to the Catalan bourgeoisie stricly.[2] Many of Terenci Moix's works reflect a clear desire for subversion, as well as evidence of writing "from a sexual margin" (*Another* 2) and are situated within camp aesthetics. Moix was also a fierce critic of homophobia and of the Catalan cultural landscape (and its homophobic reality) and alternated his literary production between Catalan and Spanish, something that put him at odds with certain Catalan literary groups, though they still recognized him with numerous prizes such as the Víctor Català Prize in 1976 and the Ramon Llull Price in 1992, in addition to the prizes he received for his oeuvre in Spanish, such as the Planeta Price in 1986.

Moix published a first novel in Spanish, *Besaré tu cadaver* (Let Me Kiss Your Corpse), in 1965. After this and until 1979, he published mostly in Catalan, self-translating into Spanish at least three of his works: *Onades sobre una roca deserta* (1969; Waves on a Deserted Rock), *Món mascle* (1971; Masculine World), and *Siro, o la increada consciència de la raça* (1972; Siro or the Uncreated Conscience of the Human Race). After 1983, he published in Spanish again with the exception of two novels: *El sexe dels àngels* (The Sex of the Angels) – published in Catalan in 1992 and translated from Catalan into Spanish by himself and his sister Ana María Moix – and *Màrius Bryon*, published in Catalan in 1995. Thus, he wrote in Catalan in the 1960s and 1970s, becoming one of the supporters of the renewal of Catalan literature at the end of Franco's dictatorship and during the transition to democracy. In the 1980s, he switched from Catalan to Spanish, a change that took place just as Catalan[3] became coofficial with Spanish in Catalonia. As in the cases of Barral, Goytisolo, and Janés, for Moix the father is vital to portraying a distinct linguistic subjectivity and to constructing affinities with linguistic and literary traditions. In Moix's case, the mocked paternal figure goes hand in hand both with the writer's desire to play with expected literary conventions by not choosing only one language and one canon to belong to and with his desire to promote other models of sexuality and masculinity, such as the one embodied by Moix's gay godfather, a man who represents an alternative for the autobiographer to follow.

The Father's Tongue

El cine de los sábados starts with a "Presentación" in media res: We are placed in Rome in 1969, and the narrator talks about his sexuality, a sexuality where queerness is evident, not so much because of the obvious homoerotic environment but because the takeaway of the scene is that the autobiographer's sexuality is one without sex. With this beginning, two things are clear: that one's sexuality is a key part of the "I" (and of the autobiographical project) and that the writer is conscious that readers might be there to find out more about his intimate life: Ultimately, Terenci Moix was a mediatic and popular author. Despite this opening, very soon the text acquires a more traditional structure, describing Moix's birth with an anecdote: His mom – pregnant with him – and her female friend and neighbour are trying to track down their husbands in the brothels of the so-called barrio Chino (Chinatown) in downtown Barcelona. It is Christmas 1941. The autobiographer concludes the scene affirming: "Es así un milagro que en vez de nacer en un cine no amaneciera en una casa de putas" (56; So it's a miracle that instead of being born in a movie theatre, I didn't first see the light of day in a whore house). With this, we are alerted to several themes of Moix's childhood memoirs: Barcelona and the neighbourhood of the Raval, his father visiting brothels, Moix's passion for cinema, and the father–mother relationship, one defined by conflict.

The autobiographer highlights from the very beginning his connection to his mother and to the female family members, and this identification breaks with the traditional alignment of the male autobiographer with the paternal figure. Through numerous descriptions of the beauty and strong personality of his mother, Moix highlights her influence and places the father and at times the self in the shadow of the maternal presence. Language is crucial in presenting the mother's personality: Moix explains that his mother arrived in Barcelona when she was young, and therefore she is "de importación" (imported) and "mestiza" (64; mixed). The mother came from Nonaspe, a village located on the border between Aragon and Catalonia, where Moix claims that the spoken language was "chapurreado" (64; mixed up). "Chapurrear," "Hablar una lengua con dificultad y cometiendo errores" (*chapurrear*: To speak a language with difficulty, and making mistakes), according to the Real Academia Española, meant in her case mixing Spanish and Catalan. Moix talks later of Nonaspe as "una franja lingüística indecisa" (an indeterminate linguistic area or zone) and explains that the mother's dialect goes back and forth between Catalan and Spanish (228–9). This beginning aligns the son with the mother's linguistic practices of alternation, subversion of rules, and unexpectedness.

Error and indecision also link the mother's and Moix's linguistic values to a linguistic reality in Catalonia: Because of the lack of education in Catalan during the dictatorship, Catalan was often spoken and written incorrectly, with interferences from Spanish – the *barbarismos* that Janés refers to in *Jardín*. As Kathryn Crameri explains, "[v]ery few Catalans born after 1936 had had any formal teaching in the language" (*Catalonia* 22), and "[b]y 1981, around half of Catalans could speak the language – which is a testament to their determination not to give up – but only 15 per cent could write it" (22). Indecision is important because Moix switched between Catalan and Spanish to write and publish, and, similarly, particularly in the urban space of Barcelona, speakers often face the dilemma of which language to speak to strangers in, Catalan or Spanish. Error and indecision also put at the forefront a parallel between language and sexuality: In a bilingual context, the child and adolescent has the potential to choose between two (linguistic) options, and in this case the self feels affectively closer to the mother's linguistic origin, a linguistic reality where the clear-cut divisions between Catalan and Spanish are erased. This potential is somehow similar for Moix to the choice between desiring men or women, an inclination that can be lived at some point as an error as well as a transgression against social rules. Yet it is important not to forget that Moix taught himself to write in Catalan and chose which language to write in, placing the subject in charge of his linguistic as well as his sexual destiny, as he also embraced his homosexuality and made it public early on.

While Moix's mother had – according to her son – "mixed" ethnic origins, the father embodies, in Moix's view, Catalan purity and authenticity; the autobiographer writes that the father's family "podía vanagloriarse una catalanidad a prueba de bombas" (*El cine* 64; could pride themselves on a bulletproof Catalan identity). In addition to transmitting a Catalan surname, Moix's father represents the traditional popular Catalan culture, a *Weltanschauung* that is represented through food, music, social events, and festivities. Moix identifies the *escudella* or Catalan Christmas soup, the father's excursions to pick mushrooms, and the sardanas, the traditional Catalan dance, as elements of Catalan culture that the father would uphold at home and that are seen in opposition to some of Moix's interests that place him closer to the mother, such as the Aragonese traditional dance, la jota (65; the jota). The father's numerous hobbies make of him a spirited person and a caricature-like image of a Catalan. Moreover, these are hobbies to which Moix feels a strong aversion, "como siempre que él insistía en una cosa, yo me resistía con todas mis fuerzas" (*El beso* 383; whenever he insisted on something, I would resist with all my will). The father's insistence on Catalan customs becomes one of the reasons Moix rejects part of his Catalan cultural legacy.

Family is essential in Moix's *Memorias* to explain one's cultural heritage. This is an element present not only in Moix's *Memorias*: As Josep-Anton Fernàndez explains in *Another Country*, by analyzing Moix's *El dia que va morir Marilyn* (1969) and *Siro o la increada consciència de la raça* (1974), in these novels, through an "oppressive familial situation," we see "the genealogical critique of an essential national identity" (47). For instance, Bruno and Jordi, the protagonists of *El dia*, reinterpret their parent's stories and their Catalan and Spanish upbringing in order to give them a meaning that makes sense to them (the sons). How languages and cultures are central to the subject's affections in complex, changing, and unexpected ways is a recurrent theme in *El dia*, as well as in Moix's *Memorias*. In the case of the *Memorias*, the father epitomizes the subject's fluctuating relationship with Catalan: From the child's admiration of his father and his language in the 1940s and 1950s to the adolescent's hatred thereof (in the late fifties and sixties). Moix describes, with critical irony, the place of Catalan under Franco's dictatorship: Catalan was turned into an unrefined language, profuse in insults and blasphemies (*El cine* 90): "el catalán utilizado para los aspectos más bastos de la vida cotidiana y el castellano como el único idioma en que se expresaban las ideas elevadas. El catalán era el dialecto del mercado. El castellano la lengua de las grandes academias del pensamiento" (283; Catalan was used for the coarsest elements of daily life and Spanish as the only language in which elevated ideas were expressed. Catalan was the dialect of the market. Spanish, the language of the great schools of thought). According to Moix, Catalan survived the Francoist censorship because of ordinary people, not because of politicians or intellectuals. Ultimately, the autobiographer points to his father to exemplify those salient to keeping Catalan alive:

> [E]l catalán surge auténtico e indomable en este bautizo mío, entre yogures, natillas y mantecados. Mientras los vencedores lo relegan a un último lugar en la vida pública y los poetas se enzarzan en lamentos sublimes, su salvaguarda callejera queda confiada a aquellos que, como mi padre, se contentaban cerrando banquetes con un verso de Pitarra que resumía el declarado amor a su oficio y la fidelidad natural a su lengua. (*El cine* 71)

> Catalan emerges authentic and indomitable in this baptism of mine, among yogurts, custards, and *mantecados* (cakes made with lard). While the victors relegated it to the bottom rung of public life and the poets engaged in sublime laments, its safeguarding in the streets was entrusted to those who, like my father, were satisfied with closing banquets with a verse of Pitarra's,[4] summing up his professed love for his craft and his innate loyalty to the language.

Not only is Catalan transmitted by the father in contravention of the norms and values of the dictatorship, but for Moix Catalan is also linked to the indomitable, the popular, and the working class to which the father belongs. In this context, Catalan bears a strong sense of authenticity, as in Barral's and Janés's writings, but in Moix it is attached to his identification with the middle-lower classes. In this setting, the father protects a language and culture facing prohibition, thus becoming a figure of admiration in the eyes of the young child, one directly linked to this safeguarding of the language in the streets. Moix reflects on how it was often the working classes who spoke Catalan, while upper-class Catalans chose Spanish as a way of showing "distinction" and their affiliation to the regime.[5] This sociolinguistic reality changed progressively in the seventies and eighties, during the period of linguistic normalization (that Josep-Anton Fernàndez dates from 1976 to 1999; *El malestar* 32) when Catalan became coofficial and was reembraced by some in the middle and upper classes – sometimes to distinguish themselves from the migrants from the rest of Spain.[6]

In Moix's *Memorias*, one side of the paternal figure is this admired Catalan father, protective of the language and intellectually nurturing. Moix confesses that the first fervour he felt for books came from his father, who would take him to the Biblioteca Central to read (*El cine* 282). The father professes deep respect for written language, a deference that he tries to instil in his sons (285). The autobiographer feels moved by his father's esteem for books, and his father's belief that all of the world's knowledge is contained in encyclopedias (286). The subject recalls how literary preferences were shared by his father and him, tracing an affiliative impulse to honour the father's legacy. For instance, Moix says that "mi infancia se había nutrido con las historias del cine que papá cogía de la Gran Biblioteca"[7] (*El cine* 76–7; my childhood was nourished by stories of the cinema that my father had picked up from the Great Library), a significant assertion if we consider the centrality of the cinema in Moix's oeuvre.[8] Yet while Moix's father venerates the written language, his ideas are bound mostly to popular culture and to an oral tradition – the Catalan tradition. In this regard, there seems to be a void, as the Catalan father transmits the importance of culture, but Moix only learns about Catalan literature and its canonical writers later in life. The father thus transmits a form of disordered culture – one that has gaps[9] but that also becomes essential to the son's literary consciousness.

Class is also important to Moix's literary consciousness: In Moix's case, the father's library is outside the home, a public library. This distinguishes Moix from Barral, Janés, and Goytisolo, who all place the library inside the home. As an indicator of socioeconomic and cultural background, the family library symbolizes tradition and prestige. Moix suppresses this association in favour of a public, communal one. The public library's name is, moreover, chief in elucidating this reality in which Catalan is unofficial. The admired father brings Moix to what the father names the "Biblioteca de Catalunya," which during the dictatorship was called "Biblioteca Central" (Central Library) and which Moix himself calls "Gran Biblioteca" (*El cine* 282; Great Library). As with gender – where a line separated girls and boys into two distinct groups – Moix perceives borders and differentiated spaces restricted to Catalan and to Spanish. The two languages had different uses, and there is an invisible boundary that gives one a prestigious position while the other is reserved for inferior uses:

> Esta dualidad entre el mundo de la calle y el mundo de las ideas se complicaba con el recuerdo de la escisión impuesta por la guerra, escisión todavía presente a la ambigüedad que rodeaba a los nombres de las cosas. Aquella sociedad de la República había dejado unos hábitos en la gente sencilla que la Dictadura no consiguió cambiar … De modo que cuando papá me llevaba a curiosear en las enciclopedias de las naves góticas, se le escapaba que íbamos a la «Biblioteca de Catalunya». Es aquí donde entraba mi extrañeza porque en la tarjeta de préstamos yo leía «Biblioteca central». (283)

> This duality between the world of the streets and the world of ideas became complicated with the memory of the excision imposed by the war, an excision still manifest in the ambiguity surrounding the names for things. That society of the Republic had left behind some habits in the common people that the dictatorship never managed to change … So that when my father took me to browse through the encyclopedias of the gothic stacks, he would say that we were going to the "Library of Catalonia". And this is where I became puzzled because on my borrower's card I read, "Central Library".

The intellectually nurturing father connects Moix with a language that was oppressed and seen as a door to the past. Moix talks about his experience with the library's names as "uno de los primeros contrasentidos idiomáticos que alcanzo a recordar" (283; one of the first idiomatic incongruences that I can remember). In *El beso* he says that he felt estrangement upon his discovery of the problem of names, giving as an example how streets and plazas often had two names, the official one of the dictatorship and the popular one in Catalan: "descubro entonces que ya en mi niñez, cuando corría por aquella plaza, los nombres estaban condenados y mi distanciamiento del mundo completamente decidido" (23; I discover then that already in my childhood, when I ran in that plaza, the names were condemned and my distance from the world fully decided).[10] Language, a first system of alienation for the subject, particularly because of this diglossic context, demonstrates how reality has been altered.

Linguistic (Dis)Affiliations

If Catalan is the oppressed language of paternal resistance in the eyes of the child, this linguistic affective reality changes, and Spanish becomes the language of fascination for Moix as an adolescent. In *El beso*, Moix explains that, during his adolescence, he was fascinated by Madrid, as a form of inverted snobbery: He defended Hispanic culture as an escape from what he perceived as a small Catalan world. This converted him into "la perfecta imagen del jovencito colonizado" (*El beso* 383; the perfect image of a colonized youth). The concept of colonization, which equates Catalonia's economic, political, and cultural status to that of Spanish America, masks Catalonia's involvement in Spain's colonial and postcolonial relationships with the Americas. Yet this idea – which I have also analysed in Barral's *Los años* – is used recurrently when explaining certain cultural dynamics between Spain and Catalonia.[11] In the case of Moix's quote, being culturally colonized by Madrid is stated with irony, given that Moix switched from writing in Catalan to Spanish and back. Like many of the members of the *gauche divine*, Moix was part in many senses of the margins and yet became part of the cultural centre, renegotiating notions between the peripherical and the mainstream in the Spanish and Catalan cultural landscape.

Gender and sexuality are not independent from Moix's feelings and choices with regard to languages. One of Moix's early realizations was that Catalonia was subjugated but was also subjugating others. In contrast to his Aragonese maternal ancestry, which was less strict and narrow-minded, Catalan culture was perceived as oppressive, a feeling directly linked to a small, provincial, and prejudiced community but also to his father's homophobia, as the father continually repeated to his son that "antes que tener un hijo maricón, preferiría verlo muerto" (see, for instance, *El cine* 139–40; rather than have a son who was a fag, I'd prefer to see him dead). Moix explains that his sexuality was the reason for the mutual distance between him and his father, as his father never accepted that he was gay, even when the rest of the family approved of it, though some with hesitation (*El beso* 189–200). Therefore, for Moix, Catalonia is not a utopian community but a place that can be as repressive towards others as Spain. Sexuality and language maintain an unbreakable bond, given that it is the father's lack of acceptance of the son's sexuality that puts the son at odds with the marginalized culture of his father. That said, this feeling that Catalan language and culture, while subjugated and marginalized, is also subjugating and marginalizing others, is useful for Moix to avoid a blind spot, to be able to speak critically about Catalan culture, and to "free" himself from any linguistic obligation.[12] At the same time, while Spanish culture and language could have been the culture to turn to, neither did Moix fully embrace a complete identification with Madrid, as he was an author who constantly tackled class and cultural dissensions in Catalonia in his literary works.

Moix calls into question the assumption of a distinct, stable border between the Catalan and Spanish cultures, highlighting that culture is hybrid even if languages are not. Nonetheless, his working system seems to profit from this cultural hybridity, which he turns into a linguistic one. Moix started writing in Spanish but quickly changed to publishing in Catalan, which could be understood as a way to affiliate his writings with the repressed language of the father. He later switched to Spanish again, embodying a linguistic alternation between two literary systems that for some have been in opposition but that to him were both useful systems, both part of the self and advantageous in constructing his literary persona, creating, being read, and selling his work.

Catalan literature has been understood by some as literature written in Catalan, and Catalan authors have been identified as those who write and publish in Catalan, excluding those authors born in or living in Catalonia who write in Spanish. This is seen differently by critics based in other areas of Spain, as Ute Heinemann points out, "des de Madrid el criteri per a aquesta classificació és l'origen, mentre que a Catalunya el criteri decisiu per a aquesta divisió és el de la llengua" (25; in Madrid, the criterion for this classification is origin, while in Catalonia, the decisive criterion for this division is that of language). Some of those for whom the language is the deciding factor in classifying Catalan literature have argued that authors born and/or resident in Catalonia but who write in Spanish (such as Eduardo Mendoza) offer a partial, false, or candy-coated vision of Catalonia, something directly related to their language choice, as they wrote in Spanish about a cultural reality that was in fact bilingual without necessarily representing this bilingualism. This happens too, as Kathryn Crameri explains, because "the reception of translated works from Catalan in the rest of Spain is much less enthusiastic than might be expected. This means that the majority of Spaniards form their impressions of Catalonia from those authors who write in Spanish" (*Catalonia* 77–8). Some critics have also accused those writers who published in Spanish after having a career publishing in Catalan of being "turncoats."[13]

Kathryn Crameri and Stewart King have challenged this notion that the Catalan and Spanish literary systems in Catalonia are mutually exclusive, and, in *Escribir la catalanidad*, King sustains that, when looking at works by Terenci Moix, Francisco Candel, Ignasi Riera, Montserrat Roig, Juan Marsé, Ramon Pallicé, or Manuel Vázquez Montalbán, "las narrativas escritas en catalán y en castellano son expresiones de la misma cultura" (3; the narratives written in Catalan and in Spanish are expressions of the same culture). King questions why it is that Spanish has been excluded as a language capable of describing, of expressing "la catalanidad." He gives examples of authors who, like Moix, have worked bilingually, another example being Andreu Martín, who drafts in Catalan and then self-translates into Spanish (75). Kathryn Crameri also considers that authors who write in Spanish but are Catalan "are a part of Catalan culture, in the broadest sense of the term" and exemplifies this with works by Juan Marsé, Eduardo Mendoza (*Catalonia* 77), and Montserrat Roig (*Language* 180). In *Construir con palabras*, Jaume Subirana advocates for considering Catalan literature as one that "incluye no catalanes que escriben en catalán y catalanes que no escriben en catalán y autores que escriben en las dos lenguas – se traducen o escriben en castellano y catalán indistintamente" (230; includes non-Catalans who write in Catalan, and Catalans who don't write in Catalan, and writers who write in both languages – those who translate themselves or write indistinctly in Spanish or Catalan). He argues that the Catalan literary system is "amplio, complejo, ambiguo a veces, mutable, sinuoso" (232; vast, complex, sometimes ambiguous, changing, sinuous). However, according to Subirana, not all of them are Catalan writers, although their literature in Spanish should be considered as Catalan literature: "¿Estoy diciendo que todos estos autores son escritores catalanes? No. ¿Creo que deberíamos contemplarlos como parte de la literatura catalana, y leer lo que acontece hoy en esta, también en lo relativo al sistema literario, teniéndoles en cuenta? Sí, sin duda" (227–9; Am I saying that all of these authors are Catalan writers? No. Do I believe that we should consider them as part of Catalan literature, and read what is happening in it today, also with regard to the literary tradition, taking them into account? Yes, without a doubt). Ultimately, the question is whether the Catalan idiosyncrasy can be expressed in Spanish and what the consequences and meanings are of expressing Catalan culture in one language or the other. Of course, as Joan Fuster argued, the literature written in Catalan is minoritarian and subaltern (*Literatura* 8) and has both a secondary position in Spain and a legacy of having been politicized by the Spanish state: "El Estado nunca supo ni pudo combatir al Catalanismo sin atacar la lengua – y, por lo tanto, la literatura – catalana. Ni la lengua – la literatura – catalana encontró hasta hoy otro recurso de defensa que el en Catalanismo" (12; The State never knew how to fight Catalan nationalism without attacking the Catalan language and, subsequently, the literature. To this day, neither the language nor the literature has ever found any means of defence other than Catalan nationalism). That said, is always the choice of one language or the other directly related to a particular ideology?

Authors who reside in Catalonia have had to navigate a politicized linguistic and literary context, particularly during the linguistic normalization period. In the end, this linguistic choice impacts not only how they work on a daily basis but also their literary production, readership, and sales. Authors born and/or who live in Catalan-speaking areas, whether they publish in Catalan, in Spanish, or both, are often asked about the reasons for their choice, and their selections become – as we see Moix's choice here – an interpretative theme. In the case of Moix, his alternation between Catalan and Spanish has been the subject of numerous readings: Because Moix won the Planeta Prize soon after his shift to Spanish in the 1980s, some critics such as Josep Maria Castellet and Carlos Ramos argued that his decision to write in Spanish was based on economics and prestige (83). When explaining Moix's language choice of Spanish, others, like the scholar Paul Julian Smith, have linked the change to Spanish to his rejection of the paternal world (44, 45). Moix's switching has also been interpreted as a positioning linked to politics but also not far from issues of sexuality, as publisher Jorge Herralde, for instance, declared that for Moix switching from Catalan to Spanish was a "multiple orgasm": "Se decide a escribir en catalán después de haber escrito primero en castellano. Luego, que es muy ambicioso y ve que la difusión de su obra en castellano podría ser muy superior, tal como decía él mismo y es obvio. También el sentirse encorsetado en la sociedad literaria catalana. Su posición siempre beligerante con la Generalitat y el gobierno de Pujol fue una constante en su vida. Bueno, pues hacer esa butifarra, ese corte de mangas de pasarse al castellano, cumplía bastantes objetivos a la vez, era un orgasmo múltiple" (349; He decides to write in Catalan after having first written in Spanish. Then, he is very ambitious, and he sees that the dissemination of his work in Spanish could be much greater, as he himself has said, and it seems obvious. Also the feeling of being straitjacketed by Catalan literary society. His ever-contentious position with regard to the Generalitat and the Pujol government was a constant in his life. Giving the middle finger by going over to Spanish, therefore, fulfilled several goals at the same time, it was a multiple orgasm). In an interview, Terenci Moix's sister, Ana María Moix, also explained Moix's language switching as related to politics as well as to his rebellious personality:

> Su ruptura con el catalán, eso lo recuerdo muy mal. Él empezó a escribir en castellano. *El día que murió Marilyn* primero se titulaba *El desorden* y la presentó al Nadal. Por aquel entonces se hizo amigo de Maria Aurèlia Capmany, Ricard Salvat, Joaquim Molas, Castellet y, por militancia, aprendió a escribir en catalán, porque antes no sabía hacerlo, ni yo tampoco, porque habíamos estudiado en castellano. O sea, que entra en la cultura catalana y es su *enfant terrible* con *La torre dels vicis capitals*, que para la cultura de la época … Francamente, aquí había unos señores muy respetables y con un bagaje clásico importante, pero él mezcló eso con la cultura de los años sesenta, había estado en Londres, y en su obra está presente la cultura y el arte pop del momento que era muy revulsivo, está la cosa descarada de su homosexualidad y sus libros sobre el sadismo, sobre el marqués de Sade, sobre la literatura anglosajona … Ésa era la mezcla. Pero ¿cuándo se pasa al castellano? De eso no me acuerdo muy bien. Sé que hubo una pelea entre él y Jordi Pujol, por cierto. ¿Por qué? Sobre eso hablamos poco. Él había obtenido una beca de la Banca Catalana o algo así. Supongo que al pasarse al castellano tuvo problemas. Ahora bien, ¿por qué se pasó? A raíz de alguna rabieta, pero no recuerdo por qué. Quizá lo hizo también para vender más libros y tener mayor proyección. Porque, a fin de cuentas, al nen le reventaba mucho la cosa pequeña de aquí. Y el mundo editorial catalán es de pagar poco porque hay que hacer patria y demás. ("Una broma amarga" 227)

> I don't remember his break with Catalan very well at all. He started to write in Spanish. *The Day Marilyn Died* was originally titled *The Disorder* and he submitted it to the Nadal Literary Prize competition. At that time, he became friends with Maria Aurèlia Capmany, Ricard Salvat, Joaquim Molas, and Castellet, and, out of a sense of political activism, he learned to write in Catalan, because previously he didn't know how to, neither did I, because we had both done our studies in Spanish. In other words, he becomes part of Catalan culture and is its *enfant terrible* with *The Tower of the Deadly Sins*, which for the cultural climate at that time … To tell the truth, here you had some very respectable gentlemen with important classical baggage, but he mixed this up with the culture of the sixties, he'd been in London, and in his work there's the culture and the pop art of the moment, which was very revulsive, there's the element of his blatant homosexuality and his books on sadism, on the Marquis de Sade, on English literature. That was the combination. But when did he transition to Spanish? I don't really remember. I know that there was definitely a fight between him and

> Jordi Pujol. Why? We never really talked about that. He'd received a grant from the Banca Catalana or something. I believe that upon switching to Spanish, he had problems. Why did that happen? Because of some tantrum, but I don't remember why. Maybe he also did it to sell more books and have greater visibility. Because, at the end of the day, he was pissed off by Catalan provincialism. And the Catalan publishing world is in the habit of paying (its authors) very little because one must write in Catalan for the nation and all that. (A Bitter Joke)

The sister's explanation – Ana María Moix publishes in Spanish – shows that the choice to alternate languages is not based on one factor alone but is related to multiple aspects, from prizes, friendships, family, education, and personal and collective history to economics and politics, and perhaps, ultimately, the issue is not worth the time, "lo recuerdo muy mal" (I remember it very poorly). Moix was probably motivated to sell more books; he was also influenced by friends and was eager to question cultural expectations as well as literary models. In the end, in Moix's autobiographical writings, his father and his weak paternal mandate set a tone that predicts the need to combat sexual normativity, an oppressive model of masculinity, and a set of accepted cultural, linguistic, and literary rules that he never sees as absolute.

The full history of Moix's *El dia* and the explanations around the novel's multiple translations attest to how, for Moix, Catalan and Spanish are not mutually exclusive but both fundamental to writing, and how he alternated between the two languages for various reasons, including advice from others, his skills, and his desire to reach an audience, receive awards, and sell his books. In *El tiempo es un sueño pop* (Time Is a Pop Dream), Juan Bonilla explains that the first version of *El dia* was written in Spanish and titled *El desorden* (The Disorder). This version was submitted to the 1965 Premio Nadal competition, winning fifth place (64). Josep Vergés, publisher and cofounder of *Destino* and of the Nadal Prize, asked Moix to visit him in his office, invited him to collaborate with *Destino,* and recommended he rewrite the novel in Catalan. According to Bonilla, Vergés said: "Su novela tiene un fallo fundamental: no se sabe en qué idioma está escrita. No es castellano ni es catalán" (63–4; Your novel has a fundamental flaw; one doesn't know in what language it's written. It's neither Spanish nor Catalan). In *Escribir la catalanidad,* Stewart King offers a somewhat similar explanation: "Moix ya había escritor una versión castellana con el título *El desorden.* Cuando el libro fue rechazado por varias editoriales, Joaquim Molas, Pere Gimferrer y Maria-Aurèlia Capmany le aconsejaron que hicera algunos retoques, incluyendo cambiar la lengua y fue publicado por

Edicions 62 en 1969" (73; Moix had already written a version in Spanish with the title *El desorden*. When the book was rejected by several publishers, Joaquim Molas, Pere Gimferrer, and Maria-Aurèlia Capmany suggested that he make some minor edits, including changing the language and it was published (in Catalan) by Editions 62 in 1969). The desire to be published– but also the opinions of friends and mentors – as well as the novel's "natural" language all contribute to the decision to self-translate the book into Catalan. It is worth mentioning here that Moix, coming from a lower-middle class background, probably wanted to live on his work as a writer and not depend economically on his father or be involved in his father's business.

Important nonetheless are the feelings narrated behind this choice. Bonilla quotes a 1972 interview with Terenci Moix published in *Diario de Barcelona* on 16 September in which Josep Faulí asked Moix how and when he learned to read and write in Catalan, to which Moix answered, "Empecé a escribir en el año 66, cuando me decidí a traducir del inglés al catalán *La torre de los vicios capitales* y del castellano al catalán *El día que murió Marilyn* – que entonces se titulaba *El desorden*. Fue claramente un caso de conversion" (64; I started to write in 1966, when I decided to translate from English into Catalan *The Tower of the Deadly Sins*, and from Spanish into Catalan *The Day Marilyn Died* – that was then entitled *The Disorder*. It was clearly a case of conversion). Bonilla also makes reference to another article in *Flashmen* in 1974 in which Moix explains that "Cuando Vergés me recomendó que escribiese en catalán yo no había leído un solo libro en catalán, así que ni siquiera tenía idea de que hubiese una cultura catalana ... Leí la *Antígona* de Salvador Espriu, si bien en español. Me quedé sorprendido de que en mi lengua, que yo creía muerta, se pudiesen expresar aquellos pensamientos" (65; When Vergés recommended that I write in Catalan, I had not read a single book in Catalan, so I had no idea that there was a Catalan culture ... I read Salvador Espriu's *Antigone*, albeit in Spanish. I was surprised that those thoughts could be expressed in my language, which I had thought was dead). Not being conscious until one's early twenties that one's language has a literary history and tradition is an experience shared by many of those who were educated under the dictatorship in Catalonia. The experience of learning that Catalan was a language of literary prestige becomes a theme in the last version Moix wrote of *El día*: "Esta experiencia personal fue básica para uno de los momentos que considero más afortunados de *El día que murió Marilyn*: el descubrimiento que hace Bruno de la lengua maternal. Lo añadí en la última versión de la novela, partiendo de mi propia experiencia, y está hecho en clave lírica: un canto clarísimo al idioma" (65; This personal experience was fundamental for one of the moments I consider to be most successful in *The Day Marilyn Died*: Bruno's discovery of his maternal language. I added it to the final version of the novel, taking it from my own experience, and it's done in a lyrical key: a clear ode to the language).

Interestingly enough, this "última versión" of *El día* is in fact a Spanish one, as King and Bonilla explain: "En 1971, la editorial Lumen publicó una traducción castellana, de José Miguel Velloso ... Moix decidió publicar catorce años más tarde, en 1984, una versión bastante revisada del texto de Velloso en la que elimina algunas secciones y añade nuevas que no habían aparecido anteriormente en las dos versiones publicadas. Esta nueva edición del libro, según la solapa, es 'la única versión que Terenci Moix considera como definitiva' Con esta afirmación, Moix favorece esta versión sobre las anteriores, incluyendo la versión catalana" (*Escribir* 73; In 1971, Editorial Lumen published a Spanish translation by José Miguel Velloso ... Fourteen years later, Moix decided to publish a heavily revised version of Velloso's text in which he removed some sections and added new ones that hadn't previously appeared in the two published editions. This new edition of the book, according to the flyleaf, is "the only edition that Terenci Moix considers as definitive." With this statement, Moix favours this edition over the previous ones, including the edition in Catalan). Similarly, Bonilla also explains that "Moix se sometió a un proceso de depuración que le permitió prescindir de muchos de los excesos de la edición original, que en la versión definitiva ... permiten que el texto tenga mayor fluidez ... La edición, pues, de *Marilyn* ... contenía una paradoja, pues siendo una traducción de la obra original, y dada la imposibilidad de corregir la obra original que se había reeditado varias veces sin que el autor tuviera la oportunidad de enmendarla, resultaba más fiel a la voluntad de este que el propio original (395; Moix submitted himself to a process of purification that allowed him to get rid of a lot of the excesses of the first edition, and that in the definitive version ... allows the text to have greater fluidity ... This edition, then, of *Marilyn* ... contained a paradox, being a translation of the original work and given the impossibility of correcting the original work that had been reissued several times without the author having a chance to emend it, it turned out to be more faithful to the author's intentions than the original itself). The concepts of originality and original language are deeply questioned by Moix in this rewriting process, and it is not only, as King explains in *Escribir*, that Moix's novel *El dia* "pertenece a las dos culturas, la castellana y la catalana" (85; belongs to two cultures, the Spanish and the Catalan one) but that this novel demonstrates that the "original culture and language" is a mix between the two, a back and forth that is necessary to its creation and construction. Josep-Anton Fernàndez considers that Moix occupies a paradoxical place in Catalan literature, "he is part of two literary institutions, the Catalan and the Spanish, which as coherent systems are mutually exclusive" (7). However, when looking at Moix's oeuvre, one sees that, to him, these two literary systems are interrelated and cannot be distinguished one from the other. In this regard, Moix not only aimed to portray a Catalan world in Spanish – in the final version of *El día* as well as in his *Memorias* – but he also portrayed his sentimental and affective relationships with the Catalan language translated into Spanish, evidencing the importance of the family, friends, and language to rethink the place of Catalan in the Spanish and Catalan society.

The *Esperpentic* Father

Characterizing his father as someone who did not respect himself or inspire much respect in his son (106), Moix affirms that his father "íbase perfilando como la figura que llenaría mis afectos con mayor cantidad de contradicciones" (106; gradually took shape as the figure who would fill my affections with the greatest number of contradictions). The father is described as a cheerful, generous fool and *tarambana* (106; scatterbrain). He professes love for his son, indulges the son's caprices, and represents a series of rules that are easy to ignore – in fact, necessary to ignore when it comes to Moix defending his sexuality. The affiliative impulse, the admiration for his father's love of books, is rapidly undone by a disaffiliative one, the father's homophobia, which makes of the father–son relationship a two-sided coin. Because of the father's homophobia, the gay son resists the paternal model and offers an *esperpentic*, distorted, and exaggerated image of the father's heterosexuality.

Moix's critics have noticed the importance of image distortion in Moix's aesthetics: Steven Forrest points out that Moix offers a disconcerting, grotesque, alienating image of reality (933), and Rosi Song persuasively argues that Moix's continuous distortions of reality situate this author's work within the literary tradition of the Spanish *esperpento* (101–2).[14] The *esperpento* projects a deformed image: It is the result of placing an image in front of a concave mirror that shows the reflected figure in all its unattractiveness, ridiculousness, absurdity, and degradation. In this case it is used to question both the father's sexuality and his Catalanness. The first way in which Moix exposes the father as an *esperpentic* is through the belittling insults on the part of Moix's mother and aunts. These women questioned Moix's father and insulted him by calling him "burdo pelagatos" (a nobody), "simplón" (gullible), and "cantamañanas" (daydreamer) (106, 107). During the familial fights, the father would shout at Moix's mother "no me provoques, que los tengo muy bien puestos" (123; don't provoke me, I have them right where they need to be), a sentence that prompted all of the women in the house to question whether Moix's father was really as "complete" as he asserted. The mother would dare the father to find another lover, while one of the aunts, Florencia, would take part in the discussion to conclude "¿lo veis? No tiene lo que hay que tener" (124; see? He doesn't have what a man needs), while insisting that the father was "un calzonazos capado" (124; pussy-whipped).[15] Thus, the father's masculinity is a theatrical argument between the father and the female members of the family – who despise him – and whose voices Moix ventriloquizes.

The father's body is also used to undermine a specific masculine prototype. This imagery is connected to the subject's class consciousness: Moix associates the underwear hanging on the balconies outside the windows of the apartments in El Raval as a symbol of the poverty of postwar Spain, a poverty that also implies moral backwardness. The autobiographer associates this moral and material poverty with his father and with the father's masculinity and body. One night, Moix catches a glimpse of his father's testicles hanging out of his underpants, an image that he says he would never be able to forget:

> Siguiendo el rastro a este recuerdo, mantengo como una de mis obsesiones permanentes la imagen de papaíto vestido de aquella guisa cierta noche que se introdujo en nuestra cama para hacernos dormir contándonos cuentos. Si quedó descalificado ante mis ojos al verle aparecer con unos calzoncillos como los que yo veía colgados en los balcones de la gente más vulgar del barrio, todavía fue peor cuando asomaron por la pernera un par de testículos muy hinchados y enrojecidos como dos pimientos. Parecían los de un perro dálmata que tuvimos décadas mas tarde. (120)

> Following the trail of this memory, I retain as one of my permanent obsessions the image of my daddy dressed this way one night when he climbed into our bed to help us fall asleep by telling us stories. He was automatically disqualified in my eyes when I saw him come in wearing underwear like the ones I would see hanging from the balconies of the most common people on the block; it was even worse when, peeking out from one of the legs, was a pair of testicles, very swollen and reddened like two peppers. They resembled those of a Dalmatian we had owned some decades later.

The father's body is animalized, a representation that demonstrates how much the son reviles him. Invoking the father's body, Moix challenges the traditional father as a noncarnal being, the one who is in power as a result of an absolute strength beyond his physical appearance. Using Freudian terminology, Moix internalizes the father not as a model of perfection that forms the *ego-ideal* – but as the opposite, a weak model to be rejected.[16] The images of the father's genitalia question the father as the bearer of the phallus, offering a counter-image to Lacanian and Freudian theories of fatherhood through the eyes of the gay son.

Moix's images also aim to be troubling by disclosing an incestuous tension between father and son. The autobiographer explains that, while he played with his father in bed, the father's testicles would hit Moix's forehead, and the son would start crying as if he had been flagellated: "jugando, jugando, aquellos atributos de una fealdad repugnante fueron a parar repetidas veces sobre mi frente, de manera que en un determinado momento me eché a llorar como si me estuviesen flagelando" (120; playing, playing, those attributes, which were of a repugnant ugliness, would end up hitting my forehead again and again, so that at a certain point I would start crying as if they were flagellating me). The undeniably sexual aspect of the scene is cardinal to Moix's subversion. The idea of flagellation points towards a moral transmitted through the strict Catholic education of Franco's regime, in which the father is responsible for punishment. This Francoist education is transgressed by placing the penitential action into what seems to be a somehow sado-masochistic practice. It is worth noting that Moix published *El sadismo de nuestra infancia* (1970; The Sadism of Our Childhood), a text that fuses the genres of theatre and sociological essay and in which a character named "Terenci Moix" meets with other protagonists of Terenci Moix's previous novels such as Bruno (protagonist of *El dia*) to discuss their sadistic upbringings. In *El sadismo* the common generational element is having been educated in a Catholic system that turned suffering and martyrdom into a form of pleasure. Father–son incest is also a theme in Moix's novel *Siro*, in what Villamados interprets as an "ajuste de cuentas con la ley del padre y la clase burguesa que representa" (75; a settling of accounts with the law of the father and the bourgeoisie that it represents). The father is also portrayed as a desired man in other parts of the *Memorias*, where we find references to his testicles again. While the mother and aunts undermined Moix's father, the dairy customers and the prostitutes praised him: "Solían tocarme los genitales para comprobar si se desarrollaban y ponían como los de mi padre, elogiadísimos tanto por algunas señoras casadas como por las putas más adictas del Barrio Chino. Ante tales expectativas, puede decirse que no hubo en la calle Ponent niño más tocado que yo" (79; They would touch my genitals to see if they were developing and becoming like my father's, which were greatly praised by several married women as well as by the hardcore prostitutes of the Barrio Chino. In view of such expectations, you could say that there was no child in Ponent Street who was more fondled than myself). It is impossible to miss the extent of the irony and the desire for subversion in Moix's representation of the paternal figure and of childhood as sexualized.

Because Moix's father is pushed out of the feminine spaces of the family, where he argues with his wife and is criticized by his sisters-in-law, the father finds refuge in and takes his son to places outside the home: The bar, the Ramblas, the library, and the brothels. The brothel is probably the central place for the father to perform and (re)construct his masculinity. Moix explains, "mi padre se definía a sí mismo como un putero, que al parecer emblema de macho de ley" (*El cine* 115; my father defined himself as a whoremonger, by all accounts the emblem of an official macho). However, Moix's images of the father in the brothel do not reinforce his manliness: In fact, the brothels are a grotesque environment where the prostitutes' deformed anatomies are used as a way to disqualify the father's behaviour. Moix explains that he started going to prostitutes when he was six (115), accompanying his father, and he compares this experience with that of going to the Biblioteca Central. Moix pictures the prostitutes and their clothing as bizarre: "allí se mostraban libremente ... piernas desnudas, llenas de morados, barrigas con peligrosas concesiones a la celulitis o brazos enrojecidos, casi despellejados a causa de una pésima depilación doméstica" (119; there they openly displayed themselves ... naked legs, full of purple bruises, bellies showing dangerous concessions to cellulitis, or reddened arms, nearly hairless owing to crude do-it-yourself depilation). Their outfits, colourful and garish, and the prostitutes' weight, bruises, body hair, and deformities, all emphasize the impossible eroticism of the scene while also showing the exaggerated and extravagant intent of Moix's writings. In *Body Images: Embodiment as Intercorporeality*, Gail Weiss emphasizes the importance of others in the processes of construction, destruction, and reconstruction that characterize the ongoing development of body image (33). Indeed, juxtaposing the father's and the prostitutes' bodies, Moix uncovers how a normative notion of virility, one based on the idea of a sexually potent man, was deceptive and could only survive because of the construction of models of women who responded to and were subjected to this masculine imagination. Aurora Morcillo points out that order and hygiene composed the essence of the Catholic ideal of women in Francoist Spain (*The Seduction* 30). Furthermore, the regime's propaganda presented the prostitute as the nemesis of the honest woman: Prostitutes were a threat not only because they enticed good men to fall from grace but also because they literally infected the Spanish citizenry with disease (97). In some ways, Moix's vision departs from this Catholic ideal but only to offer a distorted impression of it.

The father is repeatedly unfaithful to the mother, and Moix censures the father's weekly habit of achieving a new erotic victory: "cada semana debía entrañar una nueva victoria erótica, cuanto más pregonada mejor" (115; every week must lead to a new erotic victory, the more frequently boasted about the better). In this context, the father's body and morality are inseparable in Moix's criticism:

> Empecé a encontrar censurable el puterío de papá. No en sus aspectos morales, aspectos que yo era incapaz de comprender y en adelante acatar, sino por el mismo proceso de repulsión que sentí cierta noche al verle en calzoncillos y con el sexo al aire. Pero muy especialmente porque toda su actuación presentaba aspectos de un donjuanismo trasnochado. (127)
>
> I began to consider my father's whoring reprehensible. Not from a moral point of view, which I was incapable of understanding and, in the future, of abiding by, but through the same process of repulsion that I felt the evening I saw him in his underwear with his genitalia hanging out. And especially because all of his behaviour exhibited the characteristics of an old, run-down *donjuán*.

The father is perceived as arrogant and overbearing, and Moix feels that his father thereby humiliated his mother. Similarly, at the end of *El cine*, Moix explains that he used to go to the theatre to observe the dancers' dresses. His father told him that, instead of the dresses, he should look at their breasts. Moix points out the Catalan word used by his father to make reference to the women's bodies: "las 'mamelles', los llamaba él, como si la *vedette* fuese una vaca" (327; the teats, he called them, as if the vedette were a cow). Thus, the 'father's virility is defined by objectifying women in order to show off a dominating masculinity, something that the autobiographer does not relate to. The father's sexism and *donjuanismo* are intertwined with a scarcity of acceptable models of masculinity and with a model that is anything but exemplary. In *Máscaras masculinas*, Enrique Gil Calvo says the father is the one who has access to the body of the woman in a legitimate way, as opposed to the "cabrón, cornudo, amante, rufián" (jerk, cuckold, stud, thug) as the one who attains access to the female body in an illegitimate way (220) and adds that "el padre es quien, pudiendo explotar gratuitamente la sexualidad de su mujer, sin embargo renuncia a ello para fundar una familia a la que tendrá que mantener" (221; the father is he who, although able to fully exploit the sexuality of his wife, nevertheless renounces this to start a family which he will need to support). The father is in this context expected to be the moral example and educative authority (261). By presenting his father as a *donjuán*, Moix questions this expected exemplarity.

The father's *donjuanismo* also puts into question the father's Catalanness: His "catalanidad a prueba de bombas" (his bullet-proof Catalanness) is infused with the Spanish stereotype of *donjuán* and the *macho ibérico*, sexual behaviours branded and stigmatized as Spanish. In his study of the literary figure of the Don Juan, Gregorio Marañón defined him as "símbolo del conquistador de mujeres" (339; a symbol of the conqueror of women). A main issue for Marañón is precisely Don Juan's Spanishness, as he argues that "lejos de tener un carácter originariamente y fundamentalmente español, yo afirmo que el amor donjuanesco es en España una importación exótica, sin raíces nacionales y sin tradición" (346; far from having a character that is originally and fundamentally Spanish, I would argue that the prototype of the Don Juanesque lover in Spain is an exotic importation, lacking national roots and without a tradition). Similarly, Elena Soriano in *El donjuanismo femenino* explains that the word *donjuanismo* appeared in the nineteenth century with Zorrilla (21) and concurs in seeing it as a projection, a European fantasy of the Spaniard "La mayoría de las versiones de Don Juan son latinas – españolas y francesas – pero incluso las nórdicas localizan el personaje o sus aventuras en España, como único lugar propicio a semejante visión del erotismo, y en suma, un elemento más del folclore *typical Spanish*" (71; The majority of the versions of Don Juan are latinate – Spanish and French – but even the Scandinavians locate the character and his adventures in Spain, as the only suitable location for such a vision of eroticism, and therefore, one more element belonging to "typical Spanish" folklore). If indeed the literary Don Juan is an exotic projection of the Spaniard from outside of Spain, there is also enthusiastic acceptance of this figure in Spanish culture. Ramiro de Maetzu's *Don Quijote, Don Juan, La Celestina. Ensayo de simpatía* (An Essay on Sympathy), Miguel de Unamuno's *Nada menos que todo un hombre* (Nothing Less than a Complete Man), or Pérez de Ayala's *Tigre Juan* (Tiger Juan) are other examples. In fact, the Don Juan imagery has penetrated ideas of Hispanic masculinity and the Hispanic cultural tradition to turn into a concept: That of the *donjuán*. In this case, Moix uses the literary figure and concept to also subvert the father's self-praised Catalanness and to diminish the father, to make him disappear as a person. As Marañón highlights, in the end, Don Juan is in fact "*un hombre sin nombre*; es decir, un sexo, y no un individuo" (295). Alberto

Mira points out that Moix's father appears throughout *El peso* "en un segundo plano," "marginado" (in the background, marginalized). He is "un hombre que no parece estar del todo, que no llega a ser, que no llega a influir" ("El niño" 193; he's a man who doesn't seem to be entirely there, who doesn't exist, who doesn't have any influence). It is not that the father does not influence, but it is as a counter-figure: The father's machismo and his "donjuanismo trasnochado" (rundown Don Juanism) are used by Moix to make his masculinity stereotypical, normative, and rejectable.

In his early adolescence, Moix returns to the brothel and tries to perform his father's role in order to prove his own manliness. This time, the prostitutes are not loving aunts but horrendous females with poorly done make-up and reeking of cigarettes. When Moix finally enters one of the brothels to pass his "examen de hombría" (test of manliness), he finds only a mutilating, oppressive, and sickening reality: "Así recuerdo mi noche de farra como una suerte de calvario interminable, donde desparecí completamente como persona para ejercer como semental sin ninguna carta a mi favor. Se trataba de demostrar potencia, sin pensar siquiera en disfrutarla" (*El beso* 137; So I remember my night of debauchery as a kind of neverending calvary, where I completely disappeared as a person to perform as some kind of stud with no cards in my favour. It was a matter of displaying potency, with not even a thought of enjoying it). The initiation ceremony is miserable and disappointing. The asphyxiating spaces are connected to his resistance to a forced heterosexual expectation that he neither desires nor feels and that is undoubtedly oppressive.[17] After the ill-fated experience, Moix comes back to his habitual haven, the cinema, a fundamental refuge, a space where the writer can feel safe from the real world. The cinema is dominant in Moix's literary persona. As Juan Ramón Iborra has explained, cinema for Terenci Moix both started and propelled his career: Moix "Inicia su meteórica carrera literaria como crítico de cine en *Film Ideal* (1964), colaborando luego con *Presencia* (Gerona), *Destino, Nuevo Fotogramas, Serra D'Or, Tele- Estel, Tele-eXprés* y *Triumfo*" (32; He began his meteoric literary career as a film critic for *Film Ideal* (1964), later collaborating with *Presencia* (Gerona) … He also published popular books such as *Introducció a la història del cinema, 1895–1967* (Bruguera, 1967; *Introduction to the History of Film*) and the series *Mis inmortales del cine* (My Immortals of the Cinema). In addition to continuous references to film directors and movies, his narrative style often resembles melodramatic movies, and cinema can also be considered essential to Moix's subversion of cultural values related to fixed ideas of masculinity and sexuality. Robert Richmond Ellis says that it is through the "overtly heterosexist cinema of Hollywood, imposed on Spain by the cultural colonialism of the United States, that [Moix] managed to resist indigenous heterosexism" (92–3). Ellis maintains that, because in cinema masculinity is represented and interpreted, it stops being an essence to be converted into an appearance.

As Alberto Mira explains, in relation to the father, Moix "presenta una visión matrocéntrica de la vida doméstica, con el padre masculino pero débil que se desprende de las populares simplificaciones del trabajo de Freud. Aunque el padre está sexualizado y es sin duda viril, su virilidad queda cuestionada cuando se le inserta en las imágenes de la pantalla y se le asimila a actores (Clark Gable) que bien podrían ser objetos de deseo homerótico" ("El niño" 192; presents a matricentric vision of domestic life with a masculine but weak father that follows from popular simplifications of Freud's work. Although the father is sexualized and is undoubtedly virile, his virility is in question when he is placed alongside the images on the screen and compared to actors (Clark Gable) who could well be objects of homoerotic desire). In this case, the father as a Hollywood "pretty boy" can be seen as very feminized in his manners and gestures; this role is used by Moix as a counterfigure to destabilize the father's masculinity though the gay perspective of the son. Thus, the big screen projects a parallel reality that is crucial to him in order to subvert the reality of his daily life but also as a space offers the subject a reprieve from his alienating surroundings.

That said, Moix's representation of his father also contains a mockery of the *macho ibérico*. As Aintzane Rincón explains, during the sixties and seventies, the figure of the *macho ibérico* was an expression of patriotic and traditional virility, which contrasted with other forms of masculinity coming from outside Spain (256). The *macho ibérico* would embody a "masculinidad activa, fuerte y decidida en su conquista de aquellos atractivos cuerpos foráneos" (256; active, strong, determined masculinity in its conquest of those attractive foreign bodies) and was particularly visible in Spanish films of the sixties and seventies, especially those set during the tourism boom, with these men demonstrating "su hombría a través de su capacidad para conquistar a suecas, alemanas y francesas haciendo uso de su galantaría y sus dotes de atracción" (250; their manliness through their ability to conquer Swedish, German, and French women by making full use of their gallantry and their magnetism). In this context, men would be suspected of homosexuality if they remained indifferent to the feminine presence (258). In this way, Aintzane Rincón also understands "el macho ibérico era la antítesis del hombre melenudo y se caracterizó, entre otras cosas, por su instinto sexual, por su potencial viril heterosexual. El Don Juan turístico, galante y piropeador, era el más fiel representante de aquella identidad viril patriótica. Alejado de la sospecha de afeminamiento que sufrió la figura del Don Juan en el primer tercio del siglo XX, el hombre seductor y consquistador resuló la máxima expresión de la masculinidad viril desarrollista" (262; the Iberian macho was the antithesis of the long-haired young man, and was characterized by, among other things, his sexual instinct, his virile heterosexual strength. The Don Juan of the tourists, gallant and flirtatious, was the most faithful representative of that virile patriotic identity. Far removed from the suspicion of feminization that the figure of Don Juan was subjected to in the first third of the twentieth century, the seductive and male conqueror proved to be the ultimate expression of a virile masculinity during the period of the Spanish Developmentalism). Moix's father does indeed display certain elements of the Hollywood pretty boy but in fact represents more of an amalgamation, where the Spanishness is evident in the aspects of the cultural *donjuán* and its more modern version, the *macho ibérico*. By sexualizing his father, Moix claims the right to subvert gender expectations,[18] and this subversion goes hand in hand with an aesthetic statement. In fact, there is a parallel between the rejection of the abject, grotesque father in Moix's texts and the rejection of the previously hegemonic social realism found in novels of the fifties focused on Spain's postwar misery and issues of marginalization, though some of Moix's novels such as *El dia* did have numerous elements of social realism. The gay viewpoint of the son when looking at the father and describing him turns the homophobic father into a grotesque person, an *esperpento*, a ridiculous *donjuán*, a feminized Hollywood pretty boy, and mocked *macho ibérico*. This is a recurring literary theme for Moix, as he embraced in his autobiographies a much more eclectic aesthetic linked more to postmodernity than to social realism, where, as Josep-Anton Fernàndez explains, there is an effort to blur the lines between intellectual and popular culture, as well as an impulse towards hybrid forms, fragmentation, the decentring of the subject, self-reflexivity, and the ironic self-consciousness of representation (*El malestar* 91).

Masculinites, Self-Creation, and the Disorder of Culture

In Moix's *Memorias*, the father's *esperpentic* body is contrasted with the body of Moix's godfather, who is neither dirty nor polluted by women and who provides a less alienating model for the autobiographer to follow. Cornelio, Terenci Moix's godfather (who was also his cousin), is a handsome, young, gay man. The Spanish term for godfather, padrino (from Latin *pater*), contains in its etymology the idea of being a paternal substitute. The padrino is a protector, the one in charge of the upbringing (religious, educational, and moral) of a minor when the parents are not there. Yet the padrino is not the father, and he offers a different model of manhood. The autobiographer first describes Cornelio as "el finolis" (100; pretentious) and explains that Cornelio was a transgressive model who had a great influence on him:

> Mi infancia tuvo la rareza de estar asesorada por un transgresor de primera. Se trata de mi padrino oficial – en realidad mi primo – entonces un apuesto joven que, entre todas las cosas del mundo, había salido homosexual. Pero esta condición pertenecía al tipo de extravagancias que una honesta familia catalana nunca quería aceptar. Más aún: ni siquiera se hablaba de ellas. Todo indicaba que Cornelio estaba condenado a ser un maldito entre los suyos, y mi propio padre confirmaba aquella posibilidad cuando exclamaba: «Antes que tener un hijo maricón, preferiría verlo muerto.» (139–40)

> My childhood included the anomaly of being informed by a first-class transgressor. This was my official godfather – actually my cousin – then a good-looking young man who, of all things, had turned out to be homosexual. But this condition belonged to the kind of eccentricities that an honest Catalan family would never want to accept. Further, they would never even talk about these things. Everything indicated that Cornelio was condemned to be an outcast among his people, and my own father confirmed that possibility when he would exclaim: "Rather than have a son who was a fag, I'd prefer to see him dead."

Cornelio serves as a recurring counter-image to the father's heteronormative, sexist, and homophobic manliness. Although surrounded by silence – Cornelio is certainly ostracized by society – Cornelio has a relationship with another man, Alberto. While Moix describes Cornelio and Alberto as afectados (a derogatory term for gay), they are also surrounded by an aura of perfection, particularly because they belong to the upper-middle class. Cornelio's partner was a rich doctor who came from one of the wealthiest families in Barcelona. In contrast to the father's vulgarity, Cornelio and Alberto are associated with good education and taste and with the achievements of the elite. Cornelio is described as someone who used to go to the cabarets in the neighbourhood el Parallel, to high-class theatres, and to the Liceo, living a life of glamour. He was also a film lover (144), frequented the best cinemas in Barcelona, and followed specialized magazines that talked about Hollywood, such as *Primer Plano* and *Fotogramas*. In addition, he lived in an elegant neighbourhood, near la Diagonal, as opposed to Moix's father, who lived in el Raval (145). As Brice Chamouleau states in *Tiran al maricón* (Get Rid of the Faggot), class status was an essential issue when condemning homosexuality during the dictatorship and afterwards, and Moix accepts this prejudice by presenting the upper-middle-class gay as the model to follow.

Moix highlights how the bodies of Cornelio and Alberto were *really* masculine, in contrast to the father's *esperpento*-like grotesque body. He affirms that Alberto "por ser un atleta consumado parecía un macho de verdad" (140; being a consummate athlete, he seemed like an authentic macho). Cleanliness, strength, athleticism, and health are some of the adjectives used to create their hypermasculine image. Cornelio's body is also described while exercising and swimming in the sea, an image that Moix associates with the normative masculine model: "con su taparrabos negro debidamente acortado a nivel de las nalgas, y las posturas atléticas que le gustaba afectar en lo alto de las rocas, daba el pego promocionando el machismo de estampita" (242; with his black Speedo duly just covering his buttocks, and the athletic postures that he liked to assume high up on the rocks, he created the illusion of advertising the very image of machismo). In contrast, the father is described as "siempre omnipresente con sus ridículos calzoncillos de posguerra tan opuestos a los ceñidos slips de competición que solían llevar Alberto y Cornelio" (*El beso* 134; always omnipresent with his ridiculous postwar boxers so completely the opposite of the tight-fitting competitive suits that Alberto and Cornelio would wear). Cornelio and Alberto stand out in their perfection: "aparecían ostentando sonrisas irreprochables, sonrisas que no mostraban dientes llenos de musgo, como los de papá, antes bien diminutas perlas que les convertían en réplica viviente de los primeros anuncios de dentífricos" (318; they would show up flaunting irreproachable smiles, smiles that didn't show teeth full of moss, like those of my father, but rather diminutive pearls, which converted them into living replicas of the earliest toothpaste ads). On the contrary, the father, in his dirtiness, is morally unacceptable. The irony is obvious: The truly masculine, perfect, clean, strong, healthy, and athletic body is the one that the Francoist society marginalizes and condemns, that of the gay man.

Moix's comments about hygiene, strength, and virility can be read as a transgression of the Fascist ideal of the male body. Franco not only embraced Fascist aesthetics but also promoted a masculine ideal that was half-monk half-soldier (Morcillo 44), a concept of ideal masculinity appropriated from José Antonio Primo de Rivera (Pavlovic 24). Moix emphasizes how the images of athletic men were in fact more pleasing than those offered by Fascist propaganda in his childhood magazines: "No me enardecía en absoluto el vigoroso optimismo de los héroes de *Chicos* y *Flechas y Pelayos* ni, en resumen, todo cuanto oliese a camaradería, espíritu castrense y parecidos reclamos del machismo" (155; I was not at all excited by the vigorous optimism of the heroes of *Chicos* y *Flechas y Pelayos*, nor, in short, by anything that smelled of camaraderie, military spirit, and similar claims of machismo). Moix is inclined towards athletic men, body types that he associates with another culture. The bodies that attract him are those in imported American magazines and foreign movies. This early influence on Moix highlighted the heroic, classical body (32), in contrast to the more austere Francoist model of men.[19] Moix explains how the masculine body was presented with a certain freedom, while the feminine body remained completely covered until the seventies, a censorship that, according to Moix, was "una pesadilla dirigida por deficientes mentales" (54; a nightmare directed by mental deficients). Yet he discovered while writing that the magazines and publications for children and young men from the postwar era remained in his imagination and concluded "entendí hasta qué punto las imágenes que conmovieron nuestra infancia se convierten en perversas alcahuetas de nuestros deseos futuros" (156; I understood to what degree the images that moved us in our childhood turned into perverse procurers of our future desires). While magazines featured certain ideals of masculinity such as adventure and bravery, other publications represented religious figures and martyrs that connected with Moix's Catholic upbringing under Franco. Particularly influential here were Hollywood biblical epics and Italian "Sword and Sandal" films set at the time of the early Christian martyrs. According to Moix, this imagery began directing his early desires towards sadomasochism.

Cleanliness is important not only in relation to the physical but also to the moral comparison between the father and Cornelio. As Mary Douglas points out in *Purity and Danger,* "pollution has indeed much to do with morals" (130). The father's biggest source of pride – owning a house-painting business – is diminished: "empecé a despreciar a mi padre porque llevaba las manos sucias, detalle obligado por las características de su oficio" (139; I began to despise my father because his hands were always dirty, a necessary detail given the nature of his profession). Through the description of the father's dirtiness, the father's body is connected to other, larger masculine communities that Moix perceives as sexist: "y una vez más se impuso el recuerdo de papá en los lejanos días de la posguerra: una figura ridícula, en calzoncillos y camiseta y con la posibilidad de que saltasen los enrojecidos testículos que tanto asco me habían inspirado. Esta es la imagen que aparecía siempre que pensaba en una cofradía masculina" (410; and once again the memory of my father imposed itself from those long ago days of the postwar: a ridiculous figure, in his underwear and undershirt and with the possibility that his reddened testicles that had caused me so much disgust would bounce out. That is the image that appeared whenever I thought of the masculine brotherhood). In *El beso*, Moix describes the repugnance and anguish that certain men, those who liked to verbalize and show off their virility by expressing sexist attitudes towards women, would cause him. For instance, the autobiographical subject narrates how coworkers would import French magazines "con páginas llenas de tías desnudas, de buenorras, como decían mis compañeros. Yo no ignoraba que muchos se las llevaban al váter para masturbarse y, cuando les veía regresar, disimulando la revista bajo el jersey, se me antojaba que todo nuestro erotismo vivía de apaños cada vez más tristes" (39; with pages full of naked ladies, hotties, as my coworkers would say. I wasn't unaware that many of them would take them to the toilet so they could masturbate and, then when I saw them come back, hide the magazine under their sweater, and I would think that all our eroticism survived on ever sadder quick fixes). His father, some of Moix's own male friends, his father's friends from the bar, the men from the factory, and the men in the military are all a community that is linked to a series of social values related to sexism and an exaggerated virility.

In contrast, Cornelio and Alberto are an attractive alternative to these men and to the heterosexual couple, supplanting Moix's parents, whose relationship is marked by fights and unfaithfulness. Moix perceived Cornelio and Alberto's relationship as ideal, filled with friends, fashion, and prestige and considers this relationship a perfect example of the true-love stories of Hollywood cinema, even though Hollywood cinema presented love as solely heterosexual. Cornelio and Alberto lived a utopian life, eating in the best restaurants and traveling when it was very rare to do so in Spain. Being a defect-free couple in Moix's view, they became his model to imitate (318). In addition, they would dress as if they had just stepped out of a fashion magazine, which also contrasted with Moix's father's dirty clothes:

> Aquellos amantes, peripuestos y dinámicos, se erigían sin dificultad en la cara más ostentosa de una felicidad reservada a quienes eran apuestos, viriles, selectos y, sobre todo, distintos. Y el niño soñador se complacería buscando en la diversidad motivos de exaltación y, en la apostura masculina, un contraste estrepitoso con la dejadez física en que empezaba a incurrir papaíto, a quien seguía recordando con las manos sucias de pinturas y unos calzoncillos anchos, como el payaso más tonto de un circo especializado en exhibir deformidades. (319)

> Those lovers, elegantly dressed and dynamic, set themselves up without difficulty as the most ostentatious face of a happiness reserved for those

who were handsome, virile, elite, and, above all, distinct. And the dreaming boy would be happy seeking in this diversity grounds for excitement, and, in the graceful masculinity, a resounding contrast with the physical slovenliness that his daddy had begun to fall into, whom he always thought of with his hands dirty with paint and his baggy underwear, like the dumbest clown in a circus that specializes in displaying deformities.

While the father's body is presented in its deformity, the godfather is a perfect reflection of virility. Moix's attraction to Cornelio also establishes a strong relationship with a cultural context in which Hollywood aesthetics and a radically increased influx of American culture changed not only the tastes of the general public but also the strategies of Spanish writers.

In fact, "Cornelio" is a pseudonym Moix invents to protect the godfather's real identity; a name that Moix chooses because his godfather looks like the handsome Hungarian-American actor and director Cornel Wilde (140). The issue of naming cannot be overlooked: Cornelio is one of the few characters who appears with a false name in Moix's autobiographies – a name that points towards American cinema. In this way, Moix breaks with Phillip Lejeune's pact and places Cornelio outside of autobiographical law, granting him a freedom not given to others. While Lejeune maintains that proper names imply certain responsibilities for the autobiographer, "responsibility for all enunciation is assumed by a person who is in the habit of placing his name on the cover of the book" (11), Moix's responsibilities allow for exceptions. In some ways, the name of Cornelio relates to the name of the autobiographer, as Moix also changed his first name from Ramón to Terenci and thus allowed himself the possibility of living a literary life in its full sense. Here reality and literature are deliberately juxtaposed, and the change of names merges the godfather's and the writer's destinies: It gives both of them the possibility of challenging the borders of the autobiographical, self-fictional, and fictional, allowing Moix to find a porosity and flexibility in the autobiographical project. For instance, Juan Bonilla points to the similarities between Cornelio in Moix's *Memorias* and Arturu in *El día* (43), and other parallels could be drawn between the death of the younger brother in both texts or the figures of the mother and father figures in *Memorias* and the characters of Amèlia and Xim in *El dia*. This reinforces what Xavier Pla considers when looking at works by Josep Pla: That autobiographical literature cannot be read as only having a referential dimension but needs to be understood in its "existencia autónoma com a forma artística" (446; autonomous existence as an artistic form). The self is implicit or explicit always in the text: "Tota escriptura és una escriptura del 'jo', construïda sobre el 'jo' i a partir del 'jo'. L'única diferència es troba aleshores en el fet que alguns textos de ficció es presenten com a explícitament autobiogràfics ... Altres textos de ficció són implícitament autobiogràfics en el sentit que tot escriptor, quan fa la literatura, parla de si mateix" (454; All writing is a writing of the "I", built on the "I", and starting from the "I". The only difference then lies in the fact that some fictional texts are presented as explicitly autobiographical ... Other fictional texts are implicitly autobiographical in the sense that every writer, when he makes literature, speaks of himself). The point then is not to draw parallels between reality and autobiography – or between autobiography and reality – but to understand that the autobiographical project is yet another artistic project, as novels, poetry, and theatre are; a form of representation that emerges from the author's artistic sensibility, experience, thoughts, and ideas, and from the need to create.

Continuing then with this consciousness of the authorial figure, the use of the surname Moix by Terenci Moix denotes a certain deference to the father's lineage and to a patronymic system of naming, while changing Ramón to Terenci highlights the power of creating a different self for the writer than the one assigned and thus signals the power of refathering or self-fathering through the literary project. In *El cine,* Moix incorporates a traditional trope of autobiographical writing, that is, explaining the surname's genealogy. According to the father, the family's masculine ancestry and painting business date back to the Middle Ages, which proves the family's distinction (*El cine* 70). The familial business is bound to the surname Moix and to the family coat of arms. The autobiographer, however, ridicules the father's ideas, first by describing the cat that appears on the shield as "francamente feo, y que al atacar se pone jorobado" (72; really ugly, and when it attacks, it becomes hunchbacked) and later by ridiculing the surname's meaning. *Moix* in Catalan means cat, a *moixaina* means a caress, and as an adjective *moix* is used for a certain feeling of sorrow and for fruit that is ripe or rotten. Moix concludes: "Bastaría a mis intereses literarios el decir que, por ser moix, fui niño tristón como el crepúsculo, mimoso como una puta, astuto como el gavilán, solitario como el agua estancada y blandorro como la fruta a punto de sucumbir" (72; It would be sufficient for my literary interests to say that, being a *Moix*, I was a child inclined to sadness like the twilight, clingy like a whore, sharp like a hawk, solitary like stagnant water, and insipid like overly ripe fruit). The autobiographer when explaining his name says "me pusieron Ramón por los muchos que había habido en la familia. Jesús, por mi padre. César, por Julio. Montserrat, porque alguna insensata le saldría del coño" (58; they named me Ramón after the many other Ramóns who had been in the family. Jesus, after my father. César, after Julius. Montserrat, because some fool woman wanted to). Later on, he says that the name Ramón Moix had a long tradition in the family and was associated with the painting business, which was "fundada por el primer Moix de que se tiene recuerdo en una larga lista de Ramones" (71; founded by the first Moix in memory in a long list of Ramones) and which he rejected as a possible place of work. The change of name reflects his desire to break with the father's business in favour of becoming a writer.

Terenci Moix used the father's surname, merging disaffiliation, his rejection of the father's heritage, with affiliation, that is, a certain recognition of and deference towards the paternal and the familial. The surname also strengthened his ties with his sister, Ana María Moix, adding the Moix siblings, like the three brothers Goytisolo, or the Panero, to those families marked by the literary. This also happens, although in different combinations, between Josep and Clara Janés – as father and daughter – and Esther Tusquets and Milena Busquets – as mother and daughter – and impregnates these authors' literary projects. In the case of Terenci and Ana María Moix, the acknowledgments, quotes, and translations make it evident that the two Moix siblings did not want to escape from their familial relationship but that they in fact saw it as productive for their literary projects. These family relations, as in the case of the Goytisolos, also allow for another layer in analyzing how different pacts with and inspirations from reality can work in literary projects. In many ways, the familiar structure and the figure of the father in Ana María Moix's book *Julia* (1970) can be interpreted vis-à-vis Terenci Moix's reflections on the familial and the father in *El dia* or in *Memorias*. In all three texts, we find the traumatic death of a young brother, and in the case of *Julia* the protagonist has an ambivalent relationship of fascination and love for the mother, also a strong female figure, which later turns into hate and distance. The father figure in *Julia* is seen as a weak, hated, and despised character, unable to liberate himself from the mother despite having fallen in love with Eva, Julia's mentor and teacher, with whom Julia is also in love.

In many ways, Terenci Moix conceives of culture as something that resembles a familial inheritance: Something that one receives without saying much but towards which one needs to take a position. He correlates the literary family with blood relatives and a concept of culture that mirrors that of his father's, in which there are gaps and voids. For Moix, culture is a delirious and iconoclastic amalgamation of the high and the low, a hybrid blend comprised of cinema, magazines, popular music, canonic literature, and art. He mixes popular and intellectual references, making it evident that, to his mind, high culture, which is institutionalized and socially praised, needs, like the father figure, to be subverted. Moix's explanation of his discovery of literature – and his explanation of his literary affiliation – plays with the subversive incoherence at work in his texts. He affirms that the first literature in his life was film advertisements (*El cine* 95). He also loved his mother's *Figurines* – a fashion magazine – and the popular culture attained through the pleasant and intimate feminine universe of Moix's mother and aunts (*El cine* 138–9). In addition, the pleasure of reading emerged for him when he discovered that many of the scripts of his favourite movies were based on works by authors such as Kipling, Dumas, and Shakespeare (*El beso* 83). Being autodidactic in his case strengthened the process of demystification of high culture (see Forrest 931).

Several scholars, including Rosi Song, Paul Julian Smith, Carlos Ramos, Steven Forrest, Alberto Mira, Robert Richmond Ellis, and Josep-Anton Fernàndez, have considered how the destabilization of the boundaries between forms of culture situates Moix as one of the principal representatives of postmodernism and camp aesthetics in Spain. Camp aesthetics became popular in the 1960s in the United States, but in Spain it was linked with the transition to democracy in the late 1970s. In her article "Notes on 'Camp'," Susan Sontag defines it as a mode of sensibility, the essence of which is the love of the unnatural. Sontag names among its main characteristics artifice and exaggeration (275), marginality (276), innocence, and extravagance (283). In his "Introduction: Queering the Camp," Fabio Cleto defines the term in the following way: "Tentatively approached as *sensibility*, *taste*, or *style*, reconceptualized as *aesthetic* or *cultural economy*, and later asserted/reclaimed as *(queer) discourse*, camp hasn't lost its relentless power to frustrate all efforts to pinpoint it down to stability" (2). Cleto highlights what he calls "camp's affiliation to homosexual culture" (4), that is, a close relationship between the two, precisely using father–son imagery when he defines the term *affiliated* as "coming from the late Latin *affiliatus*, 'adoptive son'" (5). For her part, Caryl Flinn relates camp to the parodic and the grotesque (452).[20] Furthermore, as Josep-Anton Fernàndez explains, Moix "was in fact one of the first people to introduce pop into Spain, and perhaps the first author in Spain to cite Susan Sontag's seminal essay 'Notes on camp' (1964)" (*Another Country* 106). That Moix's writings converge with many of the characteristics ascribed to camp is evident. Camp aesthetics and philosophy are in many ways for Moix a means to subvert the hierarchical and what is inherited, mixing the foreign, the Hispanic, and the Catalan, all in one.

Literary affiliations are connected to this subversion: Moix's literary affiliations are defined by a sense of familiarity and friendship, not necessarily implying that literary affiliations substitute filiative and blood relations but that those who inspire him are like family. Moix's literary genealogy is varied and eclectic: It includes the Catalan poet Salvador Espriu, Catalan writer Josep Pla, Italian novelist Elsa Morante, anti-fascist novelist Alberto Moravia, and film director Pier Paolo Pasolini. These are not merely names invested with power or those who have an aura of the untouchable but people Moix knew and towards whom he professes warm admiration. They are "gente muy amada" (*El cine* 211; much-loved people). From his as well as previous generations and from Barcelona, he names writers Gil de Biedma, Pere Gimferrer, Maria Aurèlia Campmany, and Josep Maria Benet; the musician Joan Manuel Serrat; and the actor Pepe Martín. There is a clear sentimental character to these connections, and, when naming influences, Moix mixes Spanish and Catalan writers with musicians and TV artists.

Scholars have noticed Moix's attraction to American, French, and international film and literary classics. Steven Forrest considers how Spanish literary history "ha relegado a un lugar secundario y 'sospechoso' toda literatura exótica y cosmopolita que sobrepase las estrechas fronteras lingüísticas e ideológicas de la Península" (934; has relegated to a secondary and "suspicious" place all exotic and cosmopolitan literature that oversteps the narrow linguistic and ideological boundaries of the Peninsula) and therefore concludes that Moix positions himself in opposition to Hispanic literary tradition by embracing international cultural productions. Paul Julian Smith also comments on how Hollywood "is much preferred by Moix to interior domestic product" and how this tendency "represents a willful alienation from the homeland" (*Laws* 44). Rosi Song and Castellet read the importance of cinema in Moix's books as proof of his efforts to democratize culture (Song, Castellet 26). Parallel to these ideas, Josep-Anton Fernàndez and Alberto Mira read Moix's relationship to culture as proof of his dissatisfaction with an idea of "normality," as he denounces the tensions that existed between homosexuality and institutional culture in Catalonia during the transition and later (Fernàndez 102, Mira 340). Certainly, there is a certain favouritism towards foreign influences in Moix's writings that nonetheless coexists with specific elements of Catalan and Spanish literary traditions in his autobiography: That is, alongside an obsessive critique of the Catalan literary landscape, there is a continuous play with traditional elements of Spanish cultural figures such as the *donjuán*, the *macho ibérico*, and the *esperpento*. Yet when naming friends who are also literary influences, Moix highlights another aspect of literary affinities: To him it was often essential to meet those who would inspire him, and he was thus inspired by those who surrounded him. Both familial and friendship networks shape Moix's literary affiliation, and generational and spatial proximity are fundamental to both. Moix did not set out to be an intellectual whose primary aim was to criticize the Franco regime – as Juan Goytisolo did – or whose poetic project can be read only by an exclusive, culturally prepared group, as with the work of Carlos Barral and Clara Janés. Rather, he was a writer for the masses whose belonging to the *gauche divine* was inspired by friendship and by family ties.

Moix's autobiographies offer a partial answer to how Harold Bloom's concept of the anxiety of influence plays out in the Catalan literary tradition, in the works of a gay author, and from the end of Franco's dictatorship until Moix died of a lung-related cancer in 2003. Moix's anxiety of influence in a tradition that lacks legitimate literary fathers with whom younger writers can resolve a literary Oedipal complex is resolved by accepting diverse forms of influence, some domestic and some foreign. These influences include foreign traditions and popular cultural productions, allowing for a mixed and disordered legacy. Questioning the father figure, and both using and rejecting his legacy, is fundamental to the creation of an authorial voice that is both transgressive and legitimate in order to inherit or create a new canon, and in this regard the father is a central incursion when rethinking this Oedipal figuration of the bilingual writer.

Conclusion

Alberto Mira explains that Moix "Pertenece a una época en que la masculinidad tenía unos rasgos bien definidos" ("El niño" 185; Belongs to a time when masculinity had several well-defined characteristics). Yet, in Moix's writings, masculinities are diverse, grotesque, transgressed, admired, sexualized, and crucial for the autobiographer's self-creation. The father is pivotal when offering this kaleidoscope of masculinities: Moix's description of his father offers an exaggeration of an incongruent, paradoxical masculinity and reveals how, in fact, normative models are two-sided, alienating and also alienable. In fact, when Moix talks about his obsession with masks, he does not make reference to the cinema but rather to his father as a perfect example of one of those actors who play between reality and appearance: "Papá era un joven taciturno cuando esperaba la cena en el comedor de casa y se convertía en un alegre aventurero no bien se eregía en centro de todas las conversaciones en la mancebía de Madame Rosario" (*El cine* 181; My dad was a sullen young man when waiting in the dining room at home for his dinner, and he turned into a happy adventurer as soon as he resurfaced in the midst of all the conversations in Madame Rosario's brothel). In this way – and in his parodies of the paternal – Moix denounces gender norms as artificial. Something similar happens to the Catalan and Spanish languages: Bilingualism does not really offer a door to the outside world but is rather a system that allows Moix to change and play.

In Moix's *Memorias*, instances of genre resistance (for example, the renaming of the godfather) converge with traditional aspects of the autobiographical genre. The father is primary in this game. For Sidonie Smith, traditional autobiographies endorse not only a masculinist image of the self but also a masculine tradition, a masculine genealogy, and paternal lines, as well as reinforcing the myth of origins and asserting the primacy of patrilineal descent and androcentric discourse (see *A Poetics* 40). Moix, on the other hand, exposes the incongruity of the paternal, of tradition, of genealogy, of origins, and of linguistic divisions through the father figure. Moix's works also demonstrate how the need for transgression of authoritative models mirrors the opening up of new models of sexuality, gender identity, and performance for the democratic and multilingual Spain of the 1990s. In addition, questioning the father goes hand in hand with questioning the border between Spanish and Catalan literature and culture and is related to Moix's being an extraordinary and eccentric writer and yet also canonical, popular, and publicly recognized. Through irony, humour, and friendship, his autobiographical self diminishes the authoritative, hierarchical character of culture, as he himself dismisses the authoritative, hierarchical place of the father. Terenci Moix defended a space for authors who live in Catalonia and who shift between writing in Catalan and in Spanish. In Moix's autobiographies, the father figure is at the core of the affective fluctuation that living in a charged and changing bilingual linguistic reality produces. On the one hand, the father is a transmitter of culture, literature, and a subordinated language – the Catalan language, loved because of its resistance in a state of prohibition during the dictatorship. But the father (and his language and culture) also has another facet: A homophobic aspect that allows the writer to also question the father's cultural values, when necessary.

5 Clara Janés: Fatherhood and the Feminine

Born in Barcelona in 1940, in the immediate aftermath of the Spanish Civil War, Clara Janés is a prolific writer, poet, and translator. She has published more than 30 books and has received prizes such as the Premio Ciudad de Barcelona de Poesía (1983) and the Premio Nacional de Traducción (1997). In 2015, she became the tenth woman to occupy a seat in the Real Academia Española. Her familial context could be considered fundamental to her becoming a writer. Her father, Josep Janés, was an influential Catalan writer and publisher who started his businesses before the war and continued publishing in Spain throughout Franco's dictatorship. Josep Janés was briefly exiled in France in 1939 and sentenced to death by the dictatorship when he came back.[1] Through the father's publishing house, the family was close to Barcelona's intellectual elite. Clara Janés's surroundings were clearly privileged: Her family's broad cultural reach, symbolized by her father's library; the festive and educated atmosphere shared with personalities such as the Catalan composer and pianist Frederic Mompou, the writer Eugeni d'Ors, and the painter Emili Grau Sala; and what seemed to be a worry-free universe situated Janés in a milieu quite different from the intellectually censoring, dry, and grey Spain of the dictatorship experienced by most. The depictions of that sheltered household in *Jardín y laberinto* (Garden and Labyrinth; 1990) and *La voz de Ofelia* (Ophelia's Voice; 2005), Janés's two autobiographical texts, reveal how she grew up on a virtual island of intellectual freedom inside the Francoist state of oppression.

Despite this intellectual freedom, Janés's childhood and youthful memories are not free from difficulties: In both *Jardín* and in *La voz*, the self discloses her struggles to overcome her father's death when she was eighteen years old and to believe in herself as a writer. These two books contrast with the autobiographies written by the male authors analysed in this book: *Jardín* and *La voz* are short texts (148 and 108 pages respectively). They were published by two mid-sized and well-reputed publishing houses in Madrid, the Editorial Debate (today part of Penguin Random House Grupo Editorial) and Ediciones Siruela, reflecting Clara Janés's consciousness of her literary persona: She ensures the high level of her publications but is at the same time an author who writes for a minority of cult readers in Spain. Neither of the two books is chronological; on the contrary, each explores memory as a circular experience through fragmentation, collage, and intertextuality. Both texts are centred around the ideas of loss and recovery, the father's sudden death, and the writer's potential for simultaneously constructing bonds of filiation – those based on blood ties – and bonds of affiliation developed through intellectual affinities. Yet the tones of these two memoirs are significantly different: *Jardín* focuses on the unexpected death of her father – who died in a car accident in 1959 – and aims to recover the voices of Janés's family members and friends around the figure of Josep Janés. With Catalan fragments intercalated into the Spanish text, *Jardín* evokes Janés's infancy in the Barcelona neighbourhood of Pedralbes, an elite area of the city. Published fifteen years after *Jardín, La voz* returns to the father figure but this time through Janés's relationship with the Czech poet Vladimir Holan, a man who inspires her to write after a period of literary sterility.

One of the most striking elements of both of Janés's autobiographies is how she finds a way to establish a feminine voice in what is seemingly a masculine and patriarchal domain, the world of writing and literature. This is a tense and contradictory yet necessary negotiation that takes place in a dramatic way. The father figure occupies an importance place in this process as both a real and a symbolic figure: Mourning her father's death is essential for Janés to situate herself in a male-centred literary production. John Wilcox has highlighted that there is a clear "patriarchal hierarchic tension" in Janés's early texts (260). This patriarchal burden – and the centrality of the looming paternal figure so present in her autobiographical writings – incarcerate the self in a masculine literary environment but also give the feminine subject the means and the desire to construct an independent literary persona. At the same time, Janés's self occupies a multilingual consciousness that is crucial in her negotiating with the family's Catalan cultural legacy and with her international and intercultural literary influences. Through an exploration of the death of the father and of how the recovery of this figure is presented in relation to language and by considering Janés's encounter with the poet Vladimír Holan vis-à-vis her positioning of herself as a woman writer and translator, in this chapter I argue that in

Janés's self-writing, her father, and, later, Holan, are placed in the foreground in her construction of a heterosexual subjectivity as an author. Despite the seemingly apolitical nature of Janés's texts, her writings offer a telling example not only of how a woman writer navigates the autobiographical genre in Spain in the 1990s and 2000s but also of the place of Catalan in the work of an author born and raised in the Barcelona of Franco's dictatorship.

The Death of the Father

Janés begins *Jardín* by highlighting how she views literary creation as a state that fuses activity and passivity, death and life, observation and production: The autobiographical subject looks at a hyacinth to ask herself about the possibility of the father's return "¿qué sentido tiene la idea que me asalta a veces de su posible regreso? ¿Quién puede volver desde la muerte?" (*Jardín* 9; what is the meaning of the idea that sometimes assails me of his possible return? Who can come back from death?).[2] The hyacinth flower is named after the character Hyacinth, a prince and lover of Apollo in Greek mythology. When Hyacinth died while throwing the discus with Apollo, to mourn his lover Apollo created this flower, which symbolizes birth and resurrection. The hyacinth flower that opens *Jardín* is linked to the desire for the resurrection of her father and to the need to mourn a loved one through creativity. It is not a coincidence that the father and the process of mourning are evoked at the very beginning of the text, as these are the two elements around which the text is constructed.

Beyond granting the daughter access to Catalonia's artistic community, the father is an ambivalent figure in Janés's texts: He is a distant and absent man from whom Janés and her two sisters remain isolated. Janés recalls this divide both in *Jardín* and in *La voz*: "los datos que teníamos [de él] eran mínimos" (*Jardín* 43; the information we had about him was minimal); "el padre, ausente también de nuestro espacio por su propio cometido" (*La voz* 19–20; the father who was also absent from our space because of his own commitments). Yet her father provides security and protection in what for Clara Janés is a peaceful, solid, and confined upbringing: He is an essential figure in maintaining the equilibrium and stability of childhood. Clara Janés also speaks of Josep Janés as a person who represents the world of literature: He inspired her to write by giving her maquetas (blank books) from the publishing house and thus opened the doors of literature to her. In *Jardín*, she explains that she wrote her first poems when she was thirteen and fourteen years old. She showed them to her father, who gave her a book from Pedro

Salinas so that she would keep writing. However, the autobiographical self fears this intellectual world: "Su padre es editor. A ella le dan miedo los libros y no lee, pero, dado que vive encerrada en un jardín y no se dispersa, comunica al papel algunas sensaciones e intuiciones" (*Jardín* 11; Her father is an editor. She is afraid of books and doesn't read, but, since she lives (mostly) isolated in a garden, she communicates some thoughts and feelings to paper). The blank books that served as an incentive to write, her father's impressive roughly 25,000-book library at home[3], the literary models – many of them men – pointed out by her father or later discovered, all create an environment in which literature and art are perceived as a paternal, masculine, and alienating domain in the eyes of the daughter.

Josep Janés's death is conceived of as a turning point in Clara Janés's life, and her writing becomes an immediate reaction to reconnect with the lost father: "no recuerdo qué escribí durante los meses que sucedieron a su muerte, pero sí que era prosa" (*Jardín* 40; I don't remember what I wrote in the months following his death, but I do remember it was prose). Janés speaks of an "herencia invisible" (*Jardín* 37; an invisible legacy) that refers both to the cultural environment she was raised in and to the need to write, as her father was also a writer. In *Jardín*, the death of the father is narrated in great detail, reflecting the lucidity of the shock. The phone had rung in the Pedralbes home, and someone had informed the mother that Josep Janés had had a car accident and was hospitalized in Els Monjos, a small town in the interior of Catalonia about one hour's drive from Barcelona, between Barcelona and Tarragona.[4] Janés, her mother, and Janés's older sister went to Els Monjos, while Janés's aunts and her younger sister stayed in the house in Barcelona awaiting news and praying. Upon their arrival in Els Monjos, they found that the father had already died, as someone asked Janés, her mother, and older sister "¿van a ver a los muertos?" (*Jardín* 34; are you going to see the deceased?). The shocking words were followed by the mother's scream in Catalan "No pot ser, no pot ser!" (*Jardín* 34–5; It can't be true!).

Janés explains how she became conscious, at this moment, of the death of her father and of entering adulthood. The brutal image of the father's destroyed body, completely dismembered and inside out and narrated by the inhabitants of the town offers a merciless realism about death:

> «Mejor que no lo vea … está completamente destrozado. Una pierna suelta, la cabeza partida en dos … los sesos estaban esparcidos por el suelo. Todos los sesos fuera. ¿Hay algún médico en la familia que pueda identificarlo?». La cabeza partida, los sesos fuera, todos los sesos fuera. Y

> mamá «No pot ser, no pot ser!». Y yo, atónita ante mi mansedumbre, mi ausencia de lágrimas. (*Jardín* 35)
>
> "It's better you don't see him … he's been completely destroyed. One leg detached, his head split in two … his brains scattered all over the ground. All of them. Is there someone in the family who's a doctor? Who can identify him?" His head split in two, the brains scattered, all of his brains scattered. And mother "It can't be true!." And I, astonished by my calmness, my lack of tears.

The striking image of the father's body – his brains on the ground, his hanging leg – narrated by others but not seen, forces Janés to acknowledge his sudden death. A similar description reappears soon after, "Él estaba sentado al lado del conductor y recibió más que los otros. Quedó completamente destrozado, arrancada una pierna, la cabeza partida, los sesos esparcidos por el suelo" (*Jardín* 36; He was sitting next to the driver and he got more than anyone else. He was destroyed, one of his legs torn off, his head split in two, his brains scattered all over the ground) and is also part of *La voz*: "«Mejor que no lo vea, está completamente destrozado. Una pierna suela, la cabeza partida en dos … Los sesos estaban esparcidos por el suelo. Todos los sesos fuera»" (*La voz* 50; «Better that you not see him, he is completely smashed. One leg cut off, the head split in two … his brains strewn all over the ground. All his brains spilled out. brains were scattered on the floor. All his brains out»). These repetitions correspond to Sigmund Freud's theory of grief as a series of tests of reality, which ultimately strengthen the ego enough to overcome the loss ("Mourning" 163) but also prove the impact of the moment and how the text is constructed, as memory, as a collage.

The death of the father – and the memory of his destroyed body – is integral to the birth of the writer and to the potential to give birth to others. As Nadia Mékouar-Hertzberg has shown, the father's vertical grandeur – his physical and imagined magnanimity perceived from the point of view of a child – acquires a completely different tone after his death and through the process of writing, when the daughter is able to incorporate her father as a presence aligned with the self (33, 81). This allows Janés to establish a direct (metaphorically horizontal) dialogue with the image of the father, transforming and somehow subverting her father's real physical grandeur and symbolic importance (his verticality). In this dialogue, father and daughter meet at the same level – the level of the text – and feed each other's presence. Thus, in Janés's texts, the autobiographical act – the act of bringing oneself (in the written word) to life – is an act of double birth, in which father and daughter are born at the same time. As Nadia Mékouar-Hertzberg explains, "le père engendre la fille «écrivante» autant que la fille engendre le père en l'écrivant" (85; the father engenders the writer daughter as much as the daughter engenders her father by writing about him). Yet, this act of genesis is based on the death of the father, and there is a clear consciousness both of the textual character of mourning and of the intricate relationship between pleasure, writing and death: In *Jardín*, the subject recalls how writing "ya no era el dolor, sino la expresión del dolor" (*Jardín* 123; it was no longer pain, but the expression of pain) and how pain fuses with love – "Fue algo que vino a mí en entrega amorosa" (*Jardín* 123; It was something that came to me in a loving surrender). Thus, writing is a way to mourn her father, to recover memories of him but also to create a self inseparable from this traumatic death.[5]

In Janés's memoirs, the awareness of the self as a writing subject emerges. The father's death shapes his daughter's sense of selfhood as a writer: This death connects *Jardín* with *La voz* and with her early poetry books, particularly *Vivir* (To Live; 1983). *Vivir* offers a collection of poems – some of them dedicated to writer friends such as Victoria Atencia, Rosa Chacel, or María Zambrano – or poems inspired by the work of the Basque sculptor Eduardo Chillida. In *Vivir*, important spaces for the self such as "Pedralbes" or "Vallcarca" appear, thus highlighting the autobiographical tone of the collection. The book also contains a section subtitled "Planto" (Plaint). Introduced with the following words "Donde la hija se lamenta al padre de la ausencia del amor y a la vez se duele de su muerte" (*Vivir* 63; Where the daughter mourns the absence of her father's love at the same time as she mourns his death), "Planto" contains twelve sung poems (or twelve fragments of one long poem) that constitute a musical lamentation. One of them is a clear reference to Jorge Manrique's *Coplas por la muerte de su padre* (Couplets on the Death of His Father; 1494), titled "Río en mar es tu nombre" (*Vivir* 73; River in Sea Is Your Name). These poems all include their musical scores, and the last one is in Catalan and recalls the grave of the father: "damunt de tu la pols/ damunt de tu la cals/ damunt de tu el silence / damunt de tu el meu plany" (*Vivir* 12; above you, dust / above you, lime / above you, silence / above you, my lament). The poetic self associates the dead father and his body with the ground and envisions her own voice as covering the corpse. Thus, through the father's death and the mourning of this death, the autobiographical self goes beyond the autobiographical text: Both *Jardín* and *La voz* are explanations of how poetic projects such as "Planto" in *Vivir* or the poetry book *Kampa* (1989) were born. Self-referentiality and self-intertextuality are therefore essential to the act of writing and to the development of the poet's consciousness, while at the same time literary genres disappear to create a literary persona. In this way, Clara Janés emerges and gains consciousness as an authorial figure.

La voz, published fifteen years after *Jardín*, returns to the father's death and to Janés's mourning as a formative experience, a moment of change that forced her to overcome silence and that impelled her poetic life. Mitigated by time, the death of the father now feels less brutal but no less formative. Janés speaks of a state that exceeds the limits of grieving, a state of sterility, that is, paradoxically, the state in which writing starts. She describes it as both an end and a beginning:

> Aquel instante terrible que no sé calificar porque, siendo una muerte, fue también un nacimiento: estructuró el resto de mi vida y me estructuró a mí modificada por esa muerte; me orientó no sólo hacia la vida subterránea, sino hacia la escritura de la primera trama de recuerdos que era, fundamentalmente, la creación de un lugar de acogida, una evocación de la atmósfera en la que él, mi padre, estaba vivo. (*La voz* 48)

> That terrible moment that I don't know how to judge because, being a death, it was also a birth: it gave structure to the rest of my life and to me, modified by that death; it directed me not only toward the subterranean life, but toward writing the first section of my memories which were, above all, the creation of a place of welcoming, an evocation of the atmosphere in which he, my father, was alive.

Janés considers the death of the father as the beginning of her writing and mourning as a productive experience. Writing as a form of mourning, moreover, is seen as an experience that collects how others remember the father. Like the father's body, the family is dismembered after the father's death. In this context, the disconnect between Clara and her sisters is exacerbated: "Quedamos huérfanas de raíces, de destino, e incluso del mismo lazo que tan estrechamente nos unía" (*La voz* 19–20; We became orphaned from roots, from destiny, and even from the same bond that had once knit us so closely).

The relationship with the mother is revisited after the father's death. The mother is significant, both in *Jardín* and in *La voz*, as a figure who complements fatherhood. Presented as an antagonistic figure in some passages, Janés's mother is crucial in enforcing the Oedipal triad and in placing mother and daughter together as parallel figures in recovering Josep Janés after his death. After the father's death, Janés started writing as if she had received an invisible inheritance. This happened alongside the mother's inheritance of the father's publishing business, a change of roles symbolized by her mother's new masculine outfit, a black suit and briefcase: "Mamá cambió sus vestidos habituales por un traje negro y una cartera y empezó a ir al despacho y a plantear modificaciones de vida. Yo, por mi parte, como si hubiera recibido una herencia invisible, me puse a escribir" (*Jardín* 36–7; Mother exchanged her usual dresses for a black suit and briefcase, and started going to the office and making changes in her life. I, on the other hand, as if I had received an invisible legacy, began to write).

This invisible legacy, in addition to correlating mother and daughter, recalls the notion of the *pubilla*, a term that Janés does not use but which could signal her position as heiress, as she was oldest of the three sisters. From the Latin *pūpūllus* "pupil, under-aged," *pubilla* is a juridical term in Catalan civil law for the older daughter designated as the heir. As Llorenç Ferrer i Alòs explains, "In Catalonia the hereditary system envisaged that the eldest son in the family would inherit. When there was no male heir, the oldest daughter would inherit, and was then called the *pubilla*" (27). This system "first appeared towards the end of the eleventh century" and "a preference for male heirs had as yet not been established in this period. It was from about the seventeenth century that male primogeniture became practically universal" (30). In the modern period, this figure would guarantee the continuity of the familial patrimony when there was no male heir. Yet, it is important to keep in mind that the term designates more an exception than a common practice. As Llorenç Ferrer i Alòs says, "Having a *pubilla* was not a deliberate choice, but rather an exceptional case" (31). Isabel Pérez Molina also comments on how women could only be heirs when there were no male descendants, never in conditions of equality (73). Accordingly, women were a necessary but rarely beneficiary figure (74), and this system served to maintain the integrity and avoid fragmentation of the heritage but also to continue a patriarchal socioeconomic and juridical organization (75, 76) in what ultimately is a cultural structure reproducing patriarchal values (Pallares-Barbera, Montserrat and Antònia Casellas 69). Janés's invisible legacy does not refer to an economic, material legacy but rather to an immaterial one, a cultural legacy that is both the inheritance of culture despite her being a woman, and the right to write, a heritage veiled in patriarchal cultural forms that she is nonetheless able to claim.

That said, Clara Janés did not inherit the father's publishing house. Clara Janés's mother took over the publishing house and, because of its many debts, sold it within months of her husband's death to Germán Plaza, who turned it into Plaza & Janés.[6] In *Jardín*, Janés offers an image rarely found in Barcelona's cultural history of publishing, which often exalts publishers and is related to trade and business.

Janés's image is one in which the excitement and hopes of the father blend in a bittersweet way with her own story of sorrow when the publishing house is sold and which reveals the humanity beyond the father's project and the mother's new role as head of the family, as well as the place of women behind the scenes in a family business. The blackness of the mother's suit symbolizes mourning and the change of her role, while her losing weight and her new image turn her into a mirror of the daughter's own pain, "sus piernas, de lejos, eran apenas perceptibles; llevaba el cabello largo y liso, recogido en la nuca, y su mirada oscilaba entre la ira y la dulzura" (*Jardín* 114; her legs, from a distance, were barely noticeable; her hair was long and straight, tied back at the nape of her neck, and her gaze fluctuated between anger and sweetness). The mother's cathartic transformation is demonstrated in her new gestures as she briefly occupies the father's place in the publishing house, creating the illusion of recovery but also the painful reality of loss.

The mother and daughter's parallelism, the identification with one another, is grounded in their need to mourn through singing and writing. A fragment of Christoph Willibald Gluck's opera *Orfeo ed Euridice*, which Janés's mother, a professional clavichord player, sings and plays on the piano after Josep Janés's accident, takes on a special meaning in this process. Janés explains that her mother identified with the man who rescues Eurydice: "Curioso que mamá, cuando papá murió, tocara siempre al piano *Che farò senza Euridice*. Nunca antes se lo había oído tocar. Y ahora sí, lo tocaba, e incluso lo cantaba movida por el dolor … ¿Sentía también mamá, entonces, que existe la posibilidad de arrancar al otro de la muerte? Esto es lo que hace de Orfeo el poeta" (*La voz* 21; Strange that mother, when father died, would always play *Che farò senza Euridice* on the piano. I had never heard her play it before. And now, yes, she was playing it, and even sang it, moved by her grief … Did my mother also feel, during that time, that it was possible to pull another back from death? This is what Orpheus, the poet, does). The mother assumes the role of Orpheus: She follows her husband to Hades and in this way enters into the realm of death and of artistic production through identifying with the masculine protagonist of the myth. The Oedipal triangle that is in play in these passages equates the mother and daughter, showing that Clara Janés also felt she was entering a masculine realm when writing "y uno mismo se convierta en su propio Orfeo. Es necesario tener ese valor, ese arrojo" (*La voz* 26; and one becomes one's own Orpheus. It is necessary to have that courage, that boldness).

The two women's identification with Orpheus should not be underestimated: Mother and daughter connect with the masculine element of the myth as well as with Orpheus's capacity to produce a discourse that can resuscitate Eurydice, the silenced partner dwelling in Hades. The reworking of the myth in the text represents the transformation of the feminine subject after the husband/father's death. Mother and daughter are entangled figures that mirror each other in the process of mourning; at the same time, their mourning divides them, as each of their experiences of pain is unique. These movements of identification and separation illustrate how Janés's subjectivity is constantly reaffirming and destroying the boundaries of the self. The mother also shows that it is not only masculinity and femininity that construct and complement each other, but that maternity and paternity as notions, and the father and mother as persons, are deeply linked and in turn also allied with the daughter. In fact, in the text, maternity reinforces the place of the father and consequently the place of the female writer/daughter as the one who gives birth to the text.[7]

Crafting the Self Through Language

Jardín, like most of Janés's literary production, is written in Spanish. Clara Janés has not openly explained her reasons for choosing Spanish as her literary language, but her personal situation seems to have played an important role in her choice: In addition to growing up during Franco's regime, after her father's death she moved to Pamplona, in Navarra, where she went to university, and later to Paris and Madrid, which distanced her from the Catalan context.[8] Yet in *Jardín*, Catalan is fundamental to Janés in recovering her father. In fact, in this text, the self is crafted between multiple linguistic realities, and this multilingualism provides a sense of authenticity and reconstruction to the text. Spanish is the main language of the book, yet it is mixed with fragments in Catalan as well as quotations in French, Italian, English, and German, showing that the autobiographer's reality is anything but monolingual. As Sidonie Smith explains, every autobiographer "is constituted as a hierarchy of languages, each language being a kind of ideology-brought-into-speech" (48). Multilingualism elucidates how the subject is placed in a linguistic hierarchy but also how this subject acquires an active position within it. In addition, Janés's use of several languages shows her involvement within a very specific community: The Catalan family, her friends, and her literary influences, which turn into a collage of voices.

On the first page of *Jardín*, a note explains how the autobiographer recorded the voices of her mother, aunts, and friends of her family speaking about the father in Catalan:

> La parte del texto escrita en catalán es, casi en su totalidad, transcripción de conversaciones recogidas directamente en cinta magnetofónica. Se respetan, pues, los barbarismos y el peculiar modo de hablar de cada personaje. (*Jardín* n.p.)

> The part of the text written in Catalan is almost entirely a transcription of conversations collected directly on tape. Therefore, the barbarisms and the particular ways of speaking of each character are respected.

This fragment frames Janés's work at the same time as it gives voice to another level of authorship in the text, a sort of author who introduces the autobiographical voice, thus offering a first impression of the linguistic dynamics of *Jardín*. Likewise, the excerpt illustrates the consciousness of creating the text, of constructing her own memory, and of how the autobiographical act plays with the fictional telling – consequently, the use of *personaje* (character) to refer to those appearing in her text.

The words and sentences in Catalan scattered throughout the book seem to display the existence of a binary structure: Spanish is the *official* language of the text, while Catalan has an unofficial status. In this dual system, Catalan and Spanish are associated respectively with the oral versus the written. As the opening statement says, Catalan is spontaneous, conversational, colloquial. It is also placed outside the norms of grammar: *Barbarisms*[9] are expressions or grammar structures that come from Spanish and that Catalan speakers use when speaking Catalan instead of the grammatically correct equivalent in Catalan. This incorrectness, which is also noted by Terenci Moix, was a result of the lack of formal education in Catalan that the majority of Catalan speakers had. Moreover, the etymology of this word (from Greek βαρβαρισμός, "what the foreigners spoke, and the Greeks did not understand") shows a distance between the two languages, in which Spanish and Catalan are Others to each other. This points to a specific sociolinguistic reality of Catalonia during Franco's dictatorship: Spanish was the *official* language of education and culture, but people used Catalan with friends and family and in the street. Catalans were forbidden to live publicly in Catalan, but the language remained present and alive during those years. The fact that Catalan was officially forbidden as a language of education for almost forty years made its correct usage accessible only to an elite minority. Janés's mention of *barbarismos* on the first page of her book not only recalls this diglossia but also strives for a linguistic realism in which Catalan is alive – despite incorrectness – and points to a linguistic crafting as each language is embedded in the other.

While Catalan might seem secondary or anecdotal, the Catalan fragments in *Jardín* are essential to recovering the past and projecting the self. They are significant not because of their quantity but because of their meaning. Catalan is the language of Janés's origins, a language that celebrates life and childhood: In Catalan, she transcribes the first sentence that her father and mother exchanged when they met, "Jo a vostè la conec" (*Jardín* 122; I think I know you from somewhere). Catalan is also the language of traditional songs such as *La lluna, la pruna* (*Jardín* 72; The Moon, the Plum) and of warnings from adults "Et punxaràs" (*Jardín* 18; You will hurt yourself) as well as the language of the mother and aunts, the women who surround Janés and explain to her the myths that compose the family narrative. Catalan is also a festive language and a language of laughter: In Catalan, Clara Janés transcribes the long and somewhat incoherent dialogue between the mother and the publishing house's chauffeur. The two of them laugh together while they remember some characteristics of the father's personality that were unknown to the daughter: That Josep Janés had considerable debt and that he used to flirt with and write poems to the female butcher in order to get free pieces of ham (60–2). This laughter, suggestive as a nonverbal mode of expression, depicts relationships that ignore the class distinctions between the mother and the chauffeur as well as between the father and the female butcher. Thus, Catalan is essential in reconstructing a cheerful paternal atmosphere and a man unknown to Clara Janés.

Contrasting with laughter and joyfulness, in Catalan we also hear the unforgettable scream of Janés's mother when she discovers that Josep Janés was dead: "No pot ser, no pot ser!" (It can't be true!). This expression, in which the subject negates an undeniable reality, is repeated, structuring the text as it activates memory through the remembrance of the father's sudden death and the realization that Janés has lost her father and belongs now to the group of women who mourn him. In *Jardín*, Catalan is indeed predominantly oral and predominantly the language of women and of domains traditionally linked to the feminine (the home and raising children).[10] In this context, in *Jardín*, the relation between Catalan and Spanish resembles the divided yet mutually dependent and fluctuating relations between women and men. Somehow, the feminine world, at home, perceived as a sharing community, contrasts with the masculine one, outside, the patriarchal and hierarchical domain of books and literary tradition that is, however, kept alive by female voices and by the writing process of the female autobiographical self.

That said, if Catalan is oral, a language of voices, of singing and of hearing, it is also deeply related to writing. It is the language of Clara Janés's assertion as a writer: "Tu ho has aconseguit" (Jardín 87, 120; You have succeeded), an affirmation from Janés's uncle to his niece that appears twice in the text, indicating recognition of the Spanish writer Clara Janés and evidencing her socially legitimized achievements. Catalan is also, perhaps above all, the language of the father's books, a written language and a language of culture: In Catalan, Clara Janés quotes the titles of her father's texts, most of them written and published during the 1920s. The list of eighteen titles of texts written by Josep Janés, followed by their publication dates, shows Josep Janés's versatility as a writer, as the titles include popular short stories (*rondalles*), theatre pieces (*funcions*) and poems (*poesies*): "Las obres d'En Josep Janés son: *La Diada* (1919), *Un cop d'estaca* (1919), *En Patec* (1920) ... *Un volum de poesies* (1924), *Un volum de funcions* (1925), *Un altre volum de funcions* (1925), *Un volum de rondalles* (1922)" (*Jardín* 138; The works of Josep Janés are: *Catalonia's National* (1919), *Stake Strike* (1919), *Mr. Patec* (1920) ... *Poetry Collection* (1924), *Collection of Plays* (1925), *Another Collection of Plays* (1925), *An Anthology of Fables* (1922)). In quoting the father's titles, Janés binds her own writing in Spanish to her father's in Catalan. In addition, the hierarchized binary organization between the two languages – the cultural weight they carry, which presents Catalan as a private, interior language at once oral, spontaneous, and ungrammatical – is broken down and subverted: Catalan is ultimately the language of the father's written legacy and a language that shapes Janés's text in subtle yet persistent ways. Through the father's titles, Catalan, like Spanish, is a language of writing, publishing, and translating, a language of culture and of the celebration of culture.

The fragments in Catalan highlight the importance of the senses and the subject's debt to the memory of others, specifically Janés's mother, family friends, and those who knew the father well, such as his chauffeur. Janés offers a collage of voices that point to other voices and texts as central to reconstructing memory and her childhood. But if this collage presents memory as something fragile, a process that depends on others, the reality is that the self crafts this memory in an active way. Self-translation is basic in this process: Visually, the pages are broken by the Spanish translations of the Catalan fragments, translations done by Janés herself that appear in footnotes. Accordingly, the autobiographer is an active mediator between her Catalan childhood – cloistered at home with other women – and her adulthood as a Spanish writer, public figure, and intellectual. The autobiographer translates the Catalan into Spanish as she translates her reality to the text. These acts of self-translation in *Jardín* should not be underestimated, as Janés is a prominent translator who has translated from the French, Portuguese, English, German, and Italian, as well as from less common languages such as Turkish, Serbo-Croatian, Romanian, and Czech into Spanish. Her work as a translator is quite impressive: The Spanish National Library (the Biblioteca Nacional) entry for Clara Janés includes more than 400 titles, many of which are translations and cotranslations. In addition to translating from the Czech, particularly authors such as Vladimír Holan, Jaroslav Seifert, and Bohumil Hrabal, she has translated from the Persian, Turkish, and Japanese as coeditor of the series *Ediciones del Oriente y del Mediterráneo*, published by the Madrid-based Guadarrama. Janés has translated authors hardly known if not completely unknown in Spain, from a great variety of time periods. It is also important to highlight her work translating female authors such as Katherine Mansfield, Marguerite Duras, Mary Higgins Clark, and Sylvia Wallace. Thus, translation is indeed primary to Janés's literary persona in her autobiographical project and beyond, as it defines her sociocultural contribution to the Spanish literary landscape.

One also needs to think about the importance that translation had for Josep Janés, given that he was involved in the publishing industry and in publishing works in Spanish that were originally written and published in French, English, Italian, and other languages during the dictatorship. Josep Janés also gave translation work to exiled authors who were having financial troubles. According to Josep Mengual, "Buena parte de la literatura escrita en España en esa época (del 39 al 75) no hubiera existido sin el influjo y el estímulo de las traducciones de obras inglesas, húngaras, francesas, italianas o estadounidenses que Janés estaba haciendo accesibles a los lectores, y lo hizo en el momento en que eran convenientes y necesarias" (7; Much of the literature written in Spain from that period (1939 to 1975) would not have existed without the influence and stimulus of translations of English, Hungarian, French, or American works that Janés had made accessible to readers. He did this at a time when these works were vital). In fact, the title of *Jardín y laberinto* is a direct reference to a poem by the English poet Francis Thompson that Clara Janés quotes in *Jardín* in this way, "*The labyrinthine ways / of my mind.* Francis Thompson. La poesía inglesa. Noviembre de 1958" (*Jardín* 38; English poetry. November 1958), and for which she offers the translation: "*Le huí por los caminos laberínticos / De mi mente, y la bruma del llanto*" (*Jardín* 38; I fled from him, down the labyrinthine paths / Of my own mind; and in the mist of tears). This quote is part of an explanation of Janés's memory of a day in 1958. On that day, her father took the family to a restaurant for lunch to celebrate having published the translated collection of poems by Francis Thompson. Thus, the labyrinth of Janés's text is both her own path towards finding a literary voice after the father's demise – keeping in mind, as Colleen Culleton explains, that in Greek mythology the labyrinth is also a form of prison (41) – but also a labyrinth that connects her to the work of other poets and to the father's publishing project and the celebrations around his achievements.

In *Jardín*, Janés presents her bilingual background by staging it as a sort of theatrical display, a theatrical display where translation plays a central part: The text stages a differentiation between two languages, just as there is in theatre a difference between the text and its representation. This way of presenting her diglossic upbringing contrasts in many ways with Moix's, Goytisolo's, and Barral's autobiographies, as they all use Spanish to describe their relationship with Catalan. Through theatre and translation, Janés's representation of her Catalan past transcends genres and surpasses dualities between Catalan and Spanish, disengaging itself from the politicized linguistic ideologies of Spain, which too often consider Spanish and Catalan as languages in contention with and direct opposition to each other. As in the case of Barral, for Janés, Catalan was not a language to express her literary persona, and Janés has never been considered a Catalan writer, as she does not live in Catalonia and does not participate in the Catalan cultural milieu. As with Barral and, to a certain extent, with Goytisolo and Moix, from a Catalanist reading, Catalan could be seen as just a testimonial residue in Janés's literary legacy. Yet, even though not published in Catalan in its totality, *Jardín* shows a particular reality of Catalan deeply connected to Francoist linguistic legacies in which the subject clings and pays homage to her linguistic and cultural origins.

Janés's literary mourning for her dead father is not published until 1990, even though Josep Janés died in 1959. This temporal frame signals the elongation of pain and the importance of time in the process of mourning. Similarly, Clara Janés's literary representation of her linguistic subjectivity is affected by the double temporality in which not only the remembered time but also the historical time in which the memory is constructed have an impact. This double temporality, significant in the works studied in this book, allows Janés to represent memory as a work in progress fusing the mourning for the father with her linguistic subjectivity and crafting a bilingual text that reflects as closely as possible her Catalan childhood. As with Barral, there is a strong sense of indebtedness towards the Catalan father and thus a synergy between the recovery of the Catalan past and the father figure. Indeed, the linguistic traces of Catalan go hand in hand with the work of mourning the father. By 1990, a well-established Catalan publishing scene is in operation, and Catalan has been "normalized." In this context, Janés chooses to make reference to her Catalan past at a time in which the Catalan language has entered into a new reality, one completely different from the one she was raised in. Rather than being opportunistic or *Jardín*'s being a "somehow more Catalan exception" in Janés's production in Spanish, Janés's reference to her Catalan past in 1990 could be the result of the Transition's opening up of a discursive space in Spanish society in which the Catalan language and culture can be articulated. It can be seen also as celebration of the fact that this language had a thriving past when the father started his publishing business and that the language has survived and can be recovered. Janés has described her political and intellectual position as one of "distrust" (quoted in Faszer-MacMahon 24). In effect, Janés as a writer has never been easily drawn into simplistic political or linguistic agendas. In *Jardín*, the recovery of her Catalan origins is presented as separate from politics and as something strictly personal. Even if her desire to reclaim her childhood language is not evidently political, the Catalan fragments still have, for us as informed readers, political resonances. The Spanish dictator is not named at all, but the father's books in Catalan, his inability to continue writing and publishing in Catalan after the war, and the relegated place of her mother and aunts at home all constitute an evident reality. Catalan launches her private process of remembrance, one that seems to be disconnected from the memory of Spain's dictatorship yet points to how Catalan survived years of prohibition to finally appear as a language of recovery.

Vladimir Holan: The Lover as a Paternal Figure

A more elaborate text than *Jardín*, *La voz* offers in a refined, poetic prose a vivid account of how Clara Janés started writing again after abandoning her literary projects for six years. The autobiographer narrates how the years of silence, darkness, and bitterness were followed by a feeling of being alive when she read Vladimir Holan's poetry, started to exchange letters with him, and later met with him in Prague in the summer of 1975 (see *La voz* 53) when she visited him at his house. In these intellectual and physical encounters, writing began as "una fuerza que mueve" (*La voz* 21; a force that moves). Janés talks about a delicate metamorphosis within herself, an awakening to life, affirming that Holan rescued her from a sadness and grief bound up with the father's death: "Es que distintas muertes anidaban en mi cuerpo, distintas muertes que vigorizaban la vida subterránea y que, sin duda, se habían iniciado con la muerte real de mi padre que me había cercenado el horizonte a los 18 años" (*La voz* 27; Different deaths were nesting in my body, different deaths that gave strength to the subterranean life and that, undoubtedly, began with the actual death of my father, which had diminished my horizons when I was eighteen years old).

Born in Prague in 1905 and thus thirty-five years older than Janés and, in fact, older than Janés's father, who was born in 1913, Vladimir Holan is one of the most important Czech poets of the twentieth century. He is known for writing obscure lyrical poetry of a pessimistic nature and was connected to Spain through subtle references: He read Góngora and expressed his political concerns about the Spanish Civil War in favour of the Republic. Yet he was not a well-known author in Spain when, around 1971, Janés read his *Una noche con Hamlet y otros poemas* (*A Night with Hamlet and other Poems*), which was originally published in 1964 and translated into Spanish in 1970.[11]

Holan is a figure who evokes strong feelings in Janés: admiration, inspiration, love, and desire. Through Holan, Janés gains knowledge of a new language, Czech; a new city, Prague; and the island Kampa, located in the centre of that city, as well as the feelings of erotic love and how to express them in her writing. Moreover, Holan reminds Janés of her father in several ways: Holan acknowledges her as a writer and spurs her creativity; he also influences Janés's position as a woman writer and reawakens the filial love and admiration between Clara and Josep Janés. Holan and Janés's vital stories intersect at several levels: Holan also lost his father at a young age, he is confined to his home just as Janés remembers about her own childhood, and he establishes a literary dialogue with Shakespeare. Through a series of coincidences that seem inexplicable, Janés and Holan develop a subtle and deep intellectual and literary connection. This connection is partly based on their common interest in Shakespeare and on the strong impression felt by Janés when reading Holan's dramatic poem *A Night with Hamlet* (1964) because of its darkness, the use of harsh language in the poem, and the references to Hamlet and Ophelia. Comparing herself to Holan, Janés speaks of her own darkness, of writing as a state of reclusion, and of Shakespeare as influential her journey as a reader and writer. The impact of Holan on Janés is evident on a real and literary level, as Anne Pasero explains: "[Janés's] relationship with Holan would affect not only her writings but her entire spiritual and creative outlook" ("Introduction" 9).

The figure of Holan drives us to reflect upon several issues: the importance of men as literary inspiration for Janés; the importance of triangulation in the construction of mourning, desire, and literary subjectivity; and Janés's own veiled political stance. Holan lived in self-exile at home for political reasons. During his youth, he wrote poems in favour of the Soviet Union, and belonged to the Communist Party – Clara Janés explains that Holan wrote "verdaderos panegíricos llenos de exaltado entusiasmo como *Gracias a la Unión Soviética* (1945) *A ti* (1947) y *Soldados del Ejército Rojo* (1947)" (in "Prólogo" *Antología* 16; authentic eulogies brimming with passion like *Thanks to the Soviet Union* (1945) *To You* (1947) and *Soldiers of the Red Army* (1947). However, in 1947, when the Czech Communist Party came to power, Holan was excluded from his country's intellectual life, and the publication of his works was forbidden. The poet then isolated himself in his house on the island of Kampa (see Janés, "Holan, del otro lado del abismo" 23). In his house, he wrote at night (*La voz* 33) and engaged in a dialogue with his own shadows and phantasms (34, 87). Holan's self-exile is important for two reasons: It is similar to Janés's sensation of being intellectually exiled during her childhood, and it speaks to the need to step away from politics and society in order to accomplish a literary project.[12] The island of Kampa, the house's walls that surrounded Holan for thirty-two years of self-imposed exile, and his solitude and pain all imprison him as they, at the same time, constitute his liberation: The confinement and desolation allow him to write, to create (*La voz* 34, 87). In this way, Holan's reclusion strengthens Janés's idea that writing comes from a state of withdrawal, when the body is submerged under stagnant waters, a state of isolation that, in Holan's case, seems to have been politically caused but that is later embraced as a way of life.

Holan is cardinal in pushing Janés to self-identify as a daughter, lover, and woman writer, identifications that are presented in relation to a particular spatial imagery, including the space of the text. A series of spatial connections between Janés and Holan allow them to meet at the textual level and for Janés to discover a new space in which to cultivate her literary voice. Janés associates the garden of Pedralbes with Kampa, both spaces of self-exile but also spaces that provide the possibility of writing. Janés also links Holan with the lover that she had imagined as a child in Pedralbes (18). Moreover, Holan wrote to her in her native city, Barcelona, obliging her to come back to the paternal sphere: "el poeta de Praga, el encerrado en la isla de *Kampa*, me escribía a Barcelona" (*La voz* 11–12; the poet of Prague, he who had confined himself to the island of Kampa, was writing to me in Barcelona), thus forcing her to confront a forgotten urban landscape that is shared in *Jardín* and in *La voz*. In this context, Barcelona and Prague appear as twin cities, mirroring one another.

In *Jardín* Janés explains that the expulsion from her childhood garden after the mother's decision to move to downtown Barcelona on Muntaner Street set her in a very different landscape and rhythm of life: In the lower and interior parts of the city, taking a metaphorical fall related to her interior descent into sadness. This is the Barcelona of the 1960s, a Barcelona with few connections to the post-Olympic, touristy, and globalized city that is part of the European Union. It is instead a city of "penitence" (to use Carlos Barral's term) and cultural greyness that for Janés is full of familial memories and voices. Her move into the depths of Barcelona is intensified by her subsequent journey to Pamplona, where she goes to study. The departure for Pamplona somehow delays Janés's mourning for her father. Nonetheless, her return to Barcelona forced her to confront the new reality after her father's death: Janés felt divided between her new and old geographies: "cada vez que volvía a Barcelona una escisión se producía en mí entre la que estaba siendo en Pamplona y el anhelo de la que había sido en Pedralbes" (*Jardín* 54; every time I returned to Barcelona, a divide formed in me between who I was in Pamplona and the yearning for who I had been in Pedralbes). This split self creates an environment of receptivity in the text that permits a search for the father. The symbol of the labyrinth marks the internal search and the multiple infinite possibilities of creation in the writing process. Furthermore, the labyrinth further constructs the importance of the mythical, as not only Hyacinth – through the flower that opens the book – and Orpheus, through the reference to the mother's singing of *Orfeo ed Euridice*, are present, but the couple Ariadne and Theseus are also implicit in the image of the labyrinth, with the woman (Ariadne) as the one helping the man (Theseus) to escape it.

Janés's notion of herself as a divided, itinerant subject reappears in *La voz*. Here, Kampa is connected to Barcelona and to the garden in Pedralbes, but it is also closely linked to a space of death: Els Monjos, where Josep Janés had the car accident and was buried and where she begins her mourning. If, during her visit to Holan in 1975, Janés perceived her first poem as an intuition that took possession of her, "se adueñó de mí" (*La voz* 37; overtook me), it is when she returned to Barcelona that she started composing her first poems of love, which later turned into poems of mourning: "Después de cantar el poema que vino a mí tras mi primer viaje a Praga, en vano me había hostigado la idea de hacer aquel planto por la muerte de mi padre ... Tal vez tenía que unirse ese dolor con el de la ausencia definitiva del amado detectada en el propio cuerpo, sufrida cruelmente" (*La voz* 97–8; Once I had sung the poem that came to me after my first trip to Prague, the idea of making it an elegy for the death of my father hounded me in vain … Perhaps this pain had to merge with that of the definitive absence of the beloved, sensed in one's own body, having suffered cruelly). Thus, in *La voz*, Janés asks herself: "y yo, ¿quién soy?, ¿la de Pedralbes?, ¿la de Praga? … Sólo la de Pedralbes pudo llegar a ser la de Praga" (*La voz* 84–5; and I, who am I? The one from Pedralbes? The one from Prague? … Only the one from Pedralbes could have become the one from Prague). The split self tries to reconstruct its own identity by finding the space that allows her to look at the past but also project into the future. Prague, Pedralbes, Kampa, Barcelona, and Els Monjos are all important spaces for Janés to start singing her lament, in which she can convert her grief and love into literary expression.

After she meets Holan, writing becomes a vital necessity to her, a spontaneous need that allows Janés to incorporate the figures of the father and the lover into her subjectivity as a woman, lover, and daughter, as she is incorporated into the realm of literature. Janés writes that Holan rescued her from silence: "y yo, al leer su poesía, tras seis años de esterilidad, fui también rescatada" (*La voz* 27; and I, upon reading his poetry, after six years of sterility, was also redeemed from death). The relationship between the artist and the muse is somehow transgressed here, as the man is the one who serves as the female's literary inspiration, but at the same time their relationship is also impregnated with traditional gender norms, as the female writer is unable to produce without the man's help. For instance, for Janés, Holan is the incarnation of Orpheus, a man who comes from two worlds, the worlds of the living and of the dead. Here Janés is equated with the passive and silenced protagonist of the myth, Eurydice, whose future and salvation is in the hands of Orpheus. Janés's rewriting of the myth here does not completely convey traditional dichotomies, but it does not transgress them. The autobiographical subject is often conscious that it is necessary to fight until "uno mismo se convierta en su propio Orfeo" (*La voz* 26; one becomes one's own Orpheus).

Similarly, during her second trip to Prague, Janés dresses herself in white in order to represent herself as Beatrice of the *Divine Comedy*, to rescue Holan/Dante from the underworld (101, 124). It is well known that Beatrice was both a historical subject and a character in the *Divine Comedy* who guides the poet to heaven. Again, in the pair Dante–Beatrice, Janés identifies with the feminine element of the couple, while at the same time assuming an active role of searching. These various identifications show the subject's changeability, her power to ventriloquize through mythology and literary characters, and how the self is able to inhabit and perform many roles. Yet these various identifications also point towards the captivity and incarceration in which gender subjectivity encloses the self and the multiple attempts of the female writer to break with patriarchal traditions. Thus, in this case, heterosexuality secures and strengthens the place of the father and the patriarchal organization, while at the same time the father figure secures heterosexual desire and the triad of the daughter–father–lover. In this regard, we cannot forget that Janés's work, particularly of the eighties and nineties – her poems in *Eros* (1981), *Kampa* (1986), *Vivir* (1983), *Creciente fértil* (1989), or the novels *Los caballos del sueño* (1989) and *El hombre de Adén* (1991) – demonstrates certain idealization of heterosexual love and sublimation of masculine figures, as well as the female expression of desire towards men that has been read as both a feminine and feminist revindication.

That Janés's permeable poetic voice is filled with intertextual references underscores the fluid boundaries of her literary subjectivity, something studied by literary critics: Nadia Mékouar-Hertzberg speaks of Janés's subjectivity in *Jardín* as a "moi-dépositaire" (171; custodian-self), and Anne Pasero writes of "Janés's expression of the self as an integration of distinct and multiple elements, fluid and inconstant, in search of an ultimate union with the other" ("Introduction" 11–12). This is evident in Janés's autobiographical texts as well, where a collage made up of the voices of others constructs the self. Similarly, her autobiographical and poetic works are linked through numerous repetitions and interlocking references. As with *Vivir* and its close relationship to *Jardín* and *La voz, Kampa* is also connected to her autobiographical project: That book of poetry is dedicated to Holan and contains a series of love and erotic poems that Janés wrote between her time in Paris starting in 1975 and El Escorial in 1978.[13] In these texts, desire and heterosexual love appear vis-à-vis the remembrance of the father figure, highlighting the undeniable influence of male figures and their interrelation.

Female Mourning and the Melancholic Literary Tradition

Jardín and later *La voz* need to be understood as examples of mourning as a productive, even reproductive, experience. Sadness and grief pervade many of the passages of the two texts. In *Jardín*, Janés speaks of feelings of exhaustion (9), a state of emptiness (12) and of serene craziness (12, 13), and about feeling dead while alive (14). Janés recalls her sicknesses and diverse health problems as an adolescent, as well as her difficulties adapting to the normal rhythm of life. In *Jardín*, Janés relates this state to the father's surname, *Janés*, which derives from the Roman God Janus, "Jano bifronte que mira hacia adentro y hacia afuera" (Jardín 92; Janus with two faces who looks inward and outward) and to the familial genetic heritage, "hay gente alegre en la familia; y gente melancólica; y hay quien reúne ambos aspectos" (92; there are joyful people in my family; and melancholic people; and there are those where both characteristics are present), "Yo estoy más próxima a aquel otro aspecto de los Janés, el perderse por el bosque" (105; I'm closer to that other characteristic of the Janés, the one of getting lost in the woods). Coinciding with Sidonie Smith's notion of the father's surname as the one allowing for the (in this case female) autobiographer's inscription in a literary tradition, Janés highlights the paternal surname – a well-known one in both the Spanish and Catalan cultural contexts – as the one she identifies with. The paternal line and surname carry the genes of both a "cheerful" and a "melancholic" personality, which she relates to reclusion, silence, and literary fertility, and it is with the father's surname that Janés builds up her persona of novelist, poet, and translator. Janés is the surname used by Clara Janés to legitimize herself as an author, that is, to construct what for Julio Premat is an identity of "contradictory imperatives."[14]

In *La voz*, Janés comes back to the feelings of grief and explains that for years she was in a state of nihilism (*La voz* 19), craziness (3), and scepticism (39). Janés describes her state of silence after her father's accident as caused by "distintas muertes [que] anidaban en mi cuerpo" (*La voz* 27; several deaths [which] were nesting in my body). Even when using the term of "melancolía" to refer to the family's personality, Janés's autobiographical texts offer a telling example of literature as material evidence of the process of mourning. Following Freud's seminal work "Mourning and Melancholia," it is important to mention that, according to Freud, "mourning is the reaction to the loss of a loved person, or to the loss of some abstraction" while "melancholia instead of a state of grief develops in some people whom we consequently suspect of a morbid pathological disposition" (153). Where the process of mourning results in the subject connecting again with reality after grieving the lost one, something we see repeatedly in Janés's text, the melancholic, on the contrary, experiences "abrogation of interest in the outside world, loss of the capacity to love, inhibition of all activity and a lowering of self-regarding feelings to a degree that finds utterance in self-reproaches and self-reviling and culminates in a delusional expectation of punishment" (153). In fact, Freud associates melancholia with narcissism (161) and sadism (162), clarifying that much of the self-blaming of the melancholic is in fact directed towards the lost one.

Much has been theorized about the distinction between these two forms of grieving and, more importantly, about the importance of melancholia as a productive concept to understand the subject, as we can see in psychoanalysis (Abraham et al.). Melancholia is also seen as a central malady of the Western literary tradition – as Giorgio Agamben and Julia Kristeva have theorized – or as a way to understand gender differences and gender formation, as in the works of Luce Irigaray, Kaja Silverman, or Judith Butler. The distinction between these two forms of grief can inform how Janés's autobiographical project positions her as a woman writer who mourns the dead father and yet inherits and places herself in a line and literary tradition of (melancholic) men.

In her seminal study *The Gendering of Melancholia*, Juliana Schiesari, following the works of Sigmund Freud, as well as those of Irigaray, Silverman, and Kristeva, argues that, from Aristotle to Ficino, Tasso to Burton, Petrarch to Hölderlin, and Dostoevsky to Walter Benjamin, melancholia has been the illness experienced by great male writers. Schiesari explains that in the melancholic tradition, "an empowered display of loss and disempowerment converts the personal sorrow of some men into the cultural prestige of inspired artistry and genius" (12). Schiesari describes how, starting with Aristotle, the black bile was associated with genius:

> The melancholic temperament [was] understood by Aristotle as an unfortunate malady that invariably affected "all" great men: "Why is it that all men who have become outstanding in philosophy, statesmanship, poetry or the arts are melancholic, and some to such an extent that they are infected by the disease arising from black bile, as the story of Heracles among the heroes tells?" Among the other great *men* said by Aristotle to have been afflicted by melancholy were Ajax, Bellerophon, Empedocles, Plato, and Socrates. Given this status of "eminence," melancholy could thus become a praiseworthy attribute in its own right. (6)

Later, "Ficino thus turned melancholia into a positive virtue for men of letters and 'popularized' it to the rest of Europe" (7). Schiesari's study accurately argues that melancholia is thus a "gendered form of ethos" based on or empowered by a sense of lack. On the contrary, a "woman's lament, grievance, or suffering is seen as the 'everyday' plight of the common (wo)man, a quotidian event whose collective force does not seem to bear the same weight of 'seriousness' as a man's grief"

(12). Thus, to Schiesari, the melancholic is complicit with patriarchy: Melancholic (artists) belong to this masculine and selective group that excludes women, while women's ritual is defined by depression: Their *melancholic* state is less worthy and lacks dignity in the Western tradition.

By invoking mourning as productive and by referring to women who mourn, Janés plays with the distinction between mourning and melancholia and highlights the gendered weight of the (melancholic) literary tradition as well as the lack of women in that tradition. Janés does so by turning to the couple Hamlet and Ophelia – key figures in *La voz de Ofelia*. Hamlet and Ophelia, along with other couples in Janés's memoirs such as Orpheus and Eurydice and Beatrice and Dante, epitomize male–female differences and heterosexuality and offer room for subtle subversions of the autobiographical self in Janés's autobiographies.

As Sharon Keefe Ugalde points out, Shakespeare's Ophelia is a character who not only lends the title to Janés's second autobiographical book but is also fundamental to the construction of the writer's identity. Ugalde reconstructs Ophelia's images, from Shakespeare to the Pre-Raphaelite paintings, highlighting the (female) characteristics of this figure: Innocence, purity, passivity, and craziness. Shakespeare's Ophelia, like Janés, is a young girl overwhelmed by her father's death as well as an unrequited love. As Ugalde explains, Janés's text uses the image of the subject's immersion in subterranean waters – inspired by Ophelia's drowning in the river – as a metaphor for the writing project that connotes literary authority and alterity, and it becomes a symbol for a form of writing in which rigid borders and hierarchies are banished (11).[15] In effect, the literary production in *Jardín* is defined as a state of the body (9, 10) and is equated to an immersion in subterranean waters (see *Jardín* 10, 52, 67). This image is a leitmotiv evoked by Janés to portray her own writing and connects Janés with other writers – especially Vladimir Holan (Ugalde 8, 9) – and to the father, "tal vez también él (mi padre) sabía lo que es tener una vida subterránea" (*Jardín* 27; maybe he (my father) knew what it was to have an underground life). Yet, this hidden, secret life, while identifying her with the male artist, also needs the figure of a woman – in this case, a literary character – in order to become effective.

We must recall how, in Shakespeare's *Hamlet*, both Hamlet and Ophelia are figures overwhelmed by the deaths of their fathers. However, the two characters find themselves in very different Oedipal narratives: Hamlet is the young heir to the Danish crown, haunted by the ghost of his father. He needs to kill Claudius, the mother's lover and the assassin of his father, to recover the place of his father and thus become the rightful king.[16] A very specific impetus moves Hamlet: Vengeance, inheritance, and fighting against the one who has usurped his crown and seduced his mother. Ophelia is inserted into a very different Oedipal scenario. Her madness does not start with a ghost but with a reality: She loves Hamlet and goes mad when she discovers that the man whom she loves has killed her father. Following this discovery, she commits suicide. She is not moved by vengeance, she does not want to recover her place as an heiress, and she does not try to trick other people through her apparent insanity. Ophelia's madness is real.

Gender bias is quite evident: The young woman, crazy and lost, surrenders her life after discovering that the man she loves does not love her back. Hamlet's craziness is destructive, yet his melancholia has conceded him a superior and extraordinary status: Schiesari names Hamlet as an "exemplar of melancholic theatricality" (236), given that, "when we speak of melancholia as a cultural or discursive practice, we can no longer differentiate the affect or sense of loss from its display" (236). In effect, Hamlet is placed at the centre of a literary tradition of melancholic men (see, for instance, Schiersari 242, who explores the place of Hamlet as a melancholic in Lacan's works). While Hamlet's brilliant affirmations have turned him into a melancholic genius, Ophelia's madness constrains her as a hyper-feminine figure: Her young, dead body, floating in stagnant waters, has been presented in the Western artistic tradition as an object to gaze upon and often as a masculine fantasy. In the words of Anne Pasero, "Shakespeare's Ophelia was regarded as a passive, delicate, wan, pallid and fragile figure, an unfortunate and helpless victim of circumstance and manipulation" ("Introduction" 61).

The dynamic pointed out by Schiesari between male and female forms of melancholia/depression is at play in Janés's texts through the invoking of Ophelia and of mourning as a literary productive state. Mourning is in fact the state of many women in *Jardín*, such as the mother and Janés herself, who puts into writing female voices while she writes about her own pain. Similarly, *La voz* is centred not so much on the lost loved one but more on the process of loss itself, a process understood as a source of intellectual and artistic creativity and placed in contraposition to melancholia. Accordingly, one can interpret Janés's texts as a questioning of the place of Hamlet as the rightful heir to the literary tradition of melancholia and of melancholia as the way to become part of a privileged, elite group of male writers. As Ugalde and Pasero affirm, Janés turns Ophelia's state into a source of literary creativity (Ugalde 8–9), and Janés's Ophelia "will ultimately respond to the death of Holan and her father in just the opposite fashion, prompted to return to writing and to recover her spiritual self" (Pasero "Introduction"

60–1). Ophelia in Janés's texts is then symbolic of how women can also become representatives of the creative tradition and of mourning as one of the ways to construct a literary project, although the writer does need to refer to a literary character rather than to the real model of a female writer.

Mourning the dead father is a need, but it also becomes part of a literary agenda to incorporate the daughter's name into a large list of literary influences, a way of reclaiming the place as heir, as a *sui generis pubilla*. Ophelia is evoked as a response to Hamlet's melancholia, and Janés's literary self must be understood as an answer to how literary authority needs to be conceived beyond a masculine tradition of writers: In Janés's works, we find multiple paternal presences – the father, Janés's male professors, those canonical and noncanonical male writers who inspire her – that incarnate literary authority. All these men introduce the subject to the knowledge of foundational texts, as Nadia Mékouar-Hertzberg has pointed out (50). It is through the mourning process that begins after the father's death that Janés adds her voice into what Mékouar-Hertzberg has named "les textes des Pères" (15). Mourning helps Janés strengthen and tighten the bonds of filiation and affiliation with both her blood relations and her literary family. The mourning for her dead father allows her to engage in a dialogue with this canonical tradition: Shakespeare, Quevedo, Holan, and Góngora are named in her autobiographies. Janés also names her professors such as Alberto Blecua and Martín de Riquer and friends of her father such as Eugeni D'Ors or Frederic Mompou. In another text about her literary influences, "Secreto and Sustrato," Janés points out that her childhood reading of Santa Teresa and the *Coplas por la muerte de su padre* by Jorge Manrique, "constituyen mi asiento literario más antiguo" (9; make up my earliest literary influences) and remind her of her experience with a poem by Paul Verlaine at the age of eight and how "el poema se apodera totalmente de mí por su música y yo me apodero del poema" (9; the poem and its music completely absorb me and I absorb the poem), pointing out that her incorporation of literary influences started very early on. Women appear first sporadically on this list – to which she later adds her friendship with Rosa Chacel and Victoria Atencia – but the constant search for *another* canon, a personal one that means an exploration beyond national, linguistic, and gender borders, is a hallmark of Janés's work, and she can be considered, among the writers of contemporary Spain, to be the one who has proven to have the most diverse literary connections.

There are other examples of this tension between the female writing subject and the masculine literary canon in Janés's autobiographies.

This tension is evident in *Jardín* when Janés describes her dreams about her father's imposing library and how overwhelming it is to be surrounded by this immense quantity of books. The library's bookshelves and book spines are completely paralysing:

> Tropezaba con todo, parecía que iba a caerme, que el mismo polvo amenazaba mi difícil equilibrio entre papeles, cuando, de pronto, mis manos daban con el cuaderno de provenzal (la voz de Riquer): *Tot me desnatura, / Flor blancha vermelh'e groya me par la frejura.* Y entraba en la calma. Eran palabras mágicas como las de las jarchas. (111–12)
>
> (I stumbled over everything, it seemed like I was going to fall, like the very dust threatened my precarious equilibrium amongst the volumes, when, out of the blue, I laid my hands on the Provençal notebook (Riquer's voice) *Tot me desnatura, / Flor blancha vermelh'e groya me par la frejura.* And I became calm. They were magic words like those of the jarchas.)

Her pursuit of something unknown can be interpreted as a search for her own place and voice in this vast world full of books and titles. In her dream, she feels relieved when she finds a book with familiar content: A Provençal poetry notebook with Bernart de Ventadorn's poem, which reminds her of the medieval *kharjat*. Janés was familiar with this form, as she took a literature course at the University of Barcelona with Professor Martín de Riquer, where she read the Iberian and Provençal medieval lyrics. Janés senses a feminine voice expressing desire, a voice that prefigures Janés's own poetry of love in *Kampa*, *Eros,* and *Creciente fértil* (*Fertile Crescent*), Janés erotic poetry books published in the 1980s. This feminine lyrical voice is only encountered after coming across – and somehow overcoming – several masculine presences: The father's library, and, in it, the university professor who introduced her to medieval lyrics by reciting Bernart de Ventadorn's poems. Janés's dream symbolizes the possibility of finding a feminine voice in this masculine realm of books and literature and thus breaking down conventional and inherited divisions about masculine and feminine spaces. In this context, the father's library is an obstacle but also an opportunity to inherit her father's relationship to literature. The motive of the father's library – which connects her with other authors such as Borges and which can also be found in the works of Barral, Moix, and Goytisolo – ensures the continuity of the father's legacy inherited by the daughter. At the same time, this literary inheritance aids Janés in finding her own voice as a daughter, as a woman, and as an artist and in framing her own canon.

Literature is a collection of texts with paternal names into which Janés inserts the daughter's voice. Janés's memoirs claim the place of the daughter, of the *pubilla,* a legitimate successor to the father's business and wealth. This is a legacy that invokes responsibility: Her task is to explain who Josep Janés was by collecting broken images of the father's persona that constitute partial and fragmentary reflections of both the father and the autobiographical subject. Mourning the father fuses Janés with and gives her a space within the masculine literary tradition. Janés dignifies the feminine plaint and claims the right for the women of the family to participate in a recognized mourning. Janés's sorrow coincides with Butler's concept of grief as a process that creates a sense of community rather than as a private act (*Precarious Life* 22), in this case, a feminine community. Janés thus portrays a form of paternity that differs from the father as purely an authoritarian figure but one that is merged with the canonical male writers who are simultaneously fused in Janés's texts with the feminine and oral world of women. Accordingly, the father's death should be read in parallel with the awakening and the birth of the feminine: It is the women of the family who inherit the possibility to reconstruct Josep Janés's story.

Jardín and *La voz* demonstrate that women writers live in a paradox, a tension in which the female poetic voice is contingent on either affirming the primacy of male voices or on overcoming them. In some ways, Janés's two autobiographical texts could seem quite old-fashioned: Current feminist scholars highlight the importance of intersectionality and critique the place of white middle- and upper-class women as an elite that created a feminist discourse unwelcoming of other groups (in terms of race, sexuality, religion, or ability). In many ways, Janés's texts are in tune with the work of the French feminists of the seventies, particularly in the way she openly conveys female sexual desire and female sensuality, projecting the female body not as an object of desire but as a desiring subject. While these premises have been outpaced by other pressing priorities in the new waves of feminism and overtaken by new feminist premises, Janés's work illuminates the need on the part of a generation of Spanish female authors to challenge patriarchal structures and to convey the perceived lack of feminine literary models for those raised under the Francoist regime. Seen in context, Janés's writing situates her as a less traditional and more radical writer than previously thought. She has been a model of constancy, continuity, and independence in diverse genres and forms, and her later work has continued to follow feminist premises of expressing women's desire, touching on issues related to technologies and communication, as we see in her poetry book *Vilanos: (e-mails),* non-Western philosophy, and, in her seventies, eroticism (*Kamasutra para dormir a un espectro*, Siruela, 2019) (Kamasutra to Put a Spectre to Sleep; 2019).[17] Janés's autobiographical texts ultimately ask: What is literary authority, how do women respond to it and construct it, and to what extent do women need to make a pact with symbolic fathers and with a patriarchal structure in order to assume a position within what has traditionally been a male domain? How can a female writer adopt, adapt, and play with a masculine literary lineage and use it as a way to legitimize her own writing? Killing the father is a popular idea often used metaphorically to explain how one can overcome what was previously done. Yet it is most likely impossible to completely kill the father, even more so when he is a person who is influential and loved. The overcoming of the father figure is only possible when the self acknowledges him, mourns him, and celebrates his life, carefully finding a balance between this filial deference and parricidal defiance[18] to then experiment with other themes to find one's own artistic self.

Conclusion

Writing and longing for the father are inseparable in Janés's autobiographical texts. Josep Janés is an ambivalent figure who represents a patriarchal and masculine literary tradition, yet he is also a figure who authorizes Janés to write and to become the authority over her own poetic voice. For Clara Janés, Josep Janés is a figure whose death painfully opens the doors to adulthood, but he is also the one who permitted her to consider writing as a legitimate profession, necessary to negotiate literary inheritance and literary filiation. Janés's memoirs are a tribute to her father and a place where she negotiates the paternal burden and this "invisible inheritance" in a structure that is perceived as masculine. As a garden and labyrinth that are a prison and an escape, the Oedipal triangle traps Janés while at the same time it allows her to undo this negotiation: Through Holan, through male and female literary figures, and through mourning as a process of working through, she creates space for a birth of her own. Her appropriation of feminine voices – Ophelia, Eurydice, Beatrice – and the relationships she portrays with her mother, sister, and aunts do not exempt her from the literary need to make a pact with Hamlet, Orpheus, Dante, her father, or Holan. The feminine subject is often constructed with a deference to and admiration of the masculine, and, while this deference is sometimes viewed as an obstacle and as imprisoning, it is also an open possibility. The process of mourning is essential to establishing this dialogue with a literary tradition, to incorporating the feminine voice into a traditionally masculine literary lineage. In this sense, the father's role is presented as one that ensures Janés's induction into heterosexual femininity and also that this heterosexual femininity will find a literary space. The father is essential in Janés's perception of a literary canon and in her self-inscription in a literary genealogy and self-fashioning as a woman poet, novelist, and translator. Cultural heritage and Catalan language are visible legacies that permeate the text and remain in it. Francisco Franco is not named at all in Janés's autobiographies, but the father's books in Catalan, his inability to continue writing and publishing in Catalan after the war, and the subordinate place of her mother and aunts all constitute an evident reality. In this context, Catalan initiates Janés's private process of remembrance – one that seems to be disconnected from the memory of Spain's dictatorship yet points to a confined, elite cultural environment within the household – and to how this language survived years of prohibition. Janés's autobiographies illuminate how a female writer in Spain negotiated the consequences of sexism, linguistic policies, and privately confronted issues of historical memory and patriarchy during the Spanish democracy. The fascination with the father is undeniable in Janés's texts and clearly raises tensions between legacies and sexism that are not only complex but also never are clearly solved. Affiliation and filiation are inseparable, as are inheritance and giving birth to herself as an independent female author.

Epilogue: Bilingual Legacies

Through a close reading of autobiographical texts by four authors born in Barcelona who grew up during Franco's dictatorship, I have argued that these authors present their fathers as central figures when explaining their relationship with literary tradition. The father figure is also significant when justifying language choice in a bilingual context and when explaining how they became writers. These four authors were raised in a very particular linguistic context, with Catalan forbidden in public spheres, an official reality that contrasted with other spaces such as the household, where each family and even each family member may have adhered differently to the linguistic precepts of the dictatorship. Three out of the four authors studied here chose Spanish as their main language of literary expression, and only one of them, Terenci Moix, alternated between the two. While major authors from Catalonia wrote and published in Catalan before the war, few did so during the regime. During Franco's dictatorship, Catalan became, for many, a resistance language and a politicized choice. After the dictatorship, Catalan and Spanish underwent yet another social and political transformation in Catalonia, the so-called linguistic normalization in which Catalan became the coofficial language of the autonomous region. The autobiographical texts studied here narrate a linguistic past, but they were also immersed in a time during which authors raised in Catalonia were at times asked to justify their choice of Spanish over Catalan. None of these autobiographies were written in Catalan, but in all of them their authors thoroughly address their relationship with this language – during their childhood a language of mostly domestic life – and their families' relationships with bilingualism. All of them stress the father as crucial when acquiring a linguistic consciousness and when they became writers. Accordingly, even in the texts written in Spanish, these writers reveal the place of the Catalan language and literary tradition during the dictatorship and thereafter.

In Goytisolo's, Barral's, Moix's, and Janés's autobiographies, Catalan is at times an abyss or a remembered yet unattainable legacy that faded after the father's or the mother's death. At times, it is a language that became distant and removed after a geographical change; from time to time, it is an unpleasant language or one seen with ambivalence; and finally it is also presented as a direct path to certain familial and communal memory. That said, for the four writers, Catalan was a language that lived alongside Spanish just as Spanish coexisted with Catalan in a constant if differentiated way. Surrounded by language politics and by the occasional need to justify their choices, the decision of these authors to write and publish in Spanish stood at the forefront of their explanation of how they became writers. In the end, the language of expression is the everyday tool of any writer, and for bilingual writers this is true in an even more conscious way. These Catalans who wrote in Spanish or Spanish authors who were born in or lived in Catalonia resided within two linguistic systems, merging a sense of marginality with their privilege during the linguistic "normalization" period. Their texts illustrate the layers of the not-always-harmonious coexistence of Spanish and Catalan as two languages that at times appear in opposition and yet exist side by side and at times entangled. These autobiographies illustrate how the authors present their choice to write in Spanish in this very particular and changing bilingual context and how this choice resulted from a multifaceted decision, one that was also redefined over time. Education and an inherited literary legacy as well as sentimental attachment and familial and literary models are all present when these authors explain their choices.

If we understand these texts, even when written in Spanish, as portraying the emotional weight that stems from the prohibition and reconstruction of Catalan and its literary legacy, we can see that they are a key piece of both Catalan literature and of the literature of Spain; both literatures are interconnected in their history of voids and restorations. We can see these writers as more or less responsible, as more or less victims of circumstance, as voluntary or duty-bound heirs of their language choice. More important, these texts demonstrate how a familial heritage shapes their accounts of how they became writers and how they established relationships with two linguistic systems in their autobiographical writing.

When I started this project, the contemporary peninsular context presented a critical apparatus already avidly concerned with the father and the family. Several scholars of the literature and cinema of Spain had already signaled how the death of Franco had brought to light the extent to which the dictator resembled an authoritarian father, while in movies and literary texts the legacy of war and of the dictatorship appeared (and continues to appear) in connection with the family and fatherhood. That said, literary and cultural scholars have also highlighted the need to look beyond the omnipresence of Franco when interpreting Spanish contemporary culture, as father figures clearly go beyond the metaphor of the dictator. The writers studied here reveal a variety of attitudes towards the biological father, and, in their texts, the father undoubtedly differs from the dictator as a paternal presence, thus highlighting the distinctiveness between the two figures and the heterogeneous relations between sons and daughters and their fathers. The autobiographical genre is crucial in this regard, as the symbolism that fuses the dictator as father of the nation with the paternal figure is undone in the descriptions of their biological fathers. Instead, the father is a person who differed from the dictator, and this divergence is amplified by the Catalan bilingual context. That said, whether the father was supporting Francoist premises inside the household or not, it is impossible not to acknowledge the legacy of Francoism in these texts. In this context, if we interpret the reasonings provided by the writers in their autobiographies when explaining their adoption of Spanish as a literary language, Spanish in Barcelona's literature constitutes in many ways a consequence of Francoist language politics, one that seems to continue to be present, given that some literary structures established during Francoism and thereafter, such as publishing houses or prizes, still endure in Spain. The generation that grew up during the dictatorship and that became involved in the political transition to democracy confronted both Franco's legacy as well as the inherited values that had been transmitted through their families. They also, perhaps paradoxically, internalized certain values of the dictatorship and of their families, and accordingly it is not surprising that in the texts studied the Catalan father is presented as an absence or as unable to completely protect his language and literary legacy. In parallel, Catalan is sometimes portrayed as having feminine traits, being the secondary language, relegated to the household, to the spoken, to the land, to the sea, or to humble neighbourhoods. These authors, then, are an example of the slow machinery of change, of how resistance does not happen without a certain amount of compliance, and of how old models survive while new ones are forged.

A close reading of father figures in autobiographical texts illustrate how issues of masculinity, authorship, and canon are interrelated. In some of the studied texts, the affiliative impulse, the necessity to recognize the father's importance and legacy, goes hand in hand with a disaffiliating impulse – that is, with the necessity to judge and condemn the father. Consequently, there is a rivalry between masculinities in the autobiographies by male authors, complicated by the existence of two languages and two literary canons. In the texts studied here, we see instances in which the male authors compete for authority with the father. As the ones in charge of writing, the male authors studied here engender their writings at the same time as they give birth to themselves in the autobiographical project. These authors indeed choose their literary influences, but the link they establish with them is often a familial one, and often these influences too are not far removed from those the father or the mother had – and those that were available during the authors' childhoods. Sexual desire further complicates these relationships between authority, fathers, language, literary influences, and writing, as is evident in the works of Juan Goytisolo and Terenci Moix, two writers whose relationships with their fathers were marked by the need to confront the father's homophobia. In many ways, these authors belong to a generation that felt the need to dissolve the authoritarian model of the father figure, and questioning the father's homophobia was crucial in this process. On the other hand, the place of the daughter, shown in the example of Janés, offers yet another dynamic in the literary system: One in which the daughter receives the paternal legacy while she mourns the father – not without having to acknowledge the patriarchal reality of literary conventions and the canon or the Oedipal link established with male literary influences. In the case of both Barral and Janés, the father is the one who introduces the son and daughter to the world of writing and publishing, and the publishing industry is part of this paternal inheritance. Of course, it is not surprising that the father and not the mother is the one who transmits this legacy, and it is not surprising that Barral was heir to the father's publishing house, while Janés, the daughter, did not inherit her father's business. In this way, these texts also illustrate how father figures and paternity are yet another way to tackle the evolution of gender norms and expectations in Spain.

The authors studied in this book push the limits of (non)fiction writing in ways that often cause their autobiographies to spill over into their creative work or vice versa. Thus these autobiographies offer us the possibility of interpreting differently the authors' fiction and poetry – all as part of the same configuration of the authorial figure – and of showing that issues of paternity, language, and gender extend beyond the autobiographical. Furthermore, there is not only a coreferentiality among the texts written and published by these authors, but these authors' works are also interlaced with others by those who were their family members and also writers, such as the brothers of Juan Goytisolo, José Agustín and Luis Goytisolo; Juan Goytisolo's wife, Monique

Lange, and the wife's daughter, Carole Achache; and Ana María Moix, in the case of Terenci Moix. The texts (particularly those with an autobiographical component, whether they are fictional or not) by brothers and sisters offer yet another account of the implications of paternity, as the father was a character shared by them but who inspired them differently, thus contributing to a web of relationships between fictional and nonfictional texts by more than one author. Biological and literary legacies should in this regard not be interpreted as too far from one another.

The legacy of a sexist, patriarchal society is incontestable in these autobiographical works. Although mothers are not absent, they often appear as more veiled characters than the fathers, in the case of Goytisolo because of his mother's death and in the case of Barral and Janés as a figure that emerges more clearly when the father dies. Moix's autobiographies offer a more egalitarian portrayal in this regard, although the Catalan father continues to be the one linked to the outside world, the streets, the library, and urban space. Clearly there are nuances of time and space, in terms of personal history, that are singularly important: The death of a Catalan-speaking parent (Janés's and Barral's father, Goytisolo's mother) turns Catalan into a distant language for these three authors – yet one related to the lost father or mother and thus a masculine or feminine model, respectively. This distancing from the Catalan-speaking environment is supported in the case of Janés and Goytisolo by their leaving Barcelona in their early youth. Terenci Moix, a bit younger and with a different lived experience of the war and bilingualism from that of Barral, Goytisolo, and Janés and with both parents alive during his childhood, offers a more nuanced distribution of the importance of the two figures, father and mother, just as he does with the two languages, Catalan and Spanish. He differentiates them by giving them comparable potential when considering them as languages of literary expression. It is here that I see a parallel between mothers and Catalan language: As with Catalan in the diglossic context of the dictatorship, the mothers of the authors of this generation lived in a sexist society during the dictatorship, traditional in terms of gender norms, one that that relegated them to the household, to domestic life. Of course, many mothers did not remain willingly or completely in this interior space, and Catalan was not completely erased during the dictatorship. Yet when family members did not endorse Francoist linguistic and gender norms there was a sense of resistance and subversion. It is in this regard that *Bilingual Legacies* has stepped away from the symbolism that reads the father as an allegory of Franco to show that, when considering Spain's contemporary culture, where Oedipal narratives have been present and Oedipal readings have had an important critical impact, Spain's other linguistic and cultural realities give us yet another perspective on fatherhood that intermingles gender and language. Accordingly, the works of these four authors provide us a privileged position from which to understand how linguistic and gender subjectivities go hand in hand in their construction and change.

Notes

1. Filiations

1 John Borneman explicates in *Death of the Father* (2004) by looking at Mussolini's, Hitler's, Hirohito's, Lenin's and Stalin's, Ceaueşcu's, and Tito's regimes, whether "called 'fascists,' 'Nazi,' 'imperial,' 'cult of personality,' 'totalitarian,' 'patriarchal,' 'paternalistic,' 'communist,' or 'state socialist,'"(1), these "regimes were *patricentric* in that they attempted to unify their subjects and create a modern subjectivity through identification with a leader who becomes the general equivalent of his subjects, the standard of all value, but who himself operates outside measurement" (3).

2 Several scholars have highlighted the presence of the family and familial memory in Spanish literature and film, as well as the relationships between mothers and daughters during the dictatorship and the transition. Marsha Kinder's *Blood Cinema* (1993) and Kim Yeon-Soo's *The Family Album* (2005) are two contributions in this regard. Other references are Sara Cooper's *The Ties That Bind* (2004) and the works of Geraldine Nichols, Christine Arkinstall, and Emilie Bergmann. The works of Sandra J. Schumm's *Mother and Myth in Spanish Novels* (2015), María Asunción Gómez's *La madre muerta. El mito matricida en la literatura y el cine españoles* (2016), and Marina Bettaglio's articles are pertinent studies of motherhood and mother figures during the dictatorship and during and after the transition to democracy. Families and fathers continue to be fundamental in exploring the silenced past of the Civil War and the dictatorship, as Guillermo del Toro's *El laberinto del fauno* (2006, *Pan's Labyrinth*) and Agustí Villaronga's *Pa negre* (2010; *Black Bread*) – a movie based on Emili Teixidor's novel of 2003 – attest. In these works, fathers are crucial in the search for the protagonist's own identity vis-à-vis national history and memory, as well as in the discourse regarding legitimate

and illegitimate inheritances and generational replacement. Recent documentaries produced in Spain also exhibit links between public and private/personal stories: *Yo soy de mi barrio* (Juan Vicente Córdoba, 2002; I Am from My Neighbourhood) and *El cielo gira* (Mercedes Álvarez, 2004; The Sky Turns), the various works in the project *Entre el dictador y yo* (2005; Between the Dictator and Me), *Nadar* (Carla Subirana, 2008; To Swim), and *El horizonte artificial* (José Irigoyen, 2007; The Artificial Horizon) are all autobiographical documentaries with an "unusual historical density" (Cuevas 114), where family figures such as the father through his absence or presence grant the subject access to their family history and, in turn, to the history of the country. Indeed, as Luengo states, "La familia en el caso español es un elemento crucial en la recuperación de la memoria histórica" (26; In the case of Spain, the family figures as a crucial element in the recovering of historical memory), but we cannot forget, as Loureiro points out, that "'Family'narratives – meaning the stories one has heard in the various types of communities in which one has been involved, narratives that by nature are not historically rigorous – have much more bearing on the present than the most exacting historical knowledge" ("Pathetic" 229). Accordingly, we need to be aware that these narratives in which subjects inherit certain affections towards the past are not historical documents but are the evidence of certain affective inheritances.

3 Before the Civil War, thanks to Ortega y Gasset, Spain was one of first countries to translate the complete works of Freud, and Freud's theories were not only discussed by doctors, but they also influenced artists such as Manuel and Antonio Machado, Pío Baroja, Eugeni d'Ors, Salvador Dalí, Luis Buñuel, Federico García Lorca, and Ignacio Sánchez Mejías (see Allodi 3).

4 In fact, the small 1930s Spanish psychoanalytical establishment decamped to Argentina upon the Francoist victory, an example being the psychoanalyst Ángel Garma, the first in Spain to take patients, who with Gregorio Berman funded the Argentinian School of Psychoanalysis after his exile (Allodi 4). Doctors such as Antonio Vallejo-Nájera and other psychiatrists of the period objected to Freud's precepts and considered them "contaminación moral" (Allodi 5; moral contamination).

5 As Sánchez- Barranco explains, "[miembros de] la Iglesia Católica adoptaron un papel muy activo contra la instauración y el desarrollo de las ideas freudianas en España (algunos miembros del Opus Dei calificaban a Freud de «genio satánico»), o bien las falsificaron para asimilarlas a sus conveniencias ideológicas, promocionando bajo el epígrafe de psicoanálisis la doctrina adleriana" (170; members of the Catholic Church played a very active role against the introduction and the development of Freudian ideas in Spain (some members of the Opus

Dei called Freud a "satanic genius"), or they falsified them to integrate them to suit their own ideological interests, promoting the Adlerian doctrine under the rubric of psychoanalysis). Despite the fact that in 1954, the Regime approved the Sociedad Psicoanalítica Española (Spanish Psychoanalytical Society), which was accepted by the International Psychoanalytic Association, in 1978 there were only 200 psychoanalysts in Spain (Allodi 6).

6 In "The dissolution of the Oedipus Complex" Freud explains that "[t]he authority of the father or the parents is introjected into the ego, and it forms the nucleus of the super-ego, which takes over the severity of the father and perpetuates his prohibitions against incest, and so secures the ego from the return of the libidinal object-cathexis" (176).

7 In his analysis of Freud's works, René Girard clarifies that there is nothing passive or feminine in the son's identification with the father. To identify with the father is to want to replace him: The little boy "would like to grow like and be like him, and *takes his place everywhere*" (173, italics in text).

8 The relationships between father and daughter and father and son have been studied in several literary traditions. Striking representatives are: Yaeger and Kowaleski-Wallace's *Refiguring the Father* (1982), Bueno's compilation *Naming the Father: Legacies, Genealogies, and Explorations of Fatherhood in Modern and Contemporary Literature* (2000), and Copeland and Ramírez-Christensen's *The Father-Daughter Plot. Japanese Literary Women and the Law of the Father* (2001).

9 This includes works by Luce Irigaray, Jane Gallop, Jessica Benjamin, Judith Butler, Kaja Silverman, Nancy Chodorow, and Julia Kristeva, to name some of the most representative.

10 See Lévi-Strauss, *The Elementary Structures of Kinship* (1949) as well as Julia Kristeva, *About Chinese Women* (1977) as anthropological investigations of the father in the familial structure. As for issues of fatherhood, legitimacy, and lineage, see Laqueur's article "The Facts of Fatherhood" (in *Conflicts in Feminism*, 210).

11 Lacan's ideas about the father were mostly developed during the 1950s and are disseminated in many of his writings of this period. The readings I have considered are "The Signification of the Phallus," "Beyond the Oedipus Complex," and *Las formaciones del inconsciente. Seguido de "El deseo y su interpretación."* Elizabeth Grosz offers a useful summary of the Lacanian concepts of the father in *Jacques Lacan. A Feminist Introduction* (67–73).

12 More recently, Lolita Bosch's bilingual edition of *La familia del meu pare/ La familia de mi padre* (2008; My Father's Family) also sets forth the memory of the daughter as impossible to separate from the memory of the father,

writing, and the city of Barcelona, and Marta Marín-Dòmine, in *Fugir era el més bell que teníem* (2019; Fleeing Was the Most Beautiful Thing We Had), offers another account of the bond between father and daughter in the context of exile.

13 According to Lacan, "the father's body doesn't matter" (in Kelly, *Family Values* 4).

14 Marina Bettaglio studies, in the last recent years in Spain, the existence of a new form of "feminist fathering" that she describes as "involved, egalitarian, co-parenting, gender equitable, responsible, whether it is a mirage or something that is actually transforming parenting and Western philosophy" (3). Bettaglio urges us, nonetheless, to be suspicious of this new form of involved fatherhood taking shape in neoliberal contexts, as this allows the state to withdraw itself from many aspects of the responsibility for children (3). The four authors analysed in this book are found in between these notions of fatherhood, which range from the authoritarian, patriarchal, and sexist father to the contemporary image of a "feminist fathering," and this is why I consider their representations of their fathers to be central in the evolution that has allowed these gender changes in Spain.

15 While, as Smith and Watson explain, "the term autobiography is inadequate to describe the extensive historical range and the diverse genres and practices of life writing not only in the West but around the globe" (3), this term is not outdated when looking at my primary texts in question.

16 As Smith and Watson explain, "In contemporary parlance autobiography and memoir are used interchangeably" (274).

17 In Foucault, Michel. "Self Writing." *Ethics: Subjectivity and Truth.* The New York Press, 1997: 207–22.

18 The umbrella terms are *life writing* (as Smith and Watson define it, "a general term for writing that takes a life, one's own or another's, as its subject"; 4) and *life narrative* ("by contrast, as a general term for acts of self-representation of all kinds and in diverse media that take the producer's life as their subject, whether written, performative, visual, filmic, or digital"; 4).

19 Smith and Watson explain, "Relational life writing. This term was proposed by Susan Stanford Friedman in 1985 to characterize the model of selfhood in women's autobiographical writing, against the autonomous individual posited by Georges Gusdorf, as interdependent and identified with a community" (278).

20 Georges Gusdorf and Eakin point out that "we don't read autobiographies in the same way that we read novels" ("Foreword" x). Gusdorf talks about this "other way/other manner of reading" autobiographies in *Les éscritures du moi*, I, 245.

21 See Laura Marcus's *Auto/biographical Discourses* (5) and Shari Benstock's *The Female Self Engendered* (6) for a detailed introduction to the place of women in the autobiographical tradition.

22 This quotation, cited by Smith, comes from Julia Kristeva's *About Chinese Women*.

23 Cixous coins the term *biografille* to make reference to the relationship between daughter and father in autobiography. See Merete Stistrup Jensen's "La notion de nature dans les théories de l'«écriture féminine»" (35).

24 Sarah Ruddick considers in *Thinking about Fathers* that the basic masculine sense of self is separate: "hence the basically masculine son of a female mother will, as a father, unwittingly absent himself from his children in order to keep and defend the distance his sense of masculine/ separateness requires" (223).

25 Quoting Gusdorf, "the image is another 'myself,' a double of my being but more fragile and vulnerable, invested with a sacred character that makes it at once fascinating and frightening. Narcissus, contemplating his face in the fountain's depth, is so fascinated with the apparition that he would die bending toward himself" (32).

26 As Smith and Watson note, "While autobiographical storytelling employs fictional tactics and genres, however, autofiction uses textual markers that signal a deliberate, often ironic, interplay between the two modes" (260).

27 Concurrently, in "1960 es creà una càtedra de llengua i literatures catalanes a la Universitat de Barcelona" (33; in 1960 a Chair for Catalan Language and Literature was created at the University of Barcelona). A debate about Catalan in the Madrid-based cultural journal *Cuadernos para el diálogo* started in the mid-60s, revealing two antagonistic positions: Some wanted Spain to have a more open mindset towards the cultural diversity of the country, while others felt that Catalan should be restricted to the familial sphere only (Heinemann 21).The slow recovery that the language and culture were seeing in the sixties, however, was counteracted by the visual media, which was in Spanish until 1983 when Catalan television started. To this we must add large immigration numbers from the south of Spain: "L'any 1975, a la fi de la dictadura, el 38% dels habitants de Catalunya havia nascut fora dels Països Catalans, un alt nombre dels quals no parlava el català o en tenia un coneixement deficient" (Heinemann *Novel.la entre dues llengües* 39; In 1975, at the end of the dictatorship, 38 per cent of the inhabitants of Catalonia had been born outside the Catalan Countries, a large number of whom did not speak Catalan or had little knowledge of it).

28 Only those Catalans born after the 1960s were able to receive education in Catalan (Heinemann 23).

29 In the case of Gimferrer, "malgrat que començà la seva carrera literària en castellà, escriu des de fa temps exclusivament en català i s'oposa a les

veus que el qualifiquen d'escriptor bilingüe" (Heinemann 3; although he began his literary career in Spanish, he has been writing exclusively in Catalan for a long time and he rejects the description of a bilingual writer).

30 In Joan Ramon Resina's own words: "La manca d'Estat és, en relació amb l'imaginari mascle, tan decisiva com la castració" ("L'imaginari" 75; The lack of a State is, in relation to the male imagination, as decisive as castration).

31 In the Hispanic context, Julio Premat affirms in *Héroes sin atributos* something similar: "el autor se sitúa, frente a su obra, en las tres posiciones del triángulo edípico: es el padre, ya que le da su nombre y fija sus reglas; es la madre, la que la engenda, desde sus entrañas; es el hijo, ya que su existencia en tanto que autor está determinada por la aparición previa a la obra" (26; The writer places himself, in front of his work, in the three positions of the oedipal triangle: he's the father, because he gives the work his name and he makes the rules; he's the mother, the one who gives birth to the work, from his very depths; he's the son, given that his existence as the author is determined by the prior appearance of the work). While Premat does add the maternal element to his explanation, he underscores how the author's place in relation to the text relates the father-son relationship for the following male authors to become an author/authorial figure/figure of authority: Macedonio Fernández, Borges, Di Benedetto, Osvaldo Lamborghini, Piglia, Saer, and César Aira. He later adds: "Escribir es enfrentar al padre, es marcar la hoja con una marca transgresiva. Es inscribir, por lo tanto, al personaje que se crea en el juego de las influencias, de las filiaciones, de las rebeliones edípicas de los parricidios y las expiaciones" (27; To write is to confront the father, it's to mark the page with a transgressive mark. It's to inscribe, therefore, the character who creates himself in the game of influences, of filiations, of oedipal rebellions of parricides and atonements).

32 I borrow this term from scholar Ángel Loureiro's book *The Ethics of Autobiography* (113).

33 We cannot forget, as Fernàndez explains, that it is precisely the notion of the canon that has been a central element of debate regarding Catalan culture: "durant la segona meitat dels noranta la discussió sobre la continuïtat de la cultura s'ha convertit en un debat sobre el cànon literari. En aquest sentit, la traducció catalana del llibre *El cànon occidental* de Harold Bloom hi va tenir un paper crucial, ja que va popularitzar entre els intel.lectuals catalans el concepte de cànon. El punt culminant d'aquest debat va ser la publicació el 1999 de *El descrèdit de la literartura*, de Xavier Bru de Sala" (*El malestar* 181; during the second half of the 1990s the discussion of the continuity of culture became a debate on the literary canon. In this sense, the Catalan translation of the book *The*

Western Canon by Harold Bloom played a crucial role, as it popularized the concept of canon among Catalan intellectuals. The culmination of this debate was the publication in 1999 of *The Discredit of Literature*, by Xavier Bru de Sala).

2. Juan Goytisolo: Oedipal Dissolutions

1 Francisco Peregil's article "Goytisolo en su amargo final" ("Goytisolo in his bitter end") in the Spanish newspaper *El País* on June 7 2017, that is, three days after Goytisolo died, is evidence of this. In this article, Peregil discloses numerous details of Goytisolo's financial difficulties at the end of his life and his desire for death by euthanasia, as he was worried about the financial future of his three adoptive children – one of them being the son of his partner Abdelhadi – and the other two the children of Abdelhadi's brother (in the article Abdelhadi is named as a "great friend" ("gran amigo")). The article also explains how the suicide of Carole Achache, the daughter of Monique Lange, impacted Goytisolo, as Achache committed suicide just after having asked Juan Goytisolo for financial help.

2 While Juan Goytisolo was awarded the Spanish National Prize for Literature in 2008 and the Premio Cervantes in 2014 for his lifetime achievements, these prizes were awarded to him largely out of a sense of guilt at his not having obtained due recognition in his own country. Indeed, he was throughout his life much more highly regarded as a writer overseas than in Spain. In addition, these prizes, particularly the Cervantes, were hard for Goytisolo to accept. Francisco Peregil comments on how Goytisolo had critized the prize in 2001 when it was awarded to Francisco Umbral.

3 In Anna Caballé's own words, "la escritura autobiográfica en España estaba en mantillas" ("autobiographical writing in Spain was still in its infancy").

4 In fact, it was his brother Luis Goytisolo, also a novelist, who felt that Goytisolo was unable to distinguish between "life and literature, and "always wrote about himself" (in Rodríguez Marcos "Goytisolo explica a Goytisolo"), a comment that made reference specifically to how Juan Goytisolo interpreted Luis Goytisolo's tetralogy *Antagonía* as a work that spoke about their family.

5 Alison Ribeiro de Menezes comments on the Freudian idiom and Freudian perspective that pervades Goytisolo's autobiographies, one example being Goytisolo's use of the term "pulsión" (20).

6 Miguel Dalmau, in *Los Goytisolo*, criticizes the fact that Juan Goytisolo never explained that the Gays came from the Empordà, and that the family included important figures such as the lawyer Gay de Montellá,

something that is not mentioned in Juan Goytisolo's *Coto*, which in fact emphasizes his Basque more than his Catalan origins (50).

7 In fact, in an interview with Miguel Riera, for instance, Goytisolo said: "lo que a mí me interesa no es tener discípulos, sino tener antepasados: forjarme un linaje de abuelos o bisabuelos ilustres, y por eso miro hacia Cervantes, hacia Fernando de Rojas, hacia San Juan de la Cruz" (in O'Donoghue 304; what interests me is not having disciples, but having ancestors: forging a lineage of illustrious grandparents or great-grandparents, and that is why I look to Cervantes, to Fernando de Rojas, to San Juan de la Cruz).

8 *Nesrani* means *Christians* in the Islamic world.

9 As Fernando González Ariza explains, "By 1965, his [Goytisolo's] books had been published in more than 15 languages. Part of this success was due to the fact that Gallimard, the prestigious French publisher, had taken a chance on him, as well as the critical acclaim that his books had enjoyed in that country. During the 10 years that are examined here, Gallimard published almost everything he wrote. Goytisolo's association with Gallimard was made possible by the intervention of the American Hispanist John B. Rust, who later played an important role in launching him in the USA" (266).

10 The trope of the prison within in Goytisolo's autobiographies has been analysed by Alberto Medina (21–2 and 81–105). Medina relates this interior prison to the impossibility of being an adult in Spain and to Goytisolo's dependence on and fascination with Franco's regime. Robert Richmond Ellis (44–5) also sees Goytisolo as one of those prisoners who ultimately become the agents of their own incarceration and enslavement.

11 Goytisolo served as a bridge between politicized Spanish youth and anti-Francoist writers, and he was often seen as an ambassador of Spanish letters outside Spain (266). In *En los reinos*, he affirms that, because of his position as a representative outside the country, as a literary critic commented, he was suddenly a "globo prodigiosamente hinchado" (389; prodigiously inflated balloon).

3. Carlos Barral: Masculine Subjectivity and the Catalan Father

1 The Spanish Generation of'50 consisted of a group of authors who were born during the Spanish Civil War and who started to publish in the 1950s. Regarding the group of Barcelona, Carme Riera's *La escuela de Barcelona* (The Barcelona School) and Laureno Bonet's *Jardín quebrado: la escuela de Barcelona y la cultura de medio siglo* (Garden in Ruins: The Barcelona School and Mid Century Culture) are two major studies about the group, which included writers such as Carlos Barral, Jaime

Gil de Biedma, José Agustín Goytisolo, Jaime Ferrán, and Alfonso Costafreda.

2 As Jesús Martínez Martín explains, "hasta entonces, 1955, la editoral se había alimentado del viejo fondo escolar y material didáctico anterior a la Guerra, con sus intentos de readaptación, y de algunas colecciones de ciencias médicas o una enciclopedia de la vida Cristiana de escasa rentabilidad. Carlos Barral, desde las entrañas de la vieja editorial, cambió el rumbo hacia una edición literaria y humanística, con la idea de un catálogo planificado y de prestigio, pensando en la calidad de los textos y el sentido de la divulgación cultural" (269; until then, 1955, the publishing house had been largely supported by the old fount of school books and didactic material from before the War, with its attempts to readapt, and by several medical science collections and an unprofitable encyclopaedia on the Christian life. Carlos Barral, from within the bowels of the firm, changed its course to a literary and humanistic publisher, conceiving of a prestigious, well thought-out catalogue, and considering the quality of the texts and the sense of cultural promotion).

3 Barral explains this in *Cuando las horas veloces*: "debiera saberse que yo no publiqué *Cien años de soledad* a causa de un malentendido – a la falta de respuesta puntual de un telegrama – y no por un error editorial ni a consecuencia de una torpe lectura del manuscrito – que nunca vi – como maliciosamente se ha pretendido. Otra cosa es que a mí no me parezca esa la mejor novela de su tiempo" (*Memorias* 691–2; you should know that the reason I didn't publish *One Hundred Years of Solitude* was because of a misunderstanding – the failure to send a timely reply to a telegram; it was not because of an editorial mistake or a clumsy reading of the manuscript – that I never saw – as has been maliciously purported. Another issue is that I never thought of it as the best novel of its time).

4 As scholars Cristina Moreiras Menor ("Juan Goytisolo" 328) and Enric Bou (20) have pointed out.

5 In the 2015 Lumen edition of Barral's memorias, from where the quotes in this book come, "Memorias de infancia" appears at the very end of the volumen (pp. 871–918).

6 Part of Barral's life-writing are the numerous articles published in newspapers such as *El País*, *La Vanguardia*, *El Comercio*, *El Norte de Castilla*, *Destino*, and *Cambio 27*, which appear in *Observaciones desde la mina de plomo* (Observations from the Lead Mine; Lumen, 2002). Two themes that reappear in these articles and connect them with Barral's autobiographical works are the issues of language politics and bilingualism, as well as the destruction of the Catalan Mediterranean coast.

7 Barral spent long periods of time in Calafell. Moreover, Calafell is the place where he got married in 1954 and where his ashes were scattered after his death in 1989.

8 In *Family Values*, Kelly Oliver offers a complete and extensive analysis of Kristeva's imaginary father (see 57 and 211).

9 In *Revolution in Poetic Language*, Julia Kristeva proposes the *semiotic* (*le sémiotique*) as one of the two components of the signifying process, the other being the symbolic. According to Jacques Lacan, with his No or Name (*Nom*), the father separates the child from the maternal body and introduces him or her to the world of signifiers, the symbolic. This rupture brings the child into a process of accepting models and structures that ultimately permit socialization. Kristeva counters this clear-cut system by arguing that, before the child's entrance into language, he or she has already been in contact with the *semiotic* presymbolic maternal world. According to Kristeva, the sounds, rhythms, and gestures of the maternal body constitute a first space in which an initial *ordering* takes place (27). Kristeva's theory of the *semiotic* anticipates the binary logic of self/other, conferring the "necessary pre-symbolic dimension to signification that is bodily and drive-motivated and that lacks the defining structure, coherence and spatial fixity implied by Lacan's formulations" (Becker-Leckrone 28). Kristeva takes the term *chora* from Plato's *Timaeus* and explains that, for Plato, the *chora* is "an essentially mobile and extremely provisional articulation constituted by movements and their ephemeral stases" (*Revolution* 26). The *semiotic chora* is, then, this receptacle, an intimate space without interior or exterior, marked by the flow and stasis of bodily functions – that is, fluid and flowing – nourishing and maternal, where desire begins: "a *chora*: a non-expressive totality formed by the drives and their stases in a motility that is full of movement as it is regulated" (26).

10 In *Aquellos años del Boom* (The Boom Years), Xavi Ayén tells an anecdote about Barral that further displays how he connects the sea with sexuality: "Castellet recordaba una noche etílica en la que, en la playa, Barral quiso demostrar empíricamente a sus amigos que, para robustecer el pene, no había mejor método que golpearlo contra las rocas. Frustrado al ver que sus amigos no lo secundaban, el editor-marinero se subió la bragueta y recitó unos versos de Mallarmé … Su etapa política fue menos extravagante que aquella performance de virilidad" (293; Castellet remembers one drunken night when, on the beach, Barral wanted to demonstrate empirically to his friends that, to strengthen the penis, there was no better way than to hit it against the rocks. Frustrated when he saw that his friends didn't follow his lead, the sailor-editor zipped up his fly and recited some verses of Mallarmé … His political period was less extravagant than that performance of virility).

11 María Moliner's *Diccionario de uso del español* states that "Mar, en su acepción principal, es generalmente nombre masculino; sin embargo, en regiones del litoral o entre las gentes del mar, se usa como femenino" (1873; Sea, in its primary meaning, is usually a masculine noun; but, in coastal regions or among seafaring people, it's used in the feminine form). Ernest Hemingway, when talking about the old man in *The Old Man and the Sea*, also notices the gendered aspect of this use of the feminine article. "He always thought of the sea as la mar which is what people call her in Spanish when they love her. Sometimes those who love her say bad things of her but they are always said as though she was a woman ... The moon affects her as it does a woman, he thought (32–3).

12 Gary Cestaro explains that *infantia* "was etymologically defined by all medieval encyclopedists as the life stage characterized primarily by lack of speech" (180). The "in-fant" is called thus because he or she does not yet know how to speak (*fari*, to speak) (180–1). As Agamben explains, "it is in language that the subject has its site and origin, and that only in and through language is it possible to shape transcendental apperception as an 'I think'" (51). Agamben asserts that subjectivity is "the speaker's capacity to posit him or herself as an *ego*, and cannot in any way be defined through some wordless sense of being oneself, nor by deferral to some ineffable psychic experience of the ego, but only through a linguistic 'self' transcending any possible experience" (52).

13 "Visitas fuera de hora en la poesía de Barral" (51–68; Visits After Hours in the Poetry of Barral) in *Barralianas.*

14 Both José Vicente Saval and Carme Riera study the confluence of Barral's poetic and autobiographical texts (*Carlos Barral, entre el esteticismo* 23 and *La obra poética* 227–30). Following Riera, José Luis Ruiz also explains that in Barral's autobiographies, "la prosa actúa a modo de glosa explicativa de la poesía, ejerciendo un recurso similar a la *amplificatio*, que, dada la dificultad que entraña la expresión poética barraliana, se convierte en una leyenda más que útil para comprender gran parte de sus versos" ("La metódica inexactitud" 35; The prose serves as an explanatory annotation for the poetry, acting as a similar, amplifying force that, considering the difficulty of Barral's poetics, becomes a useful guide to understand most of his verses. "Methodical Inexactitude"). For his part, Dario Puccini highlights the narrative character of Barral's poetry (see "Carlos Barral en mis recuerdos y en su poesía" 89; Carlos Barral in My Memories and his Poetry).

15 Carlos Barral Nualart had two children, Marilí and Carlos.

16 This explanation is followed by an interesting episode: Barral and his friend Alberto Oliart were coming back from doing military service and were dressed in military uniforms when they found themselves in the middle of a

demonstration on Via Layetana. Because of their uniforms, the demonstrators viewed them angrily. In addition, they were greeted by policemen, whose greeting the two young men answered mechanically (see 318).

17 In relation to Barral's work as a publisher of the Latin American boom, see the work of Mario Santana, Xavi Ayén, Alejandro Herrero-Olainzola, Maider Dravasa, and Fernando Tola de Habich.

18 In the introduction to his complete memoirs, Barral explains that, while he was very willing to change the censored parts of the first edition of 1975, the censored version had scabbed over as a kind of scar: "Curiosamente el texto zurcido para cubrir los desgarros de la censura ha cicatrizado con el tiempo aquellas costuras y no admite sino con verdadera dificultad, como si fueran cuerpos extraños, la mayor parte de las expresiones que le pertenecieron en su primitiva redacción" (69; Strangely, with time, a scar had formed over the ravages caused by the excised, censored text. This scar did not allow the reentry – except with great difficulty, as if they were foreign bodies - the majority of the sentences that had formed the original edition).

19 Jordi Julià, in "El taller de Calafell. Sobre el mite de la infantesa a Barral, Gil de Biedma i Ferrater," considers the importance of Calafell as a space of collective creation for Barral and his friends and analyses the mystification of infancy in the worlds of Barral, Biedma, and Ferrater (137–58).

20 Calafell is also central to his class consciousness and in placing him in his relationship to the intellectuals of Barcelona, who often had a second residence. Xavi Ayén explains in *Aquellos años del Boom* that "Calafell y Cadaqués se disputarían el centro latino del siglo XX. En Cadaqués tenían casa Esther Tusquets … Carmen Balcells, Rosa Regàs, Oriol Bohigas o Federico Correa" and continues "Los visitantes de Cadaqués se acercaban a Begur, donde tenían casa Colita, Joan Manuel Serrat, Teresa Gimpera y Guillermina Motta, o a Calella de Palafrugell, a ver a Oriol Regàs" (292; Calafell and Cadaqués would be in competition for the centre of 20th century Latin culture. En Cadaqués, Esther Tusquets … Carmen Balcells, Rosa Regas, Oriol Bohigas or Federico Correa all had houses" and continues "The visitors to Cadaqués arrived by Bergur where Colita, Joan Manuel Serrat, Teresa Gimpera and Gullermina Motta had houses, or by Calella de Palafrugell to see Oriol Regas").

21 The author tries to save "un català fortament marcat pels dialectismes de la marineria" (8; a Catalan strongly marked by the dialectal expressions of seafaring).

22 The films and photographs are in fact the ones that have been used in several TV documentaries about the life of Carlos Barral, and some of them can be found in the Museu Casa Barral in Calafell.

23 In *La escuela de Barcelona*, Carme Riera explains how Barral shares with many of the members of the Generación de los 50, such as Juan and José Agustín Goytisolo and Gil de Biedma, a strong feeling of guilt for belonging to the Catalan upper class (254–5).

24 Alejandro Herrero Olaizola stresses the importance of Barral's awareness of the book as an object. He explains, for instance, how, for writers such as Donoso, Seix Barral's books became "the envy of all" Latin American writers who "had to put up with the total lack of style and the defective presentation of their novels elsewhere" ("Consuming Aesthetics" 330).

25 Barral suspects that his father was extremely protective of his library, as is proven by the fact that all his books had leather covers and an ex-libris (465).

26 For instance, according to Oliart, "(el personaje) más auténtico fue el de Carlos Barral con los pantalones arremangados hasta media pierna, la camisa abierta, la gorra marinera calada hasta los pies descalzos, andando por la playa o presentándose de esa guisa en cualquier terraza de Calafell o del puerto al que hubiera arribado con su Capitán Argüello" (18; The most authentic person was Carlos Barral with his pants rolled up past his calves, his shirt open, from the jauntily positioned captain's hat to his bare feet, walking on the beach or showing up in this guise on any terrace in Calafell or from the harbour where he would have come in on his Captain Argüello).

27 He would wear "una gorra de navegar con los oros de un banal título náutico que acumulaba al uniforme casi harapiento de los viejos pescadores del lugar. Un disfraz, en definitiva, aunque con vocación de signo mítico" (458; a captain's hat with some banal nautical title in gold, in combination with the nearly ragged uniform of the old fishermen of the region. A disguise, definitely, albeit with a mythical character).

4. Terenci Moix: Linguistic and Sexual Disaffiliations

1 Moix's popularity is attested to by books such Juan Ramón Iborra's *Detrás del arco iris. En busca de Terenci Moix* (Planeta, 2004; Behind the Rainbow. In Search of Terenci Moix) – which contains interviews with Maruja Torres, Ana María Moix, Colita, Josep Maria Benet i Jornet, Elisenda Nadal, Joan de Sagarra, Josep Maria Castellet, Eduardo Mendoza, and Jorge Herralde – and by novels such as Manel Guitart's *L'última carícia, Terenci* (Proa, 2010; The Last Caress, Terenci).

2 Neither did the writers Juan Marsé and Manuel Vázquez Montalbán. The *gauche divine* met in the late sixties and early seventies, and one of their main characteristics was a certain lack of seriousness with regard to political and social issues (see Villamados 16). In Villamados's own

words, "la principal crítica que recibieron: un elitismo que excluía en razón de clase social – con la excepción tal vez de los hermanos Moix, y especialmente de Marsé y Vázquez Montalbán" (20–1; the main criticism they received: an elitism that was exclusive on the grounds of social class – with the exception perhaps of Terenci and Ana María Moix, and especially Marsé and Vázquez Montalbán).

3 For instance, the Llei de Normalització Lingüística (Law for Linguistic Normalization) was implemented in 1983. This law led to a key improvement in the place of Catalan in the educational system as well as in public administration and the media in the region.

4 Federic Soler, also known as Serafí Pitarra, was a famous and prolific nineteenth-century Catalan playwright and poet.

5 In Moix's novel *El dia*, similar images defend the place of the middle-lower classes as the ones protecting Catalan language: "Era a dintre, que calia aguantar els pebrots. I a dintre, creieu-me, encara quedava molta gent. Homes i dones que havíen portat la llengua i la idea a un nivell d'endurança gairebé heroica, allunyant-la de les escorrialles del gran somni burgès, altrament traduït al castellà sense gaire dificultat per una part dels prohoms que la inspiraren" (281; It was inside, that you had to put up with the balls. And inside, believe me, there were still a lot of people left. Men and women who had brought the language and the idea to an almost heroic level of endurance, moving it away from the slips of the great bourgeois dream, otherwise translated into Spanish without much difficulty by some of the leading men who inspired it).

6 In 1975, "38% dels habitants de Catalunya havia nascut fora dels Països Catalans, un alt nombre dels quals no parlava el català o en tenia un coneixement deficient" (Heinemann *Novel.la entre dues llengües* 39; 38 per cent of the inhabitants of Catalonia had been born outside the Catalan Countries, a large number of whom did not speak Catalan or had little knowledge of it) – the term *Catalan* countries refers to all the areas where Catalan is spoken, and that includes in addition to Catalonia, Valencia, the Balearic Islands, parts of Aragon and Murcia, and Andorra, as well as the areas of Cerdagne, Vallespir, and Roussillon in France and the city of Alghero in Sardinia (Italy). In this context, Catalan sometimes became a form of elitist differentiation from the working-class migrants from the rest of Spain, contemptuously called *charnegos*. For a literary analysis of this figure in several works by Manuel Vázquez Montalbán, Juan Marsé, or Francisco Candel, see Villamados.

7 Today the Biblioteca de Catalunya is mostly a place for research and in-situ consultation, although some books can be borrowed and taken out. It seems, given Moix's explanation, that was it a lending library at the time.

8 Moix's father introduced him to Egypt, and, when he wrote *Terenci del Nilo* (Terence of the Nile) as his father was dying, since Moix had heard his first stories of Egypt from his father, he decided to dedicate the book to him: "redacté una dedicatoria circunstancial que era, sin embargo, la evidencia de un recuerdo y también un homenaje al maetsrazgo de ayer. Decía: 'A la memoria de mi padre, que me habló de Egipto por primera vez y también del desierto'" (76; I wrote a circumstantial dedication that was, nonetheless, proof of a memory and also an homage to the mastership of yesterday. It read: To the memory of my father, who told me for the first time of Egypt and also of the desert).

9 In *El dia*, Terenci Moix portrays Jordi Cuadreny's father as a publisher who has made money by publishing books previously forbidden by the dictatorship "Va ser així com, l'any 62, llavors que la censura obria una mica la màniga, el papà es va decider a treure al carrer, fent-les pasar per obres d'escàndol, novel.les de Stendhal, Balzac o Victor Hugo, que fins aleshores havíen estat prohibides" (168–70; This is how, in the year 1962, when censorship was lifted, Dad decided to publish, presenting them as scandalous works, novels by Stendhal, Balzac or Victor Hugo, which until then had been banned).

10 Colleen Culleton's reading of the novel by Esther Tusquets *El mismo mar de todos los veranos* (The Same Sea as Every Summer) analyses the change of names of streets and squares as creating a "maze-like narrative in which a second option (meant to be erased) always exists" and as "a bifurcated narrative" (111).

11 In *Construir con palabras*, Jaume Subirana considers that, to understand the Catalan literary system, "pensé que para hablar de todo esto sería interesante leer el sistema literario catalán a partir de parámetros poscoloniales, pero en los últimos años una y otra vez hallo ejemplos que remiten sin prefijos, al colonialismo, o imperialismo" (225; I imagined that to talk about all this it would be interesting to read the Catalan literary system from postcolonial parameters, but in recent years I have found time and again examples that refer without prefixes to colonialism, or imperialism"). As much as some Catalans feel their language and culture is "colonized" by Spain, some Spanish speakers also feel that Spanish culture is marginalized in Catalonia and thus that Catalonia can be similarly colonizing. As Josep-Anton Fernàndez puts it in *El malestar*, there is a discourse in Catalonia that Catalan society is subordinated to the power of Spain but also that Catalonia subordinates others (a fantasy, according to Fernàndez): "Segons aquesta fantasia, la llengua catalana seria imposada damunt una població castellanoparlant que, malgrat disposar de plens drets democràtics, es trobaria paradoxalment i misteriosament exclosa del joc de la democràcia" (29; According to this

fantasy, Catalan would be imposed on a Spanish-speaking population which, despite having full democratic rights, is paradoxically and mysteriously excluded from the game of democracy).

12 A critique that ends up connected to the negative connotation that Catalan acquired for some during the process of linguistic normalization, as Josep-Anton Fernàndez explains in *El malestar*, given that Catalan became the language of officialdom and had a "caràcter correctiu del programa normalitzador" (39; corrective nature of the standardization programme) and "dimensió disciplinària" (42; disciplinary dimension) that had previously been ascribed to the Spanish language.

13 As Ute Heinemann explains, "el 1986 Àlvar Valls féu una crítica plena de mordacitat a dos escriptors, Teresa Pàmies i Pau Faner, que al principi d'aquell mateix any publicaren novel.les en castellà, tot abandonant, doncs, la llengua de les seves produccions anteriors. Valls parlà de 'deserció' i els titllà de 'trànsfugues'" (24–5; in 1986 Àlvar Valls made a scathing critique of two writers, Teresa Pàmies and Pau Faner, who at the beginning of that same year, published novels in Spanish, thus abandoning the language of their previous production. Valls spoke of "desertion" and called them "turncoats").

14 See Diane M. Almeida's *The Esperpento Tradition in the works of Ramón del Valle-Inclán and Luis Buñuel* (2000) as well as Concepción Torres Begine's *España vista desde el aire. Influencia del esperpento de Valle-Inclán en el cine de García Berlanga* (2014).

15 These feminine voices resemble those represented in Moix's urban novels, such as the trilogy *Garras de astracán* (1993; Astrakhan Claws), *Mujercísimas* (1995; Super Women), and *Chulas y famosas* (1999; Cool and Famous), where sophisticated and modern women are ridiculed protagonists who question or exaggerate the masculinity of the men around them. These characters have been compared to those in Almodóvar's movies (see Mira "El niño") and also demonstrate what Caryl Flinn calls the "camp exaggeration of the female form" (448).

16 According to Freud, during the Oedipal process, the boy's identification with the father may take the form of internalizing the perfections with which he has endowed this ultimately phantasmal figure, perfections that he may (unreasonably) hope to one day acquire himself (see Weiss 25). This identification with his father helps the boy to mark a successful resolution of the Oedipal stage. In fact, the ego-ideal is depicted by Freud as "a substitute for a longing for the father" (37) in *The Ego and the Id*. This internalization of the father as a model of perfection that forms the ego-ideal has been questioned by many feminist thinkers, such as Weiss. As this scholar points out, "by describing the ego-ideal as a 'masculine ideal,' Freud (not so) unwittingly reinforces the inferiority complex that women

have already been subjected to, in his analysis, through the castration complex" (25).

17 In the case of Moix, this initiation ceremony connects the autobiographical project with the novels, as in *El dia*, when Bruno tries to "rescue" his friend Jordi from homosexuality by bringing him to the prostitutes: "Aleshores el vaig intentar salvar portant-lo al llit de la Berenice" (289; Then I tried to save him by taking him to Berenice's bed). Goytisolo, Barral, and Moix all narrate a very similar scene, illustrating that the only way to lose one's virginity in the 1950s was to spend a night with a prostitute or, in Moix's words, "una hora de sexo con la mercenaria especializada en descapullar palominos" (*El beso* 136; an hour of sex with the mercenary specializing in deflowering virgins). Barral's views on prostitutes as the ones who initiate young Spanish boys into sexuality is also quite unfavourable: "en la adolescencia [las prostitutas representaban] una peligrosa escuela de automatización de las maniobras sexuales" (*Memorias* 162; during adolescence, [the whores represented] a dangerous school of the automation of sexual moves).

18 As Rosemary Garland Thomson posits in *Extraordinary Bodies*, "the carnivalesque figure – perhaps his version of the disabled figure – represents the right to be 'other' in this world, the right not to make common cause with any single one of the existing categories that life makes available" (38).

19 Moix is similar to Goytisolo here, emphasizing how Francoist censorship would be unable to forbid desires but would shape desires. However, whereas Juan Goytisolo desires a prohibited lower-class masculine model, Moix desires the few bodies that the dictatorship allowed but that did not completely belong to Spanish culture, athletic men, and the male images imported from American popular culture.

20 For more on camp aesthetics, seminal texts are Moe Meyer's *The Politics and Poetics of Camp*; David Bergman's *Camp Grounds*; and Esther Newton's *Mother Camp*.

5. Clara Janés: Fatherhood and the Feminine

1 Josep Janés continued publishing in Catalan during the Spanish Civil War, including Catalan patriotic texts (Mengual 58, 75). He also collaborated with the Generalitat and with the Generalitat's Counsellor of Culture, Carles Pi Sunyer, during the war. In 1938, "Josep Janés y su esposa Esther Nadal salieron la madrugada del 24 de enero de Barcelona a bordo del coche en el que también viajaba Carles Pi i Sunyer" (Mengual 106; Josep Janés and his wife Esther Nadal left Barcelona at dawn on January 24 in the same car that Carles Pi i Sunyer was travelling in). Once

in France, Eugeni d'Ors convinced him to go back to Spain (Mengual 171). Josep Janés was imprisoned in Spain and sentenced to death, as Josep Mengual explains in *A dos tintas. Josep Janés, editor y poeta* (In Two Colours: Josep Janés, Publisher and Poet; 2013). After the publication of Jacqueline Hurtley's book *Josep Janés: el combat per la cultura* in 1986, Manuel de Zuloaga said in an article in *El País* that it was false that Josep Janés was condemned to death (see p. 172). Jacqueline Hurtley refuted this in the same newspaper, referring to the interviews she had done to Josep Janés's sister and wife (see Mengual 172). For more on Josep Janés's life and work as a publisher, see Jacqueline Hurtley's studies, particularly, *Josep Janés: el combat per la cultura* (Josep Janés: The Fight for Culture; 1986) as well as Josep Mengual's book.

2 All translations from *Jardín* are my own, and all translations from *La voz* are by Anne Pasero.

3 Interview between Clara Janés and Anna Casas Aguilar. 28 April 2008 in Madrid.

4 Again, the background of the scene is of great sadness, anticipating the state in which the house will remain after the father's death. Before the phone call, the mother was listening to Fauré's music, and Janés remembers a sentence from the song: "*j'ai dans mon coeur une tristesse affreuse*" (*Jardín* 33; I have an awful sadness in my heart).

5 Here I use the term in a non-Freudian sense and as synonymous with *distressing*.

6 See Xavier Moret's *Tiempo de editores. Historia de la edición en España, 1939–1975* (Time of Publishers. A History of Publishing in Spain), pp. 168–74.

7 It is important to highlight the complexity of this Oedipal scenario, given that it engages but also goes beyond Freudian theory: To start with, the literary text offers a more complicated account than the usual role of the father in separating the child from the mother. Moreover, Freud's notion, much challenged by feminist critics, that the little girl learns to separate from the mother, not by becoming the father as is the case with the boy but by desiring a child from the father and becoming heterosexual, is rewritten here by inserting the death of the father as a central element in order for the daughter to become a writer. While Janés's giving birth to the text could be interpreted as an expression of the desire to have a child by the father, giving birth to the text is also an act of identification with the mother and only takes place once the father is dead. Janés's narration shows as well the great complexity of the mother–daughter relationship and the father–mother–daughter triad, in which, in fact, each individual is interdependent on the others.

8 Janés suggests in *Jardín* that moving outside of Barcelona was the mother's decision: "Hubo una madre, viuda reciente, que alejó a su

hija mayor del núcleo familiar" (*Jardín* 53; There was a mother, recently widowed, who isolated her oldest daughter from the immediate family).

9 One definition in the Real Academia Española is "Extranjerismo no incorporado totalmente al idioma" (Foreign term not fully incorporated into the language). According to the Diccionari de la Enciclopèdia Catalana, "forma lingüística particularment lèxica, dins una llengua determinada, d'origen estranger, i normativament rebutjada" (particularly lexical linguistic form, within a given language, of foreign origin, and normatively rejected).

10 See Masanet, 207.

11 According to the autobiographical self, Janés had read Holan's *Una noche con Hamlet* four years before meeting him "primera visita a Praga en julio de 1975 … por entonces hacía cuatro años que conocía el libro" (*La voz* 37; my first visit to Prague in that July of 1975 … By then, I had known the book for four years). For more on Holan as writer and the reception of his work in Spain, see Guillermo Carnero's "Prólogo" (7–10) to Vladimir Holan. *Una noche con Hamlet y otros poemas* (Barcelona: Barral editores 1970); Janés's *Antología* of the works of Holan (Barcelona: Plazá & Janés Editores, 1983) as well as Jaume Creus i del Castillo's anthology Holan, Vladimír. *L'alè de cada nit. Antologia poètica*. (The Breath of Every Night. Poetic Anthology; Sant Esteve Sesrovires: Edicions la Guineu, 2005). Illuminating as well is Janés's article published in *Quimera*. "Holan, del otro lado del abismo" (22–5; Holan, on the other side of abyss).

12 In a 1985 interview with Helena Golanó published in *Ínsula*, Janés described the island of Kampa as a solitary inward space and a doorway to the self that no one can fully control or censor. She also explained that she shared with Holan this need for loneliness, isolation, and pain, which enabled both to write (8–9). In certain ways, Holan also resembles the self-"exiled" Spaniards during the dictatorship who neither left the country nor supported the regime but rather withdrew from society.

13 In its republication as part of the poetic anthology *Poesía erótica y amorosa*, *Kampa* includes a sung version of one of its sections, Kampa II "ar," sung by Clara Janés herself.

14 In Premat's own words in *Héroes sin atributos* (Heroes with no Attributes; 2009), "La identidad de un autor estaría caracterizada por la presencia simultánea de imperativos contradictorios (la afirmación de una singularidad y de cierta pertenencia a una colectividad, la reivindicación de una filiación y de un autoengendramiento, la ambivalencia entre la marginalidad y la integración, etc.), contradicciones que conllevan la necesidad, a cada paso de una carrera literaria, de afianzar y reconstruir el 'ser escritor'" (11; The identity of an author would be characterized by the simultaneous presence of contradictory imperatives (the affirmation

of a singularity and true belonging to a community, the claim of a filiation and of a self-begetting, the ambivalence between marginality and integration, etc.), contradictions that lead to the need, at every step of a literary career, to strengthen and rebuild "being a writer").

15 Nadia Mékouar-Hertzberg reads Cordelia and Ophelia as two interwoven figures (33). Faszer-MacMahon, on the other hand, highlights how Cordelia in *En busca de Cordelia* (Looking for Cordelia) and Ophelia in *La voz de Ofelia* are intertexual references to Holan's text *Una noche con Hamlet* and explains that "*En busca de Cordelia* posits being as a continual process of death and new life" (29–30). We cannot forget that, in Shakespeare's King Lear, Cordelia is a daughter who is treated unfairly by the father.

16 The extent to which the father's ghost and Claudius are interchangeable figures, at least with regard to Hamlet's feeling somehow relieved after Claudius has killed his father, depends on how deep we go with a psychoanalytical reading.

17 As a literary critic, Janés has also published works such as *La vida callada de Federico Mompou* (Federico Mompou's Quiet Life; 1975), *Cirlot, el no mundo y la poesía imaginal* (Cirlot, the Non-world and Imaginal Poetry; 1996), *El espejo de la noche. A Vladimir Holan en su centenario* (The Mirror of the Night. To Vladimir Holan on His Centenary; 2005), and *Las primeras poetisas en lengua castellana* (The First Woman Poets Writing in Spanish; 1986). Her work as literary critic is also remarkable; she has written about Eduardo Cirlot, Federico Mompou, Vladimír Holan, María Zambrano, and Antonio Gamoneda and has published on the place of women writers – see, for instance, her book *Guardar la casa y cerrar la boca* (Look After the House and Keep Your Mouth Shut).

18 I am borrowing these terms in conjunction – filial deference and parricidal defiance – from the work of Heather Cleary (126).

Works Cited

Abellán, Manuel. *Censura y creación literaria en España (1939–1976).* Edicions 62, 1980.

Abraham, Nicolas, Maria Torok, and Nicholas T. Rand. *The Shell and the Kernel: Renewals of Psychoanalysis.* University of Chicago Press, 1994.

Agamben, Giorgio. *Infancy and History: On the Destruction of Experience.* Verso, 1993.

Alberca, Manuel. *La máscara o la vida: de la autoficción a la antificción.* Pálido fuego, 2017.

Allodi, Federico. "Historia del psicoanálisis en España y sus contrastes con el mundo Anglófono." *Actas Españolas de Psiquiatría,* vol. 40, no. 2, 2012, pp. 1–9.

Almeida, Diane M. *The Esperpento Tradition in the Works of Ramón del Valle-Inclán and Luis Buñuel.* E. Mellen Press, 2000.

Ariza, Fernando González. "The Entry of Juan Goytisolo in the American Publishing Market." *Journal of Iberian and Latin American Studies,* vol. 19, no. 3, 2013, pp. 265–76.

Arkinstall, Christine. "Towards a Female Symbolic: Re-Presenting Mothers and Daughters in Contemporary Spanish Narrative by Women." *Writing Mothers and Daughters: Renegotiating the Mother in Western European Narratives by Women,* edited by Adalgisa Giorgio, Berghahn, 2002, pp. 47–84.

Ayén, Xavi. *Aquellos años del boom: García Márquez, Vargas Llosa y el grupo de amigos que lo cambiaron todo.* RBA, 2014.

Bachelard, Gaston. *The Poetics of Space.* Beacon Press, 1972.

Barral, Carlos. *Almanaque.* Cuatro Ediciones, 2000.

– *Catalunya a vol d'ocell.* Edicions 62, 1985.

– *Catalunya des del mar: pel car de fora.* Edicions 62, 1982.

– "Debate con Carlos Barral." *Revista de occidente,* vol. 110–11, 1990, pp. 148–60.

– *El azul del infierno.* Seix Barral, 1992.

– *La mar domèstica del llibre Catalunya des del mar.* Cyan, 1998.

– *Las aguas reiteradas.* Laye, 1952.

– *Lecciones de cosas. Veinte poemas para el nieto Malcolm.* Penísula, 1986.
– *Memorias.* Lumen, 2015.
– *Metropolitano: Diecinueve figuras de mi historia civil.* Orbis, 1985.
– *Observaciones desde la mina de plomo.* Lumen, 2002.
– *Poesía completa.* Lumen, 1998.
– "Privilegio de la galera." *Revista de occidente,* vol. 110–11, 1990, pp. 141–7.
Basilio, Miriam. "Genealogies for a New State: Painting and Propaganda in Franco's Spain, 1936–1940." *Discourse,* vol. 24, no. 3, 2002, pp. 67–94.
Becker-Leckrone, Megan. *Julia Kristeva and Literary Theory.* Palgrave Macmillan, 2005.
Benjamin, Jessica. *The Bonds of Love: Psychoanalysis, Feminism, and the Problem of Domination.* Pantheon, 1988.
Bennett, Kane. *Vibrant Matter. A Political Ecology of Things.* Duke University Press, 2010.
Benstock, Shari. "Authorizing the Autobiographical." *The Private Self: Theory and Practice of Women's Autobiographical Writings,* edited by Shari Benstock, University of North Carolina Press, 1988, pp. 10–33.
Bergmann, Emilie L. "Mothers and Daughters in Transition and Beyond." *Mirrors and Echoes. Women's Writing in Twentieth-Century Spain,* edited by Emilie Bergmann and Richard Herr, University of California Press, 2007, pp. 108–20.
Bettaglio, Marina. "Caring Masculinities and Feminist Fathering in Contemporary Spain." Article under consideration. 27 pages.
Bloom, Harold. *The Anxiety of Influence. A Theory of Poetry.* Oxford University Press, 1997.
Bonet, Laureano. *Jardín quebrado: la escuela de Barcelona y la cultura de medio siglo.* Península, 1994.
Bonilla, Juan. *El tiempo es un sueño pop. Vida y obra de Terenci Moix.* RBA, 2012.
Borneman, John. *The Death of the Father: An Anthropology of the End in Political Authority.* Berghahn Books, 2004.
Bou, Enric. *Papers Privats: Assaig sobre les formes literàries autobriogràfiques.* Edicions 62, 1993.
Bourdieu, Pierre. *Language and Symbolic Power.* Harvard University Press, 1991.
Braidotti, Rosi. *Nomadic Subjects: Embodiment and Sexual Difference in Contemporary Feminist Theory.* Columbia University Press, 2011.
Brown, Bill. "Thing Theory." *Critical Inquiry,* vol. 28, no. 1, Autumn 2001, pp. 1–22.
Buckley, Ramón. *La doble Transición: Política y literatura en la España de los años setenta.* Siglo XXI, 1996.
Bueno, Eva P., Terry Caesar, and William Hummel. *Naming the Father: Legacies, Genealogies, and Explorations of Fatherhood in Modern and Contemporary Literature.* Lexington, 2000.
Butler, Judith. *Precarious Life: The Powers of Mourning and Violence.* Verso, 2006.

– *The Psychic Life of Power: Theories in Subjection*. Stanford University Press, 1997.

Caballé, Anna. "La sinceridad de un libro." *El País*, 5 June 2017, https://elpais.com/cultura/2017/06/04/actualidad/1496600118_046253.html.

Calvo, Lluís. "El Mediterrani, l'Alguer i l'Etnografia Catalana Noucentista: Una recerca etnogràfico-lingüística a l'Alguer (1922)." *Revista de l'Alguer*, vol. 9, no. 9, 1998, pp. 11–19.

Carnero, Guillermo. Prólogo. *Una noche con Hamlet y otros poemas*, by Vladimir Holan. Translated by Josef Forbelsky, Barral editores, 1970, pp. 7–10.

Carsten, Janet. *After Kinship*. Cambridge University Press, 2004.

Caruso Mortola Gilbert, Sandra, and Susan Dreyfuss David Gubar. "Ceremonies of the Alphabet: femela Grandmatologies and the Female Autograph." *The Female Autograph: Theory and Practice of Autobiography from the Tenth to the Twentieth Century*, edited by Domna C. Stanton, University of Chicago Press, 1987, pp. 21–48.

Castañeda, Luis H. "De padres e hijos: la construcción (auto)biográfica del prestigio artístico en *Tiempo de vida*, de Marcos Giralt Torrente." *Revista Canadiense de Estudios Hispánicos*, vol. 37, no. 3, 2013, pp. 459–79.

Castellet, Josep Maria. *Nueve novísimos poetas españoles*. Barral Editores, 1970.

Catelli, Nora. *En la era de la intimidad: Seguido de El espacio autobiográfico*. Beatriz Viterbo, 2007.

Cestaro, Gary P. *Dante and the Grammar of the Nursing Body*. University of Notre Dame Press, 2003.

Chamouleau, Brice. *Tiran al maricón: los fantasmas "queer" de la democracia (1970–1988): una interpretación de las subjetividades gais ante el Estado español*. Ediciones Akal, 2017.

Chodorow, Nancy. *The Reproduction of Mothering: Psychoanalysis and the Sociology of Gender*. University of California Press, 1999.

Cleary, Heather. "Of Monsters and Parricides: The Politics of Textual Reproduction." *Hispanic Review*, vol. 83, no. 2, 2015, pp. 123–41.

Cleto, Fabio. "Introduction: Queering the Camp." *Camp: Queer Aesthetics and The Performing Subject. A Reader*, edited by Fabio Cleto, Edinburg University Press, 1991, pp. 1–42.

Clifford, James. *The Predicament of Culture: Twentieth-century Ethnography, Literature, and Art*. Harvard University Press, 1988.

Cooper, Sarah E. "Introduction: Questioning Family Dynamics and Family Discourse in Hispanic Literature and Film." *The Ties That Bind: Questioning Family Dynamics and Family Discourse in Hispanic Literature*, edited by Sarah Cooper, University Press of America, 2004, pp. 1–49.

Couser, G. Thomas "Genre Matters: Form, Force, and Filiation." *Life Writing*, vol. 1, no. 2, 2005, pp. 139–56.

Crameri, Kathryn. *Catalonia: National Identity and Cultural Policy, 1980–2003*. University of Wales Press, 2008.

– "Constructing a Bridge between Cultures: Catalan Cultural Policy and the New Immigration." *Border Crossings. Mapping Identities in Modern Europe*, edited by Peter Wagstaff, Peter Lang, 2004, pp. 145–68.
– *Language, the Novelist and National Identity in Post-Franco Catalonia*. Legenda, 2000.
Cuevas, Efrén. "El cine autobiográfico en España: una panorámica" *RILCE*, vol. 28, no. 1, 2012, pp. 106–25.
Culleton, Colleen. *Literary Labyrinths in Franco-Era Barcelona: Narrating Memory and Place*. Routledge, 2016.
Dalmau, Miguel. *Los Goytisolo*. Anagrama, 1999.
Davis, Robert Con, ed. *The Fictional Father. Lacanian Readings of the Text*. University of Massachusetts Press, 1981.
Davis, Rocío G. "Writing Fathers: Auto/biography and Unfulfilled Vocation in Sara Suleri Goodyear's *Boys Will Be Boys* and Hanif Kureishi's *My Ear at His Heart*." *Life Writing*, vol. 6, no. 2, 2009, pp. 229–41.
Davis, Stuart. "Que(e)rying Spain: On the Limits and Possibilities of Queer Theory in Hispanism." *Reading Iberia. Theory/ History/ Identity*, edited by Helena Buffery, Stuart Davis, and Kirsty Hooper, Peter Lang, 2007, 63–78.
Derrida, Jacques. *The Gift of Death*. Chicago: University of Chicago Press, 1995.
Douglas, Mary. *Purity and Danger. An Analysis of the Concepts of Pollution and Taboo*. Routledge, 1996.
Dravasa, Mayder. *The Boom in Barcelona: Literary Modernism in Spanish and Spanish-American Fiction (1950–1974)*. Peter Lang, 2005.
Eakin, Paul J. Foreword. *Autobiography*, by Philippe Lejeune, University of Minnesota Press, 1989, pp. vii–xxviii.
– *Living Autobiographically: How We Create Identity in Narrative*. Cornell University Press, 2008.
Edwards, Jorge. "El mar de la memoria." *Revista de occidente*, vol. 110–11, 1990, pp. 79–84.
Egea, Juan. "*El Desencanto*: La mirada del padre y las lecturas de la Transición." *Symposium: A Quarterly Journal in Modern Literatures*, vol. 58, no. 2, 2004, pp. 79–92.
Ellis, Robert Richmond. *The Hispanic Homograph. Gay Self-Representation in Contemporary Spanish Autobiography*. University of Illinois Press, 1997.
Engelson Marson, Ellen. "Clara Janés: Mysticism and the Search for the Female Poetic Voice." *Revista de Estudios Hispánicos*, vol. 29, no. 2, 1995, pp. 245–58
Enterline, Lynn. *The Tears of Narcissus: Melancholia and Masculinity in Early Modern Writing*. Stanford University Press, 1995
Epps, Bradley S. *Significant Violence: Oppression and Resistance in the Narratives of Juan Goytisolo, 1970–1990*. Clarendon, 1996.
Faszer-MacMahon, Debra. *Cultural Encounters in Contemporary Spain. The Poetry of Clara Janés*. Bucknell University Press, 2010.

Fernández, James. "La novela familiar del autobiógrafo: Juan Goytisolo." *Anthropos*, vol. 125, 1991, pp. 55–60.

Fernàndez, Josep-Anton. *Another Country: Sexuality and National Identity in Catalan Gay Fiction*. Maney Pub. for the Modern Humanities Research Association, 2000.

– *El malestar en la cultura catalana*. Empúries, 2008.

Fernández, Julio L. *Los enigmas del caudillo: Perfiles desconocidos de un dictador temeroso e implacable*. Nuer, 1992.

Ferrer i Alòs, Llorenç. "When There Was No Male Heir: The Transfer of Wealth through Women in Catalonia (the *Pubilla*)." *Continuity and Change*, vol. 20, no. 1, 2005, pp. 27–52.

Flinn, Caryl. "The Deaths of Camp." *Camp: Queer Aesthetics and the Performing Subject. A Reader*, edited by Fabio Cleto, Edinburg University Press, 1991, pp. 433–57.

Forrest, Gene Steven. "El mundo antagónico de Terenci Moix." *Hispania*, vol. 60, no. 4, 1977, pp. 927–35.

Foucault, Michel. "Self Writing." *Ethics: Subjectivity and Truth*, The New York Press, 1997, pp. 207–22.

Freud, Sigmund. *Civilization and Its Discontents*. Norton, 2005.

– *The Ego and the Id*. Norton, 1960.

– "Mourning and Melancholia." *Collected Papers*, vol. 4, translated by Joan Riviere, Hogarth, 1959, 152–70.

– *Totem and Taboo*. Routledge, 1999.

Freud, Sigmund, David McLintock, and Hugh Haughton. *The Uncanny*. Penguin Books, 2003.

Fuster, Joan. *Literatura catalana contemporánea*. Editorial Nacional, 1975.

Gallop, Jane. *The Daughter's Seduction: Feminism and Psychoanalysis*. Cornell University Press, 1982.

– *Thinking through the Body*. Columbia University Press, 1988.

Gámez, Fuentes M.J. *Cinematergrafía: La madre en el cine y la literatura de la Democracia*. Castelló de la Plana: Universitat Jaume I, 2004.

Garland Thomson, Rosemary. *Extraordinary Bodies*. Columbia University Press, 1997.

Gil Calvo, Enrique. *Máscaras masculinas. Héroes, patriarcas y monstruos*. Anagrama, 2006.

Gilbert, Sandra, and Susan Gubar. *The Madwoman in the Attic: The Woman Writer and the Nineteenth-Century Literary Imagination*. Yale University Press, 2000.

Gimferrer, Pere. Prólogo. *El peso de la paja. El cine de los sábados*, by Terenci Moix, Plaza y Janés, 1990, pp. 17–20.

Girard, René. *Violence and the Sacred*. Johns Hopkins University Press, 1977.

Golanó, Helena. "Entrevista con Clara Janés." *Ínsula*, vol. 461, 1986, pp. 8–9.

Gould Levine, Linda. "Resonancias literarias en *Telón de boca* de Juan Goytisolo." *Bulletin of Spanish Studies* vol. 83, no. 6, 2006, pp. 815–38.
Goytisolo, Juan. "Discurso de Juan Goytisolo en Europalia." *Anthropos. Revista de documentación científica de la cultura*, vol. 60–1, 1986, pp. 44–50.
– *Genet en el Raval*. Círculo de lectores, 2009.
– "Lectura familiar de *Antagonía*." *Quimera*, vol. 32, no. 10, 1983, pp. 38–45.
– *Memorias. Coto vedado. En los reinos de taifa*. Península, 2002.
– "In Memoriam, F.F.B. 1892–1975." *El ruedo ibérico*, vol. 46–8, Julio-diciembre 1975, pp. 160–4.
– Prólogo. *Los Goytisolo. Una próspera familia de indianos*, by Martín Rodrigo y Alharilla, Marcial Pons Historia, 2016, pp. 15–18.
– *Telón de boca*. El Aleph editores, 2003.
Goytisolo, Luis. *El sueño de San Luis*. Anagrama, 2015.
Gracia, Jordi and Domingo Ródenas. *Historia de la literatura española. Derrota y restitución de la modernidad*. Crítica, 2011.
Green, André. *Hamlet et Hamlet*. Balland, 1982.
Green, André, and Dominique Cupa, editors. *Image du père dans la culture contemporaine: Hommages À André Green*. Presses universitaires de France, 2008.
Grigg, Russell. *Lacan, Language, and Philosophy*. State University of New York Press, 2008.
Grosz, Elizabeth. *Jacques Lacan. A Feminist Introduction*. Routledge, 1990.
– *Volatile Bodies. Toward a Corporeal Feminism*. Indiana University Press, 1994.
Grugel, Jean and Tim Rees. *Franco's Spain*. Arnold, 1997.
Guenther, Lisa. *The Gift of the Other: Levinas and the Politics of Reproduction*. State of New York Press, 2006.
Gusdorf, Georges. "Conditions and Limits of Autobiography." *Autobiography, Essays Theoretical and Critical*, edited by James Onley, Princeton University Press, 1980, pp. 28–48.
Harvey, Jessamy. "The Value of Nostalgia: Reviving Memories of National-Catholic Childhoods," *Journal of Spanish Cultural Studies*, vol. 2, no. 1, 2001, pp. 109–18.
Heffernan, Carol F. *The Melancholy Muse: Chaucer, Shakespeare, and Early Medicine*. Duquesne University Press, 1995.
Heinemann, Ute. *Novel.la entre dues llengües. El dilema català o castella*. Reichenberger, 1996.
Hemingway, Ernest. *The Old Man and the Sea*. Scribner, 1952.
Herralde, Jorge. "Un deseo imposible." *Detrás del arco iris. En busca de Terenci Moix*, edited by Juan Ramón Iborra, Planeta, 2004, pp. 346–52.
Herrero-Olaizola, Alejandro. *The Censorship Files: Latin American Writers and Franco's Spain*. State University of New York Press, 2007.
– "Consuming Aesthetics: Seix Barral and José Donoso in the Field of Latin American Literary Production." *MLN*, vol. 115, no. 2, 2000, pp. 323–39.

– "Publishing Matters: The Latin American 'Boom' and the Rules of Censorship." *Arizona Journal of Hispanic Cultural Studies*, vol. 9, 2005, pp. 193–205.

Herzberger, David. *Narrating the Past: Fiction and Historiography in Postwar Spain*. Duke University Press, 1995.

Holan, Vladimír. *L'alè de cada nit. Antologia poètica*. Translated by Jaume Creus i del Castillo, Edicions la Guineu, 2005, pp. 7–10.

Hurtley, Jacqueline. *Josep Janés: el combat per la cultura*. Curial, 1986.

Iborra, Juan Ramón. *Detrás del arco iris. En busca de Terenci Moix*. Planeta, 2004.

Irigaray, Luce. "The Bodily Encounter with the Mother." *The Irigaray Reader*, edited by Margaret Whitford, Blackwell, 1991, pp. 34–46.

– *Sexes and Genealogies*. Columbia University Press, 1993.

Janés, Clara. *Cirlot, el no mundo y la poesía imaginal*. Huerga & Fierro, 1996.

– "Holan, del otro lado del abismo." *Quimera*, vol. 28, 1983, pp. 22–5.

– *Jardín y laberinto*. Debate, 1990.

– *La vida callada de Federico Mompou*. Ariel, 1975.

– *La voz de Ofelia*. Siruela, 2005.

– *Poesía erótica y amorosa*. Vaso Roto, 2010.

– Prólogo. *Antología*, by Vladimir Holan, Plazá & Janés Editores, 1983, pp. 9–49.

– "Secreto y sustrato." Université de Pau et des Pays de l'Adour. Pau, France. 13 June 2012. Conference Talk.

– *Vivir*. Madrid: Hiperión, 1983.

Jaume, Andreu. "El escritor Carlos Barral." *Memorias* by Carlos Barral, Lumen, 2015, pp. 9–28.

Jensen, Merete Stistrup. "La notion de nature dans les théories de l'«écriture féminine»." *Clio. Femmes, Genre, Histoire*, vol. 11, 2000, pp. 1–10.

Julià, Jordi. "El taller de Calafell. Sobre el mite de la infantesa a Barral, Gil de Biedma i Ferrater." *Barralianas. Homenaje a Carlos Barral*, edited by Germán Cánovas and Carme Riera, Academia del Hispanismo, 2010, pp. 137–58.

Keefe Ugalde, Sharon. "El mito de Ofelia en la obra narrativa de Clara Janés." *Myth and Subversion in the Contemporary Novel*, edited by José Manuel Losada Goya and Marta Guirao Ochoa, Cambridge Scholars Publishing, 2012, pp. 407–20.

– "La subjetividad desde "lo otro" en la poesía de María Sanz, María Victoria Atencia y Clara Janés." *Revista Canadiense de Estudios Hispánicos*, vol. 14, no. 3, 1990, pp. 511–23.

Kim, Yeon-Soo. *The Family Album: Histories, Subjectivities, and Immigration in Contemporary Spanish Culture*. Bucknell University Press, 2005.

Kinder, Marsha. *Blood Cinema. The Reconstruction of National Identity in Spain*. University of California Press, 1993.

King, Stewart. *Escribir la catalanidad. Lenguas e identidades en la narrativa contemporánea de Cataluña*. Tamesis, 2005.

Kristeva, Julia. *Revolution in Poetic Language*. Columbia University Press, 1984.

– "The Subject in Process" *The Tel Quel Reader*, edited by Patrick French and Roland-François Lack, Routledge, 1998, pp. 133–78.

– *Tales of Love*. Columbia University Press, 1987.

Labanyi, Jo. "The Construction/Destruction of the Self in the Autobiographies of Pablo Neruda and Juan Goytisolo." *Forum for Modern Language Studies*, vol. 26, no. 3, 1990, pp. 212–21.

– "Los fantasmas del pasado y las seducciones del psicoanálisis: *El desencanto* (Jaime Chávarri, 1976)." *El cine y la transición política en España* (1975–1982), edited by Manuel Palacio Arranz, Biblioteca Nueva, 2011, pp. 73–85.

Lacan, Jacques. "Beyond the Oedipus Complex." *The Seminar of Jacques Lacan. Book XVII. The Other Side of Psychoanalysis*. Norton, 2007, pp. 86–140.

– *Las formaciones del inconsciente. Seguido de "El deseo y su interpretación."* Nueva Visión, 1977.

– "The Signification of the Phallus." *Écrits. The First Complete Edition in English*. Norton, 2006, pp. 575–84.

Laqueur, Thomas. "The Facts of Fatherhood." *Conflicts in Feminism*, edited by Marianne Hirsch and Evelyn F. Keller, Routledge, 1990, pp. 205–21.

Lange, Monique. *Casetas de baño*. Taller del libro, 2015.

Latour, Bruno. *We Have Never Been Modern*. Harvard University Press, 1993.

Lejeune, Philippe. *On Autobiography*. Minnesota University Press, 1988.

Levinas. *Totality and Infinity*. Kluwer Academic Publishers, 1991.

Loureiro, Ángel G. "España maníaca." *Quimera: Revista de literatura*, vol. 167, 1998, pp. 15–20.

– *The Ethics of Autobiography: Replacing the Subject in Modern Spain*. Vanderbilt University Press, 2000.

– "Inconsolable Memory." *Hispanic Issues On Line*, vol. 10, 2012, pp. 100–22.

– "Pathetic Arguments." *Journal of Spanish Cultural Studies*, vol. 9, no. 2, 2008, pp. 225–37.

Luengo, Ana. "La última victoria del Franquismo: el *oikos* como patria, el *despot* como padre." *Hispanic Issues On Line*, vol. 19, 2017, pp. 26–43.

Mainer, José-Carlos. *Tramas, libros, nombres: para entender la literatura española, 1944–2000*. Anagrama, 2005.

Mann, Bonnie. *Sovereign Masculinity: Gender Lessons from the War on Terror*. Oxford University Press, 2014.

Mann, Susan Archer. *Doing Feminist Theory: From Modernity to Postmodernity*. Oxford University Press, 2012.

Marañón, Gregorio. *Amiel. Don Juan*. Austral, 2008.

Marcus, Laura. *Auto/biographical Discourses: Theory, Criticism, Practice*. Manchester University Press, 1994.

Martínez Martín, Jesús A. "La autarquía editoral. Los años cuarenta y cincuenta." *Historia de la edición en España* (1939–1975), edited by Jesús A. Martínez Marín, Marcial Pons, 2015, pp. 233–71.

Masanet, Lydia. *La autobiografía femenina española*. Fundamentos, 1998.

Medina, Domínguez A. *Exorcismos de la memoria: Políticas y poéticas de la melancolía en la España de la Transición*. Libertarias, 2001.

Mékouar-Hertzberg, Nadia. *Une autre écriture de l'intimité: les jardins et les labyrinthes de Clara Janés*. Harmattan, 2012.

Mengual, Josep. *A dos tintas: Josep Janés, editor y poeta*. Debate, 2013.

Mira, Alberto. "El niño queer en *El peso de la paja* de Terenci Moix." Masculinidades disidentes, edited by Rafael M. Mérida Jiménez, Icaria, 2016, pp. 185–206.

– *De Sodoma a Chueca. Una historia cultural de la homosexualidad en España en el siglo* XX. Eagles, 2004.

Moix, Ana María "Una broma amarga." *Detrás del arco iris. En busca de Terenci Moix,* edited by Juan Ramón Iborra, Planeta, 2004, pp. 226–37.

– *Julia*. Seix Barral, 1970.

Moix, Terenci. *El dia que va morir Marylin*. Edicions 62, 1981.

– *El sadismo de nuestra infancia*. Kairós, 1974.

– *Lleonard o El sexe dels àngels: una història catalana*. Planeta, 1992.

– *Memorias. El peso de la Paja. El cine de los sábados*. Plaza y Janés, 1990.

– *Memorias. El Peso de la Paja/2. El beso de Peter Pan*. Planeta, 1998.

Molero de la Iglesia, Alicia. *La autoficción en España: Jorge Semprún, Carlos Barral, Luis Goytisolo, Enriqueta Antolín y Antonio Muñoz Molina*. Peter Lang, 2000.

Moliner, María. *Diccionario de uso del español*. Gredos, 2007.

Morales Rivera, Santiago. *Anatomía del desencanto: humor, ficción y melancolía en España, 1976–1998*. Purdue University Press, 2017.

– "La imaginación desmadrada de Juan José Millás: humor y melancolía en *La soledad era esto." Revista hispánica moderna*, vol. 64, no. 2, 2011, pp. 129–48.

Morcillo, Aurora G. *The Seduction of Modern Spain*. Bucknell University Press, 2010.

Moreiras Menor, Cristina. *Cultura herida. Cultura y cine en la España democrática*. Libertarias, 2002.

– "Juan Goytisolo, F.F.B. y la fundación fantasmal del proyecto autobiográfico contemporáneo español." *MLN*, vol. 111, no. 2, 1996, pp. 327–45.

– *La estela del tiempo: imagen e historicidad en el cine español contemporáneo*. Iberoamericana-Vervuert, 2011.

Moret, Xavier. *Tiempo de editores. Historia de la edición en España, 1939–1975*. Destino, 2002.

Nichols, Geraldine. "Reproducción, familia y futuro: cuatro denuncias en clave femenina." *Mirrors and Echoes. Women's Writing in Twentieth-Century*

Spain, edited by Emilie Bergmann and Richard Herr, University of California Press, 2007, pp. 121–35.

O'Donoghue, Samuel. "Two Abortive Beginnings and the Search for a Literary Father in Juan Goytisolo's *Señas de identidad*." *Romance Notes*, vol. 55, no. 2, 2015, pp. 301–11.

Oliart, Alberto. "Carlos Barral: el hombre y el escritor (Recuerdos y consideraciones)." *Revista de occidente*, vol. 110–11, 1990, pp. 21–50.

Oliver, Kelly. *Family Values: Subjects between Nature and Culture*. Routledge, 1997.

– *Reading Kristeva*. Indiana University Press, 1993.

– *Subjectivity without Subjects: From Abject Fathers to Desiring Mothers*. Rowman and Littlefield, 1998.

Pallares-Barbera, Montserrat, and Antònia Casellas. "Social Networks as the Backbone of Women's Work in the Catalan Pyrenees." *European Urban and Regional Studies*, vol. 26, no. 1, 2019, pp. 65–79.

Parker, Andrew. *The Theorist's Mother*. Duke University Press, 2012.

Pasero, Anne M. "Clara Janés." *Spanish Women Writers: A Bio-Bibliographical Source Book*, edited by Linda G. Levine, Ellen E. Marson, and Gloria Waldman, Greenwood Press, 1993, pp. 230–41.

– Introduction. *Ophelia's Voice*, by Clara Janés, translation and critical edition by Anne M. Pasero, University Press of the South, 2011, pp. 9–72.

Pavlovic, Tatjana. *Despotic Bodies and Transgressive Bodies: Spanish Culture from Francisco Franco to Jesús Franco*. State University of New York Press, 2003.

Peregil, Francisco. *Goytisolo en su amargo final*. El País, 10 June 2017, https://elpais.com/cultura/2017/06/09/actualidad/1497010964_177086.html.

Pérez Molina, Isabel. "Pubillas y caballeras en la Cataluña moderna." *Obradoiro de historia moderna*, vol. 10, 2001, pp. 73–88.

Phelan, James. *Living to Tell about it: A Rhetoric and Ethics of Character Narration*. Cornell University Press, 2005.

Pla, Xavier. *Josep Pla, ficció autobiogràfica i veritat literaria*. Quaderns Crema, 1997.

Pope, Randolph D. "Juan Goytisolo y la tradición autobiográfica española." *Revista chilena de literatura*, vol. 41, 1992, pp. 25–32.

– *Understanding Juan Goytisolo*. University of South Carolina Press, 1995.

Premat, Julio. *Héroes sin atributos: figuras de autor en la literatura argentina*. Fondo de Cultura Económica, 2009.

Prout, Ryan. *Fear and Gendering: Pedophobia, Effeminophobia, and Hypermasculine Desire in the Work of Juan Goytisolo*. Peter Lang, 2001.

Puccini, Dario. "Carlos Barral en mis recuerdos y en su poesía." *Revista de occidente*, vol. 110–11, 1990, pp. 85–92.

Ramírez-Christensen, Esperanza. "Introduction." *The Father-Daughter Plot: Japanese Literary Women and the Law of the Father*, edited by Rebecca L.

Copeland and Esperanza Ramírez-Christensen, Hawai'i University Press, 2001, pp. 1–24.

Ramos, Carlos. "Terenci Moix. De la transición heroica a la seducción de masas." *(En) claves de la Transición. Una visión de los Novísimos. Prosa, poesía, ensayo*, edited by Enric Bou and Elide Pittarello, Iberoamericana, 2009, pp. 79–128.

Resina, Joan Ramon. "'Escribo en castellano porque me gusta' – Juan Marsé o Joan Marés: La literatura entre dos lenguas." *Escribir entre dos lenguas. Escritores catalanes y la elección de la lengua literaria. Escriure entre dues llengües. Escriptors catalans i l'elecció de la llengua literària*, edited by Arnau i Segarra, Pilar, Pere Joan Tous, and Manfred Tietz, Reichenberg, 2002, pp. 101–9.

– "L'imaginari mascle i el mascle imaginari." *Calçasses, gallines i maricons*, edited by Josep-Anton Fernàndez i Adrià Chavarria, Angle, 2003, pp. 58–77.

Ribeiro de Mendezes, Alison. *Juan Goytisolo: The Author as Dissident*. Támesis, 2005.

Riera, Carme. "Carlos Barral, entre vida y literatura: el mundo mítico de Calafell." *Barralianas. Homenaje a Carlos Barral*, edited by Germán Cánovas and Carme Riera, Academia del Hispanismo, 2010, pp. 23–7.

– "Imágenes barcelonesas en dos poetas metropolitanos." *Revista de occidente*, 110–11, 1990, pp. 57–72.

– *La escuela de Barcelona*. Anagrama, 1988.

– *La obra poética de Carlos Barral*. Ediciones Península, 1990.

– Prólogo. *Los diarios, 1957–1989*, by Carlos Barral, Anaya & Mario Muchnick, 1993, pp. 1–33.

– Prólogo. *Poesía completa*, by Carlos Barral, Lumen, 1998, pp. 7–55.

Rincón, Aintzane. *Representaciones del género en el cine español (1939–1982): Figuras y fisuras*. Universidad de Santiago de Compostela, 2014.

Rodrigo y Alharilla, Martín. *Los Goytisolo. Una próspera familia de indianos*. Marcial Pons, 2016.

Rodríguez Marcos, Javier. *Goytisolo explica a Goytisolo*. El País, 23 June 2017, https://elpais.com/cultura/2017/06/19/actualidad/1497886741_700543.html. Accessed 3 Aug. 2019.

– *Muere el escritor Juan Goytisolo a los 86 años en Marrakech*. El País, 5 June 2017, https://elpais.com/cultura/2017/06/04/actualidad/1496579528_592092.html. Accessed 20 Nov. 2020.

Rovira, Joan Castelló. "Entrevista a Carlos Barral, escriptor." *Impactes*, Ràdio Barcelona, 2 February 1981. Radio Interview.

Ruddick, Sarah. "Thinking about Fathers." *Conflicts in Feminism*, edited by Marianne Hirsch and Evelyn F. Keller, Routledge, 1990, pp. 222–33.

Sánchez-Barranco Ruiz, Antonio, et al. "Una contribución a la historia del psicoanálisis en España." *Apuntes de Psicología*, vol. 30, no. 1–3, 2012, pp. 165–74.

Sánchez Santiago, Tomás, and José Manuel Diego. *Dos poetas de la generación de los 50: Carlos Barral y José Ángel Valente*. Antonio Ubago, 1990.

Santana, Mario. *Foreigners in the Homeland: The Spanish American New Novel in Spain, 1962–1974*. Bucknell University Press, 2000.

Sausse-Korff, Simone. "Père biologique, père sexué, père symbolique." *Image du père dans la culture contemporaine: Hommages à André Green*, edited by André Green and Dominique Cupa, Presses universitaires de France, 2008, pp. 281–9.

Saval, José Vincete. *Carlos Barral, entre el esteticismo y la reivindicación*. Fundamentos Editorial, 2002.

– "Carlos Barral i la qüestió del llenguatge." *Journal of Catalan Studies*, vol. 14, 2011, pp. 165–72.

– "Carlos Barral's Publishing Adventure: The Cultural Opposition to Francoism and the Creation of the Latin-American Boom." *Bulletin of Hispanic Studies*, vol. 79, no. 2, 2002, pp. 205–11.

Schiesari, Juliana. *The Gendering of Melancholia: Feminism, Psychoanalysis, and the Symbolics of Loss in Renaissance Literature*. Cornell University Press, 1992.

Seco, Manuel. *Diccionario del español actual*, vol. 2. Aguilar, 1999.

Sieburth, Stephanie. *Inventig High and Low: Literature, Mass Culture, and Uneven Modernity in Spain*. Duke University Press, 1994.

Silverman, Kaja. *Male Subjectivity at the Margins*. Routledge, 1992.

Smith, Paul J. *Laws of Desire: Questions of Homosexuality in Spanish Writing and Film, 1960–1990*. Clarendon Press, 1992.

Smith, Sidonie. *A Poetics of Women's Autobiography: Marginality and the Fictions of Self-Representation*. Indiana University Press, 1987.

Smith, Sidonie, and Julia Watson. *Reading Autobiography. A Guide for Interpreting Life Narratives*. University of Minnesota Press, 2010.

Song, Rosi H. "From *Enfant Terrible* to Prodigal Son: Terenci Moix's Embrace of a Literary Tradition." *Journal of Spanish Cultural Studies*, vol. 5, no. 1, 2004, pp. 83–95.

Sontag, Susan. *Against Interpretation and Other Essays*. Farrar, Straus & Giroux, 1966.

Soriano, Elena. *El donjuanismo femenino*. Península, 2000.

Stafford, Katherine O. "Recuerda que soy tu criatura: de "francosteins" y su memoria." *Hispanic Issues On Line*, vol. 19, 2017, pp. 13–25.

Stallybrass, Peter, and Allon White. *The Politics and Poetics of Transgression*. Cornell University Press, 1986.

Stanton, Domna C. "Autogynography: Is the Subject Different?" *The Female Autograph: Theory and Practice of Autobiography from the Tenth to the Twentieth Century*, edited by Domna C. Stanton, University of Chicago Press, 1987, pp. 3–20.

Stistrup Jensen, Merete. "La notion de nature dans les théories de l'«écriture féminine." *CLIO* (blog). *Histoire, femmes et sociétés*, 9 November 2007, http://clio.revues.org/218.

Subirana, Jaume. *Construir con palabras. Escritores, literatura e identidad en Cataluña (1859–2019).* Cátedra, 2018.

Thiollière, Pierre. *Carlos Barral poète: la nature et la mer, miroirs du moi.* Presses universitaires de Franche-Comté, 2011.

Tola de Habich, Fernando, y Patricia Grieve. *Los españoles y el Boom.* Editorial Tiempo Nuevo, 1971.

Torres Begines, Concepción. *España vista desde el aire. Influencia del esperpento de Valle-Inclán en el cine de García Berlanga.* Universidad de Málaga, 2014.

Tubert, Silvia. "Introducción." *Figuras del padre,* edited by Silvia Tubert, Cátedra, 1997, pp. 7–30.

Tusquets, Esther. *Habíamos ganado la guerra.* Bruguera, 2007.

Vilarós, Teresa M. *El mono del desencanto. Una crítica cultural de la transición española (1973–1993).* Siglo Veintiuno, 1998.

Vila-Sanjuán, Sergio. *Otra Cataluña. Seis siglos de cultura catalana en castellano.* Destino, 2018.

Vilaseca, David. *Hindsight and the Real. Subjectivity in Gay Hispanic Autobiography.* Peter Lang, 2003.

– *Queer Events. Post-Deconstructive Subjectivities in Spanish Writing and Film, 1960s to 1990s.* Liverpool University Press, 2010.

Villamados, Alberto. *El discreto encanrto de la subversión. Una crítica cultural de la Gauche Divide.* Laetoli, 2011.

Weiss, Gail. *Body Images. Embodiment as Intercoporality.* Routledge, 1999.

Wilcox, John C. *Women Poets of Spain, 1960–1990.* University of Illinois Press, 1997.

Yaeger, Patricia, and Beth Kowaleski-Wallace, editors. *Refiguring the Father. New Feminist Readings of Patriarchy.* Southern Illinois University Press, 1989.

Yildiz, Yasemin. *Beyond the Mother Tongue: The Postmonolingual Condition.* Fordham University Press, 2012.

Index

Toronto Iberic

1 Anthony J. Cascardi, *Cervantes, Literature, and the Discourse of Politics*
2 Jessica A. Boon, *The Mystical Science of the Soul: Medieval Cognition in Bernardino de Laredo's Recollection Method*
3 Susan Byrne, *Law and History in Cervantes'* Don Quixote
4 Mary E. Barnard and Frederick A. de Armas (eds), *Objects of Culture in the Literature of Imperial Spain*
5 Nil Santiáñez, *Topographies of Fascism: Habitus, Space, and Writing in Twentieth-Century Spain*
6 Nelson Orringer, *Lorca in Tune with Falla: Literary and Musical Interludes*
7 Ana M. Gómez-Bravo, *Textual Agency: Writing Culture and Social Networks in Fifteenth-Century Spain*
8 Javier Irigoyen-García, *The Spanish Arcadia: Sheep Herding, Pastoral Discourse, and Ethnicity in Early Modern Spain*
9 Stephanie Sieburth, *Survival Songs: Conchita Piquer's* Coplas *and Franco's Regime of Terror*
10 Christine Arkinstall, *Spanish Female Writers and the Freethinking Press, 1879–1926*

11 Margaret Boyle, *Unruly Women: Performance, Penitence, and Punishment in Early Modern Spain*
12 Evelina Gužauskytė, *Christopher Columbus's Naming in the* diarios *of the Four Voyages (1492–1504): A Discourse of Negotiation*
13 Mary E. Barnard, *Garcilaso de la Vega and the Material Culture of Renaissance Europe*
14 William Viestenz, *By the Grace of God: Francoist Spain and the Sacred Roots of Political Imagination*
15 Michael Scham, Lector Ludens*: The Representation of Games and Play in Cervantes*
16 Stephen Rupp, *Heroic Forms: Cervantes and the Literature of War*
17 Enrique Fernandez, *Anxieties of Interiority and Dissection in Early Modern Spain*
18 Susan Byrne, *Ficino in Spain*
19 Patricia M. Keller, *Ghostly Landscapes: Film, Photography, and the Aesthetics of Haunting in Contemporary Spanish Culture*
20 Carolyn A. Nadeau, *Food Matters: Alonso Quijano's Diet and the Discourse of Food in Early Modern Spain*
21 Cristian Berco, *From Body to Community: Venereal Disease and Society in Baroque Spain*
22 Elizabeth R. Wright, *The Epic of Juan Latino: Dilemmas of Race and Religion in Renaissance Spain*
23 Ryan D. Giles, *Inscribed Power: Amulets and Magic in Early Spanish Literature*
24 Jorge Pérez, *Confessional Cinema: Religion, Film, and Modernity in Spain's Development Years, 1960–1975*
25 Joan Ramon Resina, *Josep Pla: Seeing the World in the Form of Articles*
26 Javier Irigoyen-García, *"Moors Dressed as Moors": Clothing, Social Distinction, and Ethnicity in Early Modern Iberia*
27 Jean Dangler, *Edging toward Iberia*
28 Ryan D. Giles and Steven Wagschal (eds), *Beyond Sight: Engaging the Senses in Iberian Literatures and Cultures, 1200–1750*
29 Silvia Bermúdez, *Rocking the Boat: Migration and Race in Contemporary Spanish Music*
30 Hilaire Kallendorf, *Ambiguous Antidotes: Virtue as Vaccine for Vice in Early Modern Spain*
31 Leslie Harkema, *Spanish Modernism and the Poetics of Youth: From Miguel de Unamuno to* La Joven Literatura
32 Benjamin Fraser, *Cognitive Disability Aesthetics: Visual Culture, Disability Representations, and the (In)Visibility of Cognitive Difference*
33 Robert Patrick Newcomb, *Iberianism and Crisis: Spain and Portugal at the Turn of the Twentieth Century*

34 Sara J. Brenneis, *Spaniards in Mauthausen: Representations of a Nazi Concentration Camp, 1940–2015*
35 Silvia Bermúdez and Roberta Johnson (eds), *A New History of Iberian Feminisms*
36 Steven Wagschal, *Minding Animals in the Old and New Worlds: A Cognitive Historical Analysis*
37 Heather Bamford, *Cultures of the Fragment: Uses of the Iberian Manuscript, 1100–1600*
38 Enrique García Santo-Tomás (ed), *Science on Stage in Early Modern Spain*
39 Marina Brownlee (ed), *Cervantes'* Persiles *and the Travails of Romance*
40 Sarah Thomas, *Inhabiting the In-Between: Childhood and Cinema in Spain's Long Transition*
41 David A. Wacks, *Medieval Iberian Crusade Fiction and the Mediterranean World*
42 Rosilie Hernández, *Immaculate Conceptions: The Power of the Religious Imagination in Early Modern Spain*
43 Mary Coffey and Margot Versteeg (eds), *Imagined Truths: Realism in Modern Spanish Literature and Culture*
44 Diana Aramburu, *Resisting Invisibility: Detecting the Female Body in Spanish Crime Fiction*
45 Samuel Amago and Matthew J. Marr (eds), *Consequential Art: Comics Culture in Contemporary Spain*
46 Richard P. Kinkade, *Dawn of a Dynasty: The Life and Times of Infante Manuel of Castile*
47 Jill Robbins, *Poetry and Crisis: Cultural Politics and Citizenship in the Wake of the Madrid Bombings*
48 Ana María Laguna and John Beusterien (eds), *Goodbye Eros: Recasting Forms and Norms of Love in the Age of Cervantes*
49 Sara J. Brenneis and Gina Herrmann (eds), *Spain, World War II, and the Holocaust: History and Representation*
50 Francisco Fernández de Alba, *Sex, Drugs, and Fashion in 1970s Madrid*
51 Daniel Aguirre-Oteiza, *This Ghostly Poetry: Reading Spanish Republican Exiles between Literary History and Poetic Memory*
52 Lara Anderson, *Control and Resistance: Food Discourse in Franco Spain*
53 Faith Harden, *Arms and Letters: Military Life Writing in Early Modern Spain*
54 Erin Alice Cowling, Tania de Miguel Magro, Mina García Jordán, and Glenda Y. Nieto-Cuebas (eds), *Social Justice in Spanish Golden Age Theatre*

55 Paul Michael Johnson, *Affective Geographies: Cervantes, Emotion, and the Literary Mediterranean*
56 Justin Crumbaugh and Nil Santiáñez (eds), *Spanish Fascist Writing: An Anthology*
57 Margaret E. Boyle and Sarah E. Owens (eds), *Health and Healing in the Early Modern Iberian World: A Gendered Perspective*
58 Leticia Álvarez-Recio (ed), *Iberian Chivalric Romance: Translations and Cultural Transmission in Early Modern England*
59 Henry Berlin, *Alone Together: Poetics of the Passions in Late Medieval Iberia*
60 Adrian Shubert, *The Sword of Luchana: Baldomero Espartero and the Making of Modern Spain, 1793–1879*
61 Jorge Pérez, *Fashioning Spanish Cinema: Costume, Identity, and Stardom*
62 Enriqueta Zafra, *Lazarillo de Tormes: A Graphic Novel*
63 Erin Alice Cowling, *Chocolate: How a New World Commodity Conquered Spanish Literature*
64 Mary E. Barnard, *A Poetry of Things: The Material Lyric in Habsburg Spain*
65 Frederick A. de Armas and James Mandrell (eds), *The Gastronomical Arts in Spain: Food and Etiquette*
66 Catherine Infante, *The Arts of Encounter: Christians, Muslims, and the Power of Images in Early Modern Spain*
67 Robert Richmond Ellis, *Bibliophiles, Murderous Bookmen, and Mad Librarians: The Story of Books in Modern Spain*
68 Beatriz de Alba-Koch (ed), *The Ibero-American Baroque*
69 Deborah R. Forteza, *The English Reformation in the Spanish Imagination: Rewriting Nero, Jezebel, and the Dragon*
70 Olga Sendra Ferrer, *Barcelona, City of Margins*
71 Dale Shuger, *God Made Word: An Archaeology of Mystic Discourse in Early Modern Spain*
72 Xosé M. Núñez Seixas, *The Spanish Blue Division on the Eastern Front, 1941–1945: War Experience, Occupation, Memory*
73 Julia Domínguez, *Quixotic Memories: Cervantes and Memory in Early Modern Spain*
74 Anna Casas Aguilar, *Bilingual Legacies: Father Figures in Self-Writing from Barcelona*